encycleopedia

Pedal-power is a priceless asset for our fragile planet. Bicycles aren't part of the gridlock growing on the world's roads, so by definition they're part of the solution. That's true for all bikes, and today there are more bikes to choose from than ever. Encycleopedia celebrates this new diversity in bicycle design and technology.

Our aim is to delight you with machines you might never otherwise see. It's a book of answers, of ingenious and practical responses to a whole range of real needs. We hope it gives an idea of what can happen when we combine the astonishing potential of the pedal and the wheel.

Cycling is more than a sport. It's more than just transport. It's a way of finding a new, life-changing freedom. Rarely is it so much good fun to help make the world a better place in such an effective and visible way.

page 3

The international guide to alternatives in cycling

The Overlook Press
Woodstock & New York

Encycleopedia

©2000 Alan Davidson and Jim McGurn.
This is the sixth edition.
Encycleopedia was first published in Great Britain in October 1993 by Open Road Ltd, The Danesmead Wing, 33 Fulford Cross, York, YO10 4PB
Tel: +44 1904 654654 Fax: +44 1904 654684
Email: melanie@bcqedit.demon.co.uk
Website: www.encycleopedia.com

Published in the UK, in English and German versions, by Open Road Ltd, and distributed by subscription and through cycle stores worldwide by them and their agents.

First published in the USA in 1998 by The Overlook Press, Peter Mayer Publishers Inc, Lewis Hollow Road, Woodstock, New York, 12498
Encycleopedia is distributed by the Overlook Press and their agents through bookstores in North America.

A CIP Cataloging-in-Publication Data for this book is available from The Library of Congress.

Open Road Edition ISBN: 1 898457 06 9
Overlook Press Edition ISBN: 1 58567 086 3

Open Road, publishers of Encycleopedia, also publish Bike Culture Quarterly and Bycycle magazine. Encycleopedia is also published in the German language. Details on how to order Open Road publications are on page 138-139.

Conceived and compiled by Alan Davidson and Jim McGurn

Co-publishers: Jim McGurn and Alan Davidson
Editors: Peter Eland and Dan Joyce
Editorial team: Peter Eland, Dan Joyce, Jim McGurn, Tony Hadland, Simon Levermore; Extra Energy section by Hannes Neupert of Extra Energy
Design and art Direction: Creative Partnerships, Tel +44 1904 330366, Fax +44 1904 338470, Email info@creativepartnerships.co.uk Website www.creativepartnerships.co.uk
Art Editor: Vince Danks
Product care and assembly: Mike West
Studio Photography: Paul Batty, 6 Derwent Park, Wheldrake, York, YO4 6AT, UK
Tel/Fax: +44 1904 448 663
Additional Photography: Jason Patient and Sue Darlow

Moving images
Camera Work: Amy Davidson

Printed by **William Gibbons & Sons Ltd, PO Box 103, 26 Planetary Road, Willenhall, West Midlands, WV13 3XT**

Translated into German by Ralph Schneekloth, Doro Siebecke. German to English translations by Peter Eland. German proofreading by Silke Feldhusen.

Encycleopedia 2001:
The Guide to Alternatives in Cycling

RRP: UK £12, USA $19.95, Germany DM 35

Welcome to Encycleopedia

Encycleopedia is a platform for imaginative cycle-makers who are trying to change the world for the better by offering real practical transport alternatives.

Behind it all is our conviction that pedal-power has an enormous contribution to make in bringing this planet back from the brink towards a more human-scale, sustainable future. Cycling harms no one and benefits everyone. Human-powered transport is more than getting from A to B: it's a way of life.

Who's behind Encycleopedia?

Our firm is called Open Road. We're a bunch of bike fans based in York, England, although our agents and correspondents are scattered around the world. We're supported by a broad base of reader-shareholders. Encycleopedia is also published in a full German-language edition.

Do manufacturers pay for space in Encycleopedia?

Yes, although neither we nor they see it as advertising. They take part by invitation only. We write the text for each entry, in consultation with the manufacturer, and we design the pages. The fee (which we keep deliberately low to give smaller manufacturers the chance to take part) just covers our costs: as well as the editorial work there is photography, translation and co-ordinating the manufacturers' sales information to hundreds of Encycleopedia-affiliated cycle shops around the world.

Getting hold of the products

Your first port of call should be one of the bike shops listed towards the end of this Encycleopedia. A good network of specialised, local bike shops is vitally important for the future of cycling. Please do support your local bike shop, even if it does sometimes cost a little bit more than mail-order.

You may find that they stock the product you're looking for, but it's more likely that the dealer will have to source it for you. We provide all of our affiliated shops with ordering information about each of the products in Encycleopedia. It may be, though, that for a variety of reasons they're unable or unwilling to get hold of the product without a firm order. In such cases you should approach the manufacturer directly.

In some cases the manufacturer only ever sells direct. We explain this on the page itself and give you, where relevant, the details of the company. If they have agents or distributors in other countries, we've indicated that as well – and contact addresses for these countries are listed on page 144-145. When you contact manufacturers or shops, let them know that you saw their product in Encycleopedia. Incidentally, some of the more specialised shops may run hire services, so that you can try out some of the bikes before you decide to buy.

What will the products cost?

It's very difficult to give an idea of the price of a product beyond its country of origin. Not only is it expensive to send bicycles around the world, but insurance, import duties, local taxes and the overheads involved all mean that you can expect to pay significantly more outside the country of origin – often twice as much if the product comes from another continent.

For this reason, we've given the price of products in the country of origin, in the currency of that country (with some rare exceptions). Encycleopedia is read in so many countries that no other approach makes sense.

The Encycleopedia website

All Encycleopedia products and more are on our website: www.encycleopedia.com. This website will be constantly expanded with new products and editorial, so visit it regularly.

Bike Culture Quarterly

If you enjoy Encycleopedia, you'll also enjoy Bike Culture Quarterly, our magazine for the open-minded cyclist. It's a colourful, ads-free celebration of the diversity of cycling, and amongst other things, it's a 'breeding ground' for products which could appear in future Encycleopedias, but which are not yet commercially available or are just prototypes. There's much more too – history, art and campaigning. To order, see pages 138-139.

Bycycle

Sharp reporting and features with bite define Bycycle, our bi-monthly magazine primarily aimed at the UK reader – though readers anywhere will find much of interest. Bycycle is available worldwide.

Contents

DIE ERSTAUNLICHE MASCHINE
THE AMAZING MACHINE
LA MACHINE MERVEILLEUSE

On a bicycle you are over 15 times as efficient as a horse rider, in terms of energy consumed per kilometre travelled, and you can travel faster and further. [1]

On a bicycle you can travel up to 1037 kilometres on the energy equivalent of a litre of petrol. [1]

On a bicycle you weigh about six times more than your vehicle. In a car your vehicle weighs around 20 times more than you do.

On a bicycle you protect yourself against the 'Western diseases' of heart disease, high blood pressure, obesity and stress. [2]

On a bicycle you provide a motor which improves its own strength and efficiency – and even its working life – the more it is used.

On a bicycle you use less energy in riding than a car uses to power its headlights. A mere 37.3W (0.05hp) will propel a cyclist at around 13km/h; a single car headlight uses around 60W. [1]

On a bicycle you can expect to be as fit as an average person ten years younger, if you use it regularly. [2]

On a bicycle you can travel four times faster than you can walk using the same amount of energy. [1]

On a bicycle you can have your cake and eat it. A moderate half-hour each way commute will burn 8 calories a minute, or the equivalent of 11kg of fat in a year. [3]

[1] Bicycling Science, by Whitt and Wilson, The MIT Press. [2] Cycling: Towards Health and Safety, The British Medical Association, Oxford University Press. [3] Beer, J, Bycycle magazine #9, Open Road

NEW YORK · AMSTERDAM · SEVILLE · LONDON · PRAGUE
BUDAPEST · DUBLIN · MADRID · WASHINGTON · ROME
YORK · BERLIN · VIENNA · MILAN · LOS ANGELES
RIO · PEKING · MEXICO CITY · TOKYO · BUENOS AIRES

MIT RAD IN DER STADT

MIT RAD IN DER STADT

MIT RAD IN DER STADT

CITY CYCLING

VÉLOS EN VILLE

VÉLOS EN VILLE

VÉLOS EN VILLE

STREETS AHEAD

More cycling is done in cities than anywhere else. Yet unsuitable bikes are still pouring out of bike shops and into the hands of unsuspecting customers who will try to use them for riding in the city. There are limits to what you can do with fat, knobbly tyres, no mudguards (fenders), no racks, no chainguard and no lights.

If you're concerned mainly with getting to work on time in all weathers, you want a bike that's reliable, robust and simple to maintain. Fortunately, you now have that choice. Manufacturers have wised up! They've realised that city riding presents its own set of demands, and some superb city bikes have begun to appear in the product ranges of bike manufacturers worldwide.

It's obvious that a lot of thought has been put into them. Low-maintenance, weatherproof components, including the new generation of hub gears, have been matched with well-designed, lightweight frames to provide machines ideally suited to urban use. Good acceleration along with swift, reliable gear changes and confidence-inspiring braking all help a cyclist to integrate with urban traffic and remain safe.

But that's only part of the story. What if you have to travel to the city first by train, bus, car or plane? Or what if you live in the city and want to get out? If you live in a country that has a good integrated transport policy in operation then you're one of the lucky ones. For the rest of us, we'd do well to carry our own integrated transport with us, in the form of a folding bike.

Forget the old image of the folder as a heavyweight bundle of loose fitting tubes, dripping with oil, and that you need a degree in mechanical engineering and a spare weekend to fold. Today's folders are light, tight and just right! The best of them ride like conventional uprights and fold in seconds to a compact bundle considerably smaller than the sort of suitcases your fellow travellers will be wheeling along the railway platform. The use of new materials and new frame designs means they are light and responsive. Kitted out with quality components, and often with suspension, you can ride them comfortably all day.

The only problem with them is, you're likely to draw such an admiring crowd when you deftly unfold your pride and joy at a busy station that the time you've saved by having one may well be spent answering the questions of awe-struck onlookers.

City cycling isn't all about moving swiftly through busy streets unfettered by baggage. Sometimes you need to carry a load. A regular shopping trip or a visit to the recycling plant may mean recourse to the car if you can't face several journeys with loaded panniers. But here, too, you have a choice. Developments in cycle technology have resulted in load-carrying devices which swallow huge payloads with ease and yet are light and manoeuvrable. Everything from small detachable trailers designed to carry 30kg up to four-wheeled recumbent HGVs that will carry a quarter of a tonne.

In the business communities of Europe and North America there has been a resurgence in the use of pedal-power to carry loads around cities. Courier companies now exploit the speed and versatility of recumbent trikes, quadricycles and cycles with trailers to get goods swiftly into the heart of the city. They bypass the gridlocked traffic and the parking space nightmares, and deliver goods door-to-door cheaply and efficiently. Recent trials in London have shown that pedal-powered deliveries are not only far more economical than their petrol-powered counterparts but are up to a third quicker and are far more popular with the customers, too.

With more choice than ever, life for the city cyclist has never been so exciting.

Some roads in Dutch and German cities have been converted to 'bicycle streets', where cyclists have absolute right-of-way over the entire breadth of the road. Cars may use bicycle streets but are prohibited from rushing bicyclists or otherwise interfering with them. In addition, many lightly-travelled streets are one-way for cars but two-way for bicyclists, thus increasing their route choice.

Cycling is the most neglected means of travel in the US; less than one per cent of all trips in American cities are by bicycle. By contrast, cycling accounts for 28% of urban trips in the Netherlands, 20% in Denmark, 12% in Germany, and 10% in Switzerland. According to a 1995 Rodale Press Survey, 6% of all commuters in Texas would prefer to cycle to work over any other means, all other things being equal.

When the Danish Cyclists Federation launched a national 'Cycle To Work' campaign, supported by the Ministry of Environment, 30,211 people took part and cycled to work for three weeks. Altogether, they cycled 3.5 million kilometres, preventing the pollution from 300,000 litres of fuel. One in ten participants was a 'new' cyclist, and had previously used the car, and 94% of the participants said that they would continue cycling.

In Palo Alto, California, all road-patching must adhere to high standards for smoothness. Bicycle-detecting sensors, clearly marked so that cyclists can easily activate them, are used to change traffic lights. The city pays its employees a mileage rate for business travel by bicycle, maintains a police bike squad and funds an on-road cycling course for middle-school students. All new developments except single-family homes must provide secure bicycle parking, and all new office buildings 10,000 square feet or larger must provide showers for employees.

In Freiberg, Germany, 29% of all shopping trips to the centre take place on foot, 24% by bicycle, 26% by public transport, and only 14% by car. Ninety per cent of the population of Freiburg live in areas where speed is limited to 30km/h. The authorities are building a new 'Bicycle Centre' next to the train station, with secure parking, repair/retail shop, convenience store, café, etc.

Most developed cities devote at least one third of their land to parking lots and roads. One city in Japan has built a 12-story bicycle parking lot, using cranes to lift and park up to 1,500 bikes at a time.

The Dutch population travelled 191.5 billion kilometres within the Netherlands in 1998. Train journeys increased, while travelling by car fell slightly compared with 1997. 12.6 billion kilometres were covered by bicycle, almost 1 billion less than the year before. It's thought this was probably due to the bad weather in 1998. Holland has over 19,000km of bike lanes.

Community bike loan schemes are cropping up all over Europe and North America. In some schemes you pay a deposit to borrow a bike for as long as you need. In others you simply take a bike, use it, and leave it at your destination for someone else to use. Places where such schemes operate include California, Colorado, Florida, Oregon, Denmark, Holland, Norway, Switzerland, Germany, Denmark and Canada.

David Steed of Tucson, Arizona set the record for the longest track-stand in history. He remained balanced on his bike, with both feet on the pedals and without either of his wheels making a full revolution forwards or backwards, for 24 hours and 6 minutes between 10 and 11 March 1986. You'd think by then he'd have realised the traffic lights were stuck on red!

There's nothing like a bicycle for threading your way through today's clogged streets. Cycle couriers the world over can vouch for it, but sometimes the load is bigger than a normal bike can manage. Enter the Bike Best!

With a lockable and waterproof luggage compartment securely mounted in the tubular steel subframe, the Bike Best (Bicycle Extending Shopping Trolley) mounts securely to most mountain-bike frames. A standard hub bolts into the rear dropouts, and the subframe attaches to this hub and to the seatpost of the bicycle. The rear wheels and derailleur are transferred to the back of the subframe, and a second chain connects the new, central, hub to the rear gears. This is an easy job for any experienced cycle mechanic, and extends the machine to about the length of a conventional tandem.

The steel subframe weighs 10kg and the 10kg moulded plastic container provides a 120-litre secure cargo area. With the load below the saddle and between the wheels, the bike is very stable on the road and also when you're loading up: a spring-loaded two-point stand will easily keep the laden machine upright.

The box comes with a lockable lid, but can be adapted to take a car child seat and a clear rain hood; it's called the Bike Best Guardian.

The rigid subframe provides considerable protection for any passenger, and looking backwards gives a clear view of the world going by. At present the Bike Best is only available in blue, with a light or dark blue carrier, but other colours are available to special order. And soon, even the largest of pets may be able to join the ride: a ventilated plexiglass cover for animal transport is under development.

bike best

Michael Brigden works from his own workshop in Norwich. He invented and patented the Bike Best subframe to help him carry home an average weekly shop on a bike, and believes that with more than three-quarters of modern traffic involving shopping, the bicycle must be able to carry serious loads if it is to compete.
After investigating various ideas, Mike has gone into production himself. He's concentrated on the extension kit rather than complete bikes, because he's found that most cyclists prefer to keep their own favourite gearing, brakes and riding position, adding the subframe when extra load-carrying is needed. The Bike Best is already popular with members of the Norwich Cycling Campaign, and the local Greenpeace shop are also interested in Mike's developments.
Bike Best is actively seeking partnerships with manufacturers and agents both in the UK and abroad. Manufacturers interested in licensing or agents with an existing distribution network who wish to add the Bike Best to their range should contact Mike.

Bike Best Ltd, 71 Wroxham Road, Sprowston, Norwich NR7 8TW. Tel/Fax +44 1603 405 918 Email info@bikebest.co.uk Website www.bikebest.co.uk

In the UK, the Bike Best conversion kit costs around £340 retail, and prices will vary worldwide.

GOTHAM CITY

The roughest ruts and the deepest potholes hold no fear for the Gotham City, Dahon's new flagship folding bike. With a custom Marzocchi-designed front fork and a rear air shock, the bike is designed to take the worst urban environment in its stride.

The riding position is quite high and upright, so that you can see over traffic, and also enjoy a comfortable position with no back-strain. The WTB saddle is particularly comfortable, and was chosen with the riding position in mind.

With full suspension, ride quality is excellent: unsurfaced tracks or cycleways are no problem, and the Ritchey Speedmax tyres can even tackle some light off-roading. It's an adaptable bike: different riding styles and rider tastes are catered for with the height-adjustable stem and pressure-adjustable rear air shock.

The Gotham City's frame is made from custom-drawn 7005 aluminum tubing, and the bike weighs 13.0kg. Seven-speed SRAM ESP 7.0 twist-grip gearing is always to hand, and the range is just right for city riding – a good low for acceleration, and a high gear big enough to keep up with the traffic. Ritchey bar ends give an alternative riding position for longer stretches, and powerful ProMax V-brakes operate smoothly on machined-sidewall 20" (406) rims.

Folding is easy, and uses Dahon's patented Lite-Touch system. Large levers open or close easily with little hand force – yet lock absolutely solid and play-free. The folding procedure is simple: saddle down, stem up, fold down the handlebars, then fold the main frame. Both frame and handlebar latches are secured with safety catches when the bike is being ridden.

The fold takes just 10 seconds, and the bike then fits into an optional hard case, safe for use on even the most bike-unfriendly of airlines.

dahon

Dr. David Hon, who founded the company over 17 years ago, sees the Gotham City as a logical development: "We've been interested in suspension for many years. As demonstrated so elegantly by Sir Alex Moulton, suspension allows smaller wheels to reach the efficiency of larger wheels." Another benefit is, he points out, the increased comfort.

Dahon are the world's largest producer of portable folding bicycles, folding frames, and folding components, and have made well over a million machines, from compact 16" commuters to full-sized 26" mountain bikes. Their Speed, a fast 20 (406)-wheeled folder, was featured in Encyclopedia 99.

With their headquarters in California, Dahon have factories and offices in Taiwan and China. Dahon have dealers in many countries. In case of difficulty, contact the headquarters in Los Angeles: Tel +1 818 305 5264 Fax +1 818 305 9153 Website: www.dahon.com Email dahon@ficnet.net

In the USA, the Gotham City costs around $900, and prices will vary worldwide.

Wait a while at any major railway station and sooner or later a Brompton will be wheeled past, folded and lifted onto a train. This vanishing act once used to surprise both passengers and train staff. No longer. Like the laptop computer, years of use have made the Brompton a popular traveller's accessory.

How do you improve such an established and successful product? By degrees. While the Brompton's ultra-compact folded frame remains unchanged, components have been upgraded to push the riding performance of the bike still further.

Tyres are now a slicker skinwall design made specially for Brompton. Rated at 6.8 bar (about 95psi), these reduce rolling resistance, making trips swifter and easier. The brakes have been improved, too. Up front, the Brompton is checked by a more powerful dual-pivot calliper. The dynamo system on T-types now features a halogen front lamp and a bright rear light with six LEDs. For L-types, there's a battery light option. The once-optional folding left-hand pedal is now standard on the L3, T3, L5 and T5. You can order these models with a different gear range – 14% higher or 7% lower on the five-speeds, 12% or 18% lower on the three-speeds. And you can buy them with any accessories factory-fitted. There are even more colours to choose from now: the standard palette includes red, yellow, ivory, green, black, silver, blue and Turkish green.

New for 2000 is a budget model: the C-type has the standard Brompton frame, but economises on the peripherals. You can add any Brompton accessories later. Take your pick from lights, quick-release front bags for shopping or touring, extra-long seat posts, alternative tyres for unfriendly roads, and a rainproof luggage cover.

The C3 and L3 both weigh in at 25lb (11.4kg). The extras on the T-types add weight but not bulk: all five Bromptons pack into the same 22.2" x 21.5" x 9.8" (565 x 545 x 250mm) space in just 15-20 seconds. A folded Brompton is convenient as well as compact: the chain is hidden away where it won't rub on your clothes, and thanks to rollers underneath, the package is easy to stow or wheel around.

brompton bicycle ltd

Though commonly seen on commuter trains, 'planes, or buses, Bromptons have been much further afield – even to the South Pole. Scientist André Philips has used his at the Antarctic base for riding between the main accommodation dome and the research telescopes. Meanwhile, Julie Pick rode her Brompton 2,215 miles from Kings Lynn, UK, to Istanbul in 45 days.

That the Brompton is so versatile is a testament to Andrew Ritchie's design, which has been painstakingly revised over 25 years. He struggled in the early days, after being ignored by the bicycle industry, but production is now flat out and the company has received the Queen's Award for Export Achievement: Bromptons are sent all over the world – in very small boxes, naturally.

Brompton Bicycle Ltd, Kew Bridge Distribution Centre, Lionel Road, Brentford, Middlesex, TW8 9QR, UK. Tel +44 20 8232 8484 Fax +44 20 8232 8181 Website www.bromptonbicycle.co.uk

In the United Kingdom, prices range from £353 to £613, and will vary worldwide.

The Limbo is a bike with a secret. Take a close look at the picture… seen it yet?

At first glance you might miss the secret trick, but you won't fail to appreciate that this is a seriously comfortable recumbent. The seat is carefully shaped, with a foam base for support and mesh back for ventilation. Custom-tuned RockShox coil-over rear suspension below the seat absorbs road shock with no pedal-induced bobbing. The 20" (406) front wheel and 26" (559) rear wheel gives a wide range of tyre and gearing options: the standard derailleur set-up gives a range of 23-123" gears. Conventional Shimano and SRAM bicycle components are used throughout, so that any professional cycle dealer can service the Limbo.

Comfort requires a perfect fit: the Limbo adjusts to suit. Both the height and the angle of the steering mast can be tweaked, and the seat angle and position on the large diameter cro-mo main tube can be varied to suit riders from 5'0" to 6'4" (152 to 193cm). The seat height adjusts between 24"-26" (610-660mm), which gives good visibility and easy balancing.

The main frame-tube is custom-formed cro-mo steel, and the curve makes for a low step-over height. The complete bike weighs around 37lb (16.5kg).

And the secret? At the twist of a few hex keys the Limbo's forks relocate, making a nimble short wheelbase recumbent. The conversion is done in about 15 minutes: front forks come out of their forward position, the steering linkage rod is removed, and the forks are then slotted into the rear head-tube, directly below the steering column. No adjustment of the chain is necessary. In short-wheelbase mode the handling is still excellent – it's just a slightly different feeling, perhaps a little more suited for urban riding, while the longer option is always there for leisurely country touring.

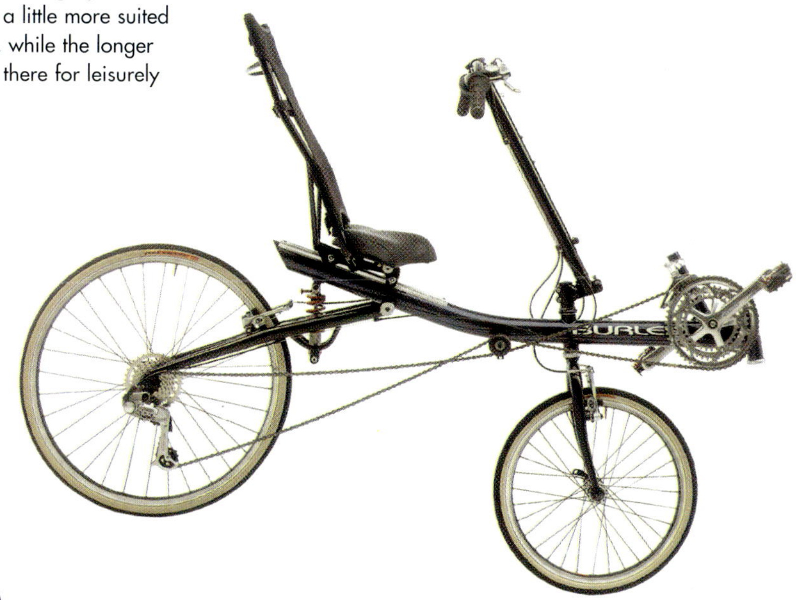

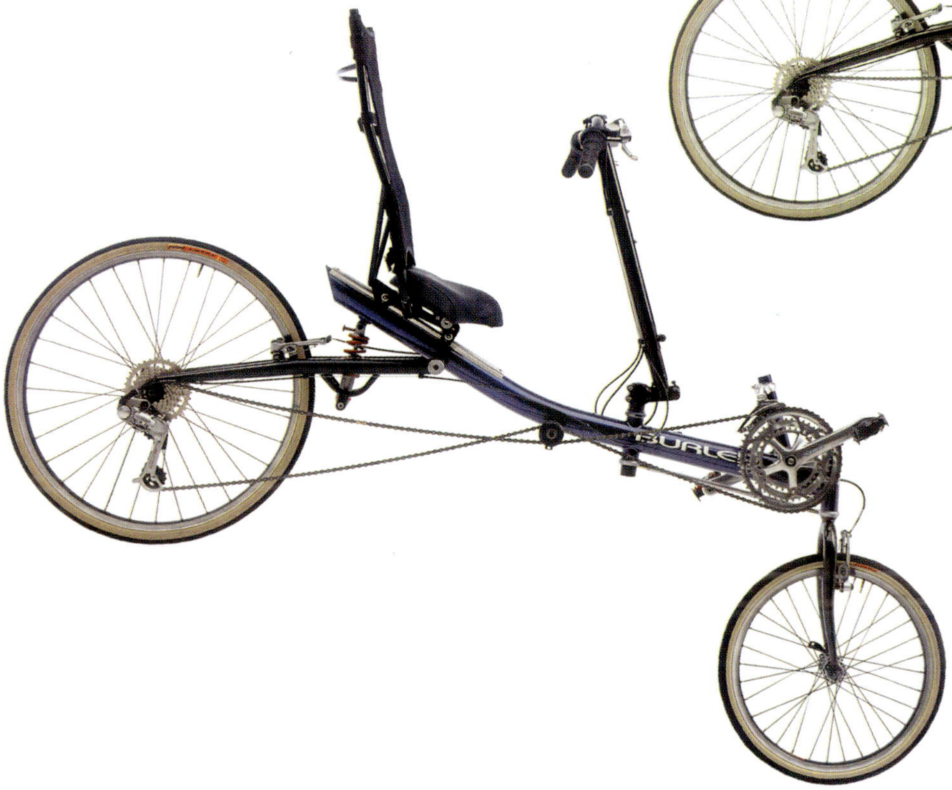

burley design cooperative

Burley pride themselves on offering one of the widest ranges of family solutions for cycling enthusiasts: their trailers, Piccolo trailerbike and tandems are featured elsewhere in this Encycleopedia. They are also the US importer for the Birdy folder (also featured in this issue), and produce a line of quality rainwear.
Burley stand out in one other important respect: the company is run as a co-operative, so that each worker has a share of the business, and all earn the same wages. Burley are strong advocates for the co-operative way of working, and the business is often used as a model example of how it should work in practice.

Burley Design Cooperative, 4020 Stewart Road, Eugene, OR 97402-5408, USA. Tel +1 541 687 1644 Fax +1 541 687 0436
Email burley@burley.com Website www.burley.com

In the USA, the Limbo costs around $3750.

Some rickshaws are low-tech – and some are space-age. The Cycles Maximus Trishaw has gone for quality and performance; the aim, according to the designers, is to make simply the finest load- and people-carrier in the world.

They have not stinted with the specification: the steel chassis uses aircraft grades for high-stress parts, and the forks are specially made by BMX frame-building experts Curtis – who know exactly how to make robust and lightweight forks. The brakes are all-hydraulic: balanced Hope disks on each 23" rear wheel, and Magura rim brakes on the 20" (406) front wheel, complete with parking brake.

Twin chainrings can be combined with a variety of gearing systems to give the wide range necessary for a load-carrier: the SRAM 3x7 is fitted as standard, with Rohloff 14-speed or SRAM 7-speed options. A chain-driven differential unit is the final stage in the transmission, with specially developed 19mm hollow axles to the rear wheels.

The chassis can be fitted with one of four modular units: for people-carrying (with a rain/sun hood), a high-sided delivery box, a fully lockable box to fit Eurocrates, or a flatbed base. The overall length is 2.30m, and width can be chosen at either 1.20m or 1.08m. The chassis weighs 40kg, and the seat unit 17kg. Weights for the load-carrying bodies vary according to the design but are usually less than 20kg.

Cycles Maximus are working with Lynch Motors, whose electric-assist conversion kit is featured elsewhere in this Encycleopedia. The Trishaw is available with Lynch electric-assist for those heavy jobs – one less truck.

cycles maximus

Tom Nesbitt and Ian Wood have been fanatical about bikes for as long as they can remember. Ian is the landlord of two of Bath's most musical pubs (the Bell and the Hat & Feather), and for several years promoted music of the highest calibre at the 'Hub Club', where he soon became known as Ian 'Bike Boy' Wood.

Tom has a long history of bike-building: ever since he graduated in Design and Technology he's been building special bikes, often for circus use or stunt machines, and in 1996 he was commissioned by Cycle Bath, a local cycle group, to build a cycle car, which would be good on local fun rides.

Soon afterwards Tom and Ian started working together to create a rickshaw service for Bath. Unhappy with the vehicles they tested they retired to the workshop; the first prototype Cycles Maximus 'One Less Car' Trishaw emerged in Spring 1998. Since then these machines have done sterling work replacing many unnecessary local car journeys.

Cycles Maximus, The Bell, 103 Walcot St, Bath BA1 5BW, UK. Tel +44 1225 319 414 Fax +44 1225 334 494 Email sales@cyclesmaximus.com

In the UK, 'One Less Car' trishaws cost £2700 plus delivery.

The EP-X pulls off a remarkable trick: it has the consumer-goods appeal to awaken design-conscious non-cyclists to the joys of cycling – yet offers real performance and practical value to the most experienced rider. The company logo 'One day all bikes will be made like this' may seem ambitious, but they do have a point: it's high time for new thinking in bicycle design.

The EP-X is built on new ideas: the chassis is moulded from aerospace composites around a foam core, with aluminium inserts for dropouts and bearing attachments. A synchronous belt replaces the chain, so city suits or going-out clothes won't get greased up. The belt requires little or no maintenance: it never rusts, and is little affected by water or mud. The Roadster uses a SRAM seven-speed hub gear. Disk brakes on the front wheel, and a SRAM drum brake on the back, make for sure stopping whatever the weather, and low maintenance.

When you've returned home, the Roadster has several tricks up its sleeve. First, the one-piece chassis is easily wiped down, and a once-over with a damp cloth is enough to ensure that it won't leave any nasty marks over the rest of your possessions. Then, just flip it over so it stands on bars and saddle, remove a quick-release, and the rear end swings right over, leaving the EP-X standing stable and small in a corner or under the stairs. The folding mechanism also provides the pivot for unobtrusive but effective suspension for the rear swing-arm. A carrier rack fits to the seatpost, and mudguards are under development.

The EP-X range goes beyond the Roadster, and beyond roads, with the Terra-Shark, a mountain-bike which combines the same level of style with full-performance long-travel suspension. Further models are in the pipeline.

epmb uk ltd

The EP-X range has only just come onto the market – yet it's already gathering awards. Even before it was launched, the work of the EPMB Design Centre, in Western Australia, which carried out the CAD design and analysis for the frames, was honoured with an Australian Design Award. EPMB are an English and Malaysian group with a reputation for, amongst other things, leisure products and motorcycle components. Distribution of the EP-X bikes is handled through EMPB UK, based in Warwick.
When they took the EP-X range along to the big UK dealer show in Birmingham in March 2000, the EP-X team were delighted to win both first and second places in the 'Best new adult cycle' category. They even won the Fashion and Clothing award – even though they don't (yet!) make a single stitch of clothing!

EP-X, The Manor, Haseley Business Centre, Warwick CV35 7LS, UK. Tel +44 2476 247 264 Fax +44 2476 247 265 Email info@ep-x.com Website www.ep-x.com

In the UK the EP-X Roadster costs around £1500. Prices will vary worldwide.

Take a ride in the city. You stop, you start, you cruise. All three activities put specific demands on a bike – and riese und müller have met those demands in a radical new way with the Equinox.

With the upright riding position, and pedals well forward, there's no problem putting feet flat on the floor when you stop: the 'balancing act' as you poke for the ground on tiptoe is a thing of the past. The high riding position is good in traffic, and the multi-position handlebars are positioned on a height-adjustable stem so that the back is straight, arms are relaxed and neck unstrained.

You can concentrate on enjoying the ride – or on the traffic – as the automatic four-speed Shimano hub gearing selects the correct gear – bottom gear for starting off, then switching up as you pick up speed. The fully-enclosed chain drive runs hidden inside the rear swing-arm, keeping the chain protected from dirt and away from your clothes.

Comfort is further enhanced by the quick-adjust suspension. This lets the rider 'stiffen' the suspension by 22% in an instant to adjust for loads on the rear carrier, or to accommodate two different riders. Suspension lets you use high-pressure tyres on the 20" (406) wheels, which are robust enough to withstand the most potholed city streets or cyclepaths.

The frame is made from 7005 T6 TIG-welded aluminium, and the compact design is handy for parking or public transport. Overall weight is around 16.8kg. A pannier adapter, and a quick-release basket, are available as options. As befits any city bike, top-quality dynamo lights and mudguards come as standard.

page 18

riese und müller

The Equinox is the newest bike in the riese und müller stable: their other machines are the Birdy folder (see elsewhere in this Encycleopedia), the Culture and Avenue city bikes, and the Delite, a sporty full-suspension 'street-bike'. Full suspension is a riese and müller trademark – their motto is 'suspended cycling', and the company's founders, Markus Riese and Heiko Müller, firmly believe it's the way of the future. In a few years' time, they predict, only the cheapest and most basic of bikes will be without suspension.

riese und müller: Tel 0049 6151 366 860 Fax 0049 6151 366 8620 Email team@r-m.de
Website www.r-m.de

In Germany, the Equinox costs around DM 3199, and prices will vary worldwide.

The Birdy is an ingenious synthesis of touring bike and compact folder, blurring the boundaries of what you can do with a portable bike. It offers a conventional riding position with a stiff frame, while the elastomer suspension provides an exceptionally smooth ride. Much of the responsiveness is due to the way the front and rear wheel suspension swing-arms form part of the folding mechanism, eliminating the need for hinges in the main frame.

The Birdy's frame is powder-coated 7005 T6 aluminium. The suspension uses easily-changed elastomers, colour-coded to suit your weight and comfort requirements. The frame is 'one size fits all' but with a choice of two handlebar stems. The 'comfort' stem is more upright and has vertical adjustment, whereas the lighter and racier standard 'allround' stem is a fixed height.

This year carrying luggage on the Birdy is easier than ever. All models are now fitted with threaded bosses to take a low-rider front carrier capable of carrying 10kg. At the back you can fit the SL carrier to the swing-arm, or opt for the frame-mounted pannier rack – either will carry another 12kg. The pump stows safely out of sight in the seatpost. Other accessories include lighting kits, mudguards and a propstand.

The Birdy's makers offer specially-commissioned tyres for better performance. The 1.5" high-pressure Road Reflex uses the latest skinwall technology, has reflective sidewalls and a Kevlar anti-puncture band. A chunkier MTB tyre is available for off-road use.

To fold the Birdy, first swing the rear wheel under, then fully lower the seatpin. Next swing back the front wheel, and finally fold down the handlebar stem. This reduces the bike to a 78x56x28cm package in as little as 15 seconds, ready to go into the optional carrying bag. Or you might prefer the convertible rucksack with its pull-out compartment designed to conceal and protect the bike.

Thousands of Birdys have been produced over the last five years. They've been used for everything from commuting through touring to off-road and even triathlon. There's the entry-level Red (7-speed Shimano Deore derailleur), the low-maintenance Green (Shimano Nexus 7-speed coaster hub) and the touring-oriented Blue (wide-ratio SRAM 3x7 hybrid gear with Shimano Deore derailleur). Now, replacing the Elox, there's the new lightweight Black (9-speed Shimano Deore XT). At just 9.2kg this Birdy is truly a featherweight.

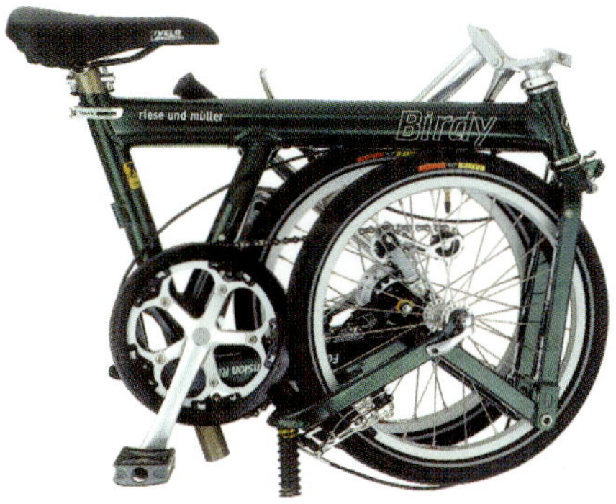

riese und müller

A sure sign of the Birdy's impact is the coverage it attracts on the Internet. Naturally, the manufacturers, riese und müller, have a website (at www.r-m.de) but there's a lot of other information from a variety of sources in English, German and Japanese. The independently-produced Birdy Bicycle Information pages include general reviews, product news and features on components and modifications. You'll also find links to discussions and comments by owners, together with reports on touring with the Birdy. You can get to these pages from the Folding Society's homepage at www.foldsoc.co.uk
The Equinox, an innovative town bike, and other models from riese und müller are featured elsewhere in this Encycleopedia.

riese und müller, Erbacher Str. 123, D-64287 Darmstadt, Germany. Tel +49 6151 366 860 Fax +49 6151 366 8620 Email team@r-m.de Website www.r-m.de

In Germany, Birdys cost from DM 1999 for the Red to 3199 for the Black. Prices will vary worldwide.

The Pacy leaps into the folder market with a whole series of superlatives. It's claimed as the smallest 20"-wheeled folding bike, with a lightning-fast fold, tremendous torsional stiffness, excellent comfort and unsurpassed luggage-carrying capacity.

The riding position is as spacious as a normal bike's, and the ride is full-size, too. The front end of the cro-mo frame has been particularly designed for stiffness, so leg-power is translated directly into forward motion, rather than absorbed by frame flex. The Pacy has such well-behaved and stable handling that it can easily be ridden hands-off. The well-sized 20" wheels with high-pressure tyres offer easy-rolling performance.

The folding process has two stages: the first step is to fold the rear swing-arm and the seatpost. This is usually sufficient for taking the bike on public transport, and takes just five seconds. To reach the fully-folded size of 71x69x28cm, the handlebar is pulled up by the stem, the quick-release front wheel is removed and attached to the frame on a special mounting. That takes another 15 seconds.

Unfolding takes no longer, and unlike many folders you don't have to re-adjust the seat height – the saddle folds back into position, ready to go. The same quick-release clamp which folds the seatpost also folds the Pacy luggage rack – a lightweight and robust design, which gives the luggage full benefit from the suspension. There's the option of extra luggage capacity via the front fork low-rider braze-ons.

The standard rear suspension smooths both big shocks and jarring vibrations, and along with the comfortable saddle and Pacy handlebars, allows extended rides without discomfort.

The equipment options are as versatile as the Pacy itself: a suspended front fork and a carrying bag are available, along with various seven-speed hub gears, which can be combined with the Swiss Mountain-Drive. And if you want a superlative transmission to match the bike, there's a luxury 14-speed Rohloff hub-gear version.

thomas poreski spezialfahrräder

The Pacy is designed and made by Hubert Meyer and Thomas Poreski. Hubert runs an auto workshop and metalworking shop, and they have been making the unique Culty recumbent trike for three years now (it's featured elsewhere in this Encycleopedia). The Pacy was invented of necessity: Thomas commutes regularly from his home to Berlin, 700km away, where he works as a scientific consultant to a German member of parliament. The idea for the Pacy was conceived on a long train journey, as Thomas mulled over folding bikes, and how they could be improved. He'd tried the rest, and thought he and Hubert could do better! The Culty team are particularly proud that their bikes are 'Made in Germany', yet remain perfectly affordable.

Information for public and dealers: Thomas Poreski Spezialfahrräder, Charlottenstr. 39, 72764 Reutlingen, Germany. Tel +49 177 2777592 Fax +49 7121 204085 Email thomas.poreski@culty.de Website www.pacy.de
Manufacturer: Hubert Meyer GmbH, Birkenfelderstr. 11, 75180 Pforzheim-Büchenbronn, Germany. Tel +49 7231 972810 Fax +49 7231 972812 Email hubert.meyer@culty.de

In Germany, a version with quality components and a seven-speed hub costs from DM 1799.

Few cycling concepts are as radical as the Culty. With front wheel drive and rear steering, and independent lean-steering, the differences go beyond the visual. The ride is uniquely different, and brings unique benefits.

You lean into the curves at any speed, just like a bicycle. This gives huge reserves of cornering safety, despite the narrow overall width and pleasantly high seating position. No other recumbent can tackle difficult terrain, with a full load, with such aplomb. The leaning technology makes the Culty a great off-roader: you stay upright, even as the Culty chassis absorbs extreme undulations – without disturbing the steering! All three wheels are suspended.

A full load on the Culty means what it says. Alongside the rider you can carry up to two children and a crate of beer, and an additional transport box, without overloading. The forward centre of gravity gives good traction on climbs, and the Culty has proved itself on ice and snow in winter, just as it has in hot desert regions.

'Unusual' isn't a put-down when applied to the Culty: it's a statement of fact. Riding the Culty gives a uniquely relaxating yet dynamic sensation. Newcomers learn the technique in just a few minutes.

Everyday transport of large-volume luggage, sporty evening relaxation rides or extended tours are equally possible with the Culty. Alongside many transmission variations and upgrades, an electric-assist system and weather-protection cover are also available. The standard frame fits riders from 4′8″ to 6′5″ (145 to 195 cm) tall, and there's an extra-long version for those up to 7′ 3″ (220 cm) in height.

thomas poreski spezialfahrräder

Three years after its launch, the Culty has found a following not just in Germany and Europe, but in North America and even Australia. Wherever it hits the streets it's the natural centre of attention.

Thomas Poreski and Hubert Meyer, the inventors of the Culty, are as versatile as their product. Hubert runs an auto workshop and own metalworking shop.Thomas is a scientific adviser to a German member of parliament. The Culty has now been joined by a folding bike, the Pacy, which is described elsewhere in this Encycleopedia.

Information for public and dealers: Thomas Poreski Spezialfahrräder, Charlottenstr. 39, 72764 Reutlingen, Germany. Tel +49 177 2777592 Fax +49 7121 204085 Email thomas.poreski@culty.de Website www.culty.de
Manufacturer: Hubert Meyer GmbH, Birkenfelderstr. 11, Tel +49 7231 972810 Fax +49 7231 972812 Email hubert.meyer@culty.de

In Germany, a version with quality components and a seven-speed hub costs from DM 3989. prices will vary worldwide.

Full suspension transforms the ride of small-wheeled folding bikes. Borrowing high-end technology from the world of mountain bike racing, Peregrine Bicycle Works make very practical 'suitcase' bikes with some of the most tried-and-tested suspension units around: a Cane Creek AD-5 air shock at the rear, and all PBW bikes can be supplied with Ballistic front suspension forks.

You can change the suspension's spring and damping to suit you, or even pump it up hard to lock it out. But the customisation of your bike goes further. PBW supply your bike with an adjustable stem, so that you can move the handlebars up, down, forward or back. Once you've found your favourite position, whether aero tuck or sit-up-and-beg, PBW will custom-make a rigid stem for you, and the adjustable stem goes on to the next customer.

There are six models in the PBW range: two trekking bikes, for everyday riding or commuting; two mountain bikes, for rougher rides; and two road bikes. All are made in the USA from high-strength 4130 cromoly steel, and feature rear suspension and quality components from Sachs, SRAM, Rohloff, Dia Compe and Shimano. Weight starts at 23.5lb (10.6kg) for the 9-speed Knockabout trekking bike, up to 32.75lb (11.6kg) for the fully-featured Voyageur long distance road bike.

A PBW bike can folded in less than a minute to under 30x30x12" (76x76x30cm), and the package is held together by the way the bike is folded. The rear wheel tucks under the frame, separating at the shock, and the seatpost pushes right down. The stem is then removed. By further removing the pedals and wheels, each bike packs into a 29" hard-shell suitcase in under 20 minutes.

pbw bikes

"All my life I'd ridden a bicycle, and I decided it was my calling to make useful bikes." So says one-time computer programmer Hugh Kern. He switched careers, confident that two engineering degrees and an advanced engineering degree would be a sound basis for bike design.

"I worked in bike shops and with other manufacturers, but was unhappy and figured the only way to have a job in the bike business was to make bikes myself. So I learned welding at a vocational technology college. I collected some tools, worked on a design and began to build. I went to the United Bicycle Institute frame building class to find out how real bike builders do it. I reworked my tooling and started out in business as PBW Bikes."

PBW bikes are distributed in the USA and Germany; Hugh would be happy to hear from potential distributors in the UK, Scandinavia and Holland.

PBW Bikes, PO Box 2809. Athens, GA 30612, USA, Tel/fax: +1 706 548 1179.
E-mail info@PBWbikes.com, website: www.pbwbikes.com
Germany: Voss Spezialrad GmbH: Tel +49 4821 7 80 23 fax +49 4821 796 93 Email voss-spezialrad@t-online.de
Website www.voss-spezialrad.de

Prices start at $995 in the USA, and will vary worldwide.

With a Skoot, the dream of integrated transport becomes a practical proposition. Ride where you want to go, and fold the Skoot away, in seconds, into its case. Then carry it into offices, restaurants or hotels, or take it further on trains, buses, trams, or taxis. All without hassle, loss of dignity or greasy hands. It packs away neatly in 30 seconds, even on a crowded pavement.

Unpacked, it's a street-legal cycle with an adult-size frame for road use, with 12" (203) pneumatic tyres, front and rear lighting, reflectors and calliper brakes. The single-speed transmission has a 5:1 pedal ratio and the chain is completely enclosed to protect your clothing. If you Skoot to work, you can carry a stylish briefcase or lap-top computer inside the frame. There's no need to lump a lock around: the Skoot never needs to be left outside a building where it could be stolen.

Packed away, a Skoot is as unobtrusive as a small suitcase and will fit neatly under a desk at work, or in a cupboard at home. It weighs around 31lb (14.5kg) and has large roller wheels for pulling it along. Folded dimensions are 569x797x138mm. The rigid space-frame is made of rugged TIG-welded cro-mo tubing, with custom-machined stainless steel and aluminium parts. The colourful ABS shell mouldings are available in many designs, from corporate grey (with your own company logo) to canary yellow, or even zebra stripes!

The Skoot is a great combination of fun and practicality, giving instant mobility without the drawbacks usually associated with taking along a bike. Take it on holiday to explore towns and cities, or just to get down to the beach as quickly as possible. You could even take it on a cruise liner or yacht, to explore interesting ports of call.

skoot international limited

Vincent Fallon is a product designer who has been working freelance with European manufacturers for 20 years. He teamed up with some friends who are consultants in aerospace engineering and between them they came up with Skoot 'from scratch'. The brief they set themselves was to come up with a form of personal transport which could be taken inconspicuously into buildings. Vincent and his son Vaughan set up a company in Colchester to manufacture the Skoot and market it worldwide. The team's lack of preconceptions led to some unconventional design solutions – such as the removable cranks and handlebars which fold to become only 130mm wide. Importantly for such a radical design, it conforms to British Standards BS6102/1 for strength, safety and impact tests.

A range of Skoot branded attaché and lap-top cases, waterproof clothing and helmets is also available. The Skoot is available direct from the manufacturers, and can be ordered online through their website.

Skoot International Limited, 24 Peartree Business Centre, Stanway, Colchester, Essex, CO3 5JN, UK.
Tel: +44 1206 542 543 Fax: +44 1206 542 543 Email enquiries@skoot.net Website www.skoot.net

In the UK, the Skoot costs around £850.

"Perhaps the most remarkable design of machine in the long history of the bicycle." That's how Alex Moulton described the original Pedersen bicycle. Its unique feature is the use of small diameter thin-walled tubes in a lightweight triangulated structure to support the comfortable hammock saddle.

Mikael Pedersen was a Danish engineer who came to England and spent much of his working life at Dursley, Gloucestershire. He filed the first British patent for his improved bicycle in 1893 and went on to make thousands of beautifully finished Dursley Pedersens. The London to Brighton and back unpaced record was broken on a Pedersen, showing that this smooth-riding bike was no slouch. Production ceased in 1917 but in recent years discerning cyclists have again come to appreciate the special merits of the Pedersen – comfort, lightness and elegance. Enter Copenhagen blacksmith Jesper Sølling.

Jesper discovered the Pedersen in the late 1970s and is now the world's largest manufacturer of these fine machines, having supplied more than 6,000 to 25 different countries. You can buy a solo, tandem or even a triplet. Solos are available in five standard frame sizes and every CrMo tubed frame has more than 50 brazed joints. As Jesper puts it, "There is a full day's work of my hands in one frame." The tubes are CrMo by Potte & Pothoff and are paired throughout. This improves the lateral stability of the machine and helps stop the frame flexing under pedal pressure.

The hammock saddle is extremely durable and has a very different feel from a conventional seat. Used with the upright Royal handlebars, it offers a particularly comfortable and anatomically beneficial posture for many riders with back problems. But don't forget that the Pedersen is also a performance machine, as the early record-breakers proved. A century on, and fitted with the latest in triple chainsets and V-brakes, the Pedersen makes a superb tourer.

jesper sølling cykelproduktion

Jesper's agent for Germany, Switzerland and Austria, Kalle Kalkhoff, and his wife Gaby, have toured extensively on their Pedersen tandem. Kalle's company, KGB, also markets Woodguards, a range of cycle components, hand-crafted from timber by Johannes Rességuier of Bremen. These include mudguards, rims, carrier racks, chainguards, grips and even lights.

Wood is a fine material for mudguards: strong, light, and with a timeless elegance. Johannes carefully laminates his from nine layers of Swedish birch. He even makes a double-curved version that follows both the tyre profile and the wheel – no easy matter in wood.

Woodguards components are most often seen on Pedersens, but bestow a functional distinction on almost any quality bicycle.

Pedersen of Denmark and Woodguards, c/o KGB, Donnerschweerstr.45, Oldenburg 26123, Germany. Tel +49 441 885 0389 Fax +49 441 885 0388 Email kgb.kalle@nwn.de Website www.pedersen-fahrrad.de

In Germany, Pedersens of Denmark cost from DM3500, and prices will vary worldwide.

Pashley have long had a reputation for building classic, traditionally British roadsters. Since the company was formed in the 1920s, their elegant and reliable machines have become an institution, part of the British way of life.

Joining forces with another great institution, Harrods, was a natural move. When the famous Knightsbridge store celebrated its 150th anniversary last year, a visit to the store's archives revealed a long history of supplying cycles to its distinct clientele, not only from the best manufacturers of the day, but also under Harrods' own brand. The time seemed right for a new range of traditionally-handcrafted Harrods-branded cycles, and Pashley were the obvious choice to develop the Gentleman's Light Roadster, the first of this new range.

Pashley's brief was simple – to use the best combination of modern equipment and classic styling to create a flagship for the range. This bicycle was to be built up to a specification, not down to a price!

The result is an elegant, comfortable and easy-rolling machine with a hand-brazed lightweight frame. Built from Reynolds 531 butted tubing, it has quality touches such as taper gauge stays and fork blades, a precision cast fork crown and forged drop-outs. Embellished with leather and stainless steel detailing, the look is unashamedly 1950s. In the best roadster tradition, the GLR has the latest in Sturmey-Archer hub gears, the Sprinter 7-speed. The lighting system combines the low maintenance dependability of a Shimano hub dynamo with automatic light-sensitive headlamp switching and battery back-up. At the rear there's a powerful LED lamp. And forget the rod brake systems of old: the GLR's Magura hydraulic rim brakes provide a lot more stopping power.

The saddle is a Brooks Champion Flyer, complemented by leather-covered handlebar grips. Stainless steel components include the handlebar, wheel rims, spokes,

mudguards, seat pillar, hydraulic brake hose and even the gear cable. The puncture-resistant tyres are an easy rolling yet comfortable 700 x 35c – the modern equivalent of 28" roadster tyres – and have a reflective safety band.

pashley cycles

At a time when other cycle manufacturers are consolidating their product range and outsourcing their production, Pashley are doing the opposite. Managing Director Adrian Williams believes that Pashley's small size and in-house production facilities give it the advantage of quick response with complete end-to-end control. He has a strong belief in being involved in the whole process from start to finish.

Adrian is always open to new ideas. In his seven years at Pashley, he has revitalised the Moulton APB range, acquired the Brilliant collection of family bikes and folders (including the Micro and the Fold-it), introduced a range of Land Rover bikes, brought in the PDQ recumbents, and launched the TVSeries of trials and BMX bikes. Yet he has not deserted Pashley's old markets, such as tricycles and carrier cycles. The mail delivery bike has been re-engineered for greater comfort and reliability, with hub brakes and 3-speed gears, and the Post Office remains Pashley's biggest commercial customer.

Pashley Cycles, Masons Road, Stratford-upon-Avon, Warwickshire, CV37 9NL, UK.
Tel +44 1789 292 263 Fax +44 1789 414 201
E-mail info@pashley.co.uk
Website www.pashley.co.uk

In the UK the Gentleman's Light Roadster costs around £850-900.

When you're riding through city streets, an upright sit-up-and-beg position is one of the most practical, elegant and comfortable ways to cycle – unless you're riding over cobblestones or potholes. Then the jolts which the crouched sports rider absorbs with his bent knees and elbows travel up your spine. For maximum comfort you need some form of suspension, and that's just what Kettler's CityShopper provides.

The Kettcom Comfort System is a spring rear suspension unit, and this is combined with SunTour suspension forks at the front. Both are fully adjustable for rider weight and conditions, ensuring that you roll over irregularities in the road without your tyres leaving the tarmac – a more efficient as well as more comfortable way to travel.

The CityShopper features a rust-proof aluminium frame, as do all Kettler bikes. Aluminium is less dense than steel, and is built into larger-diameter tubes to achieve frame stiffness without adversely affecting weight. Kettler pioneered all-aluminium bikes, and their current range of tubing uses a unique asymmetric cross-section developed in-house for their own use.

Components have been well chosen to meet the needs of the city cyclist. Mudguards and a chainguard will keep both bike and rider clean, while the halogen dynamo lighting is dependable and always there. A sprung saddle adds further to rider comfort, while the integral rear rack will carry panniers full of groceries or a briefcase with equal ease. Gearing comes from the all-weather Shimano Nexus 7-speed hub gear, with a back-pedal roller brake. Tyres have a puncture-proof strip. There's even a propstand so you don't have to lean the bike against walls. Separate ladies' and gents' models are available.

kettler

Kettler launched their first all-aluminium frame bicycle in 1977. All Kettler bikes since have used aluminium frames. Their other models include the unsuspended CityCruiser, the derailleur-geared CityTour, and the fully-suspended CityComfort.
Kettler's brand name, which dates from 1949, is well known in Germany, Europe and throughout the world for leisure goods, and the company has representatives in many different countries. Kettler produce sports and fitness equipment, table tennis tables, casual furniture, tanning centres, and outdoor play equipment, as well as bicycles. Of particular interest to cyclists, they also produce three models of rear childseat.

Heinz Kettler GmbH & Co., Postfach 1020, D-59463 Ense-Parsit, Germany. Tel +49 02938 810 Fax +49 02938 2022
E-Mail: alu-rad@heinz-kettler.de. Website www.heinz-kettler.de

In the UK, Kettler bikes are available from: Kettler (GB) Ltd, Merse Road, North Moons Moat, Redditch, Worcestershire, B98 9HL. Tel: 01527 591901. Fax: 01527 62423. Email: kettler@btinternet.com. For Kettler agents in other countries, see pages 144-145.

Versatility has made the Christiania transporter trike an enduring success. You name it, this trike will carry it. Children, groceries, building materials, gas bottles, animals, one child in a wheelchair – all of these and more will go into the 35"x24" load platform. Now Christiania Bikes have unveiled a model that's more versatile still. Called the Light-Split, it's billed as having three-and-a-half wheels!

Strictly speaking there are four, but the fourth wheel is just a little castor. It's there because the frame splits in half – to give you a large and stable handcart. So you don't need to struggle across pedestrianised city centres, parks or beaches with heavy bags or small children hanging off your arms: you can wheel your passengers or load along instead. It's easier and faster, and you even have twin drum brakes on the handcart. The separability has other benefits: the Light-Split can more easily be transported by train, and of course it can be stored in a smaller space.

The Light-Split has a carrying capacity of 80kg (180lb) and weighs under 40kg. Depending on your local terrain, you can specify various hub gearing options. Typically, the front wheels are stopped with twin hydraulically-actuated drum brakes, while the rear wheel has a back-pedal roller brake. Other options – such as the rain-proof cover, luggage carrier and childseats – will depend on your intended use.

Whatever option you choose, the trike handles securely. The rear half tilts when cornering, so you won't lift a wheel. It also has steering damping on the front wheels.

The Christiania trike is becoming increasingly popular as a commercial vehicle. Long part of the Danish post office fleet, Christiania trikes are also used by Danish brewers Carlsberg as mobile vending platforms. In Britain, Andrea Casalotti uses them in his load-carrying business to deliver everything from wholefoods to medical supplies. Studies have shown that transporter cycles are faster and cheaper than motorised vans in congested urban areas.

christiania bikes

Christiania Bikes have been produced for 10 years on the beautiful Danish island of Bornholm, in the Baltic Sea, and founder Lars Engstrom ensures that it's a strongly community-based business. The workshop is Lars' old farm in the countryside. The company ran out of space after a few years, and his neighbours began to take over some of the production for parts of the trikes. Lillian and Gunnar next door have since become experts in wheel production, while the next farmers along, Jonna and Knud Erik, have turned a pig shed into a assembly workshop for the wheels. In an old supermarket nearby, Ole takes care of the the wood for the boxes. In Østerlars, farmers Lise and Kenn handle the sewing of the covers, child seats and the like. Now Lars is planning to move the main workshop into Rønne, the main city on the island.

Christiania Bikes, Dammegardsvej 22, DK-3782 Klemensker, Denmark. Tel +45 5696 6700 Fax +45 5696 6708. Email info@christianiabikes.com. Website www.christianiabikes.com

Looking for a leisurely tourer that combines full suspension with the elegance and practicality of a continental city bike? Something capable of soaking up the bumps on forest trails, farm tracks and bridleways, yet easy to propel on the tarmac? Then your search is over – meet the Vektor from Utopia.

Designed for gentle rides of up to 100km a day, the Vektor majors on comfort. It's got the long wheelbase of a Dutch roadster and an easily-adjustable handlebar stem for an upright or slightly forward-leaning riding position. The frame is available in three sizes with top-tube, and two with a step-through option.

The Vektor is designed so that you can tune the suspension precisely to your taste. No tools are needed to adjust the telescopic front suspension: the oil-damped rear suspension is also adjustable and you can choose a spring matched to your own weight. The Vektor can carry plenty of luggage: low-riders bolt onto the lower front suspension, and the rear pannier rack is mounted on the rear suspension swing-arm.

The Vektor's main frame tubes are CrMo with an ovalised cross-tube, and the rear suspension's chunky swing-arm is hard-anodised aluminium. For ease of maintenance, moving parts use special plastic bearing bushings and the sub-assemblies are bolted together. Have no worries about the structural integrity of the unorthodox frame – with typical German thoroughness, it's been checked by Manfred Otto's respected testing-house, EFBe of Bochum.

The weight of this comprehensively-equipped bike is about 20kg, and depends on the equipment options selected. There's a staggering choice. For example, you can have a Shimano or Spectro 7-speed hub, the Shimano 4-speed hub, 21-speed Spectro 3x7 hybrid gearing or the 14-speed Rohloff Speedhub. There are similarly wide choices for handlebars, saddles, carriers and lighting systems. A positively Utopian situation.

utopia

Utopia was established by Inge Wiebe and Ralf Klagges in 1982. Their aim was sustainable development, minimising production of toxic chemicals and the pollution caused by unnecessary long-distance transport. Consequently, they source 90% of their equipment in Europe, from manufacturers such as Continental, Lepper, Brooks, Spectro, Rohloff, Magura and Busch & Müller. Likewise, they prefer steel for frames because of its durability and the greater elasticity compared to frames of aluminium. They refuse to use solvent-based paints.

Passionate believers in the upright riding position, Utopia stress its benefits, such as good visibility, an unstrained neck and lightly-loaded wrists. Their component selection reflects this stance: if an item is not compatible with the upright riding position, Utopia won't specify it.

RadRatgeber (Cycle Guide) is an informative and educational guide to the Utopia philosophy and to bikes in general published by the company in German. You can browse this publication on their website, where you can also specify and price a bike on screen. Apart from the Vektor, Utopia produce nine other bikes, including the Nirorad featured in Encycleopedia 99.

Utopia, Kreisstr. 134F, 66128 Saarbrücken, Germany.
Tel +49 681 970360 Fax +49 681 9703611
Email utopia@saarmail.de Website www.utopia-fahrrad.de and www.radratgeber.de

In Germany, a typically-equipped Vektor would cost around DM 4800, or DM 5400 with the Rohloff hub, and prices will vary worldwide.

It's small and, at under 10 kilos, it's light, but like its namesake the Ant Bike can carry many times its own weight. Those 12" wheels don't sacrifice strength; all things being equal, small wheels are structurally stronger than large wheels. And the Ant Bike's rigid frame gives it a ride quality comparable to large-wheeled bikes.

The folding mechanism is among the most user-friendly on any folding bike. There is no cycling origami to wrestle with: with one push of a button the bike collapses in on itself. The manoeuvre is no more complex than folding an umbrella: even the least mechanically-inclined cyclist is comfortable with the Ant Bike. Compacted, the prototype shown here measures 82x72x19cm: the production model will be a little smaller. Unfolding is as simple as folding: the self-locating push-button release mechanism just clicks into place when it reaches the fully open position. Handlebars and stem swivel through 180 degrees and also self-locate.

The Ant Bike is designed as a short- to medium-range commuter and city bike, especially for mixed mode travel – it will go in cars, trains, or boats without problems. When folded, it's easy to trundle along if you don't want to carry it. On the road, the geometry of the bike allows children as well as adults to ride the bike comfortably. The fat slick tyres insulate the rider from lumps and bumps, and if you want even more comfort, a rear-suspension model is available.

The Ant Bike is built from 7000 series double-butted aluminium. The single-speed version has a reasonable gear of 52", and there's also a Shimano 4-speed Auto-D hub gear version, with a gear range from 50 to 92" or 57 to 104", depending on the sprocket size chosen.

One Dot

One Dot P/L are an Australian company dedicated to developing and marketing new product ideas. The original Ant Bike was invented 10 years ago by Perth inventor Jamie Herder. Just over a year ago, One Dot gained the rights to the invention, and since then Aldo Contarino and David Officer of One Dot have been working with Jamie Herder to bring the bike to its present form. Prototypes went on display at the Interbike trade show in 1999. It was thought that consumers might object to the small 12" wheels, yet many people were attracted to the bike for just that reason. With the recent craze for small scooters, small wheels are in vogue.

One Dot P/L, 113 Anzac Hwy, Ashford, Australia 5035. Tel: +61 8 8371 4439 Fax: +61 8 8371 1686 Email: info@one-dot.com

The price of the Ant Bike was still to be arranged at the time of going to press.

Practical rather than heedlessly hedonistic is the Anthrotech philosophy: it's fun to ride, but above all it's a useful transport solution, for families, shopping, touring and more.

The seating position is relatively high for a recumbent tricycle, so that the rider's eyes are level with those of car drivers. The steering geometry isolates the handlebars from road shock and gives light, controlled handling, and the balanced drum brakes on the front 20" wheels give all-weather stopping power. The drums can, optionally, be hydraulically-activated using Magura components – or replaced with Sachs disk brakes for huge reserves of stopping power.

Riders of all sizes and ages feel comfortable on the AnthroTech, and the gearing gives plenty of low ratios. You can decide between the Sachs 3x7 system, or a seven-speed SRAM hub-gear. Clothing is protected by a plastic tube on the top chain run.

The frame is made of steel, sand-blasted and powder-coated, and the main boom, carrier and bottom-bracket housing are all stainless steel. The position of the bottom-bracket can be quickly adjusted for leg-length without having to alter the length of the chain – thanks to a second tensioner below the cross-beam. The AnthroTech weighs around 21.2kg.

Its carrying capacity makes it a fine tourer, and the carrier at the back could easily take a full expedition rucksack and tent – load capacity is up to 30kg. There's also a pannier adapter available for standard cycle panniers, and another adapter can be used to mount a Römer Jockey childseat. Alternatively, a trailer hitch for the popular Weber coupling can also be fitted. Other options include a folding seat which makes getting through doorways easier, a lockable rear fairing, 160W electric-assist, a front fairing, and adaptations for riders with special needs.

The AnthroTech uses mostly standard cycle components, so finding spares away from home is straightforward.

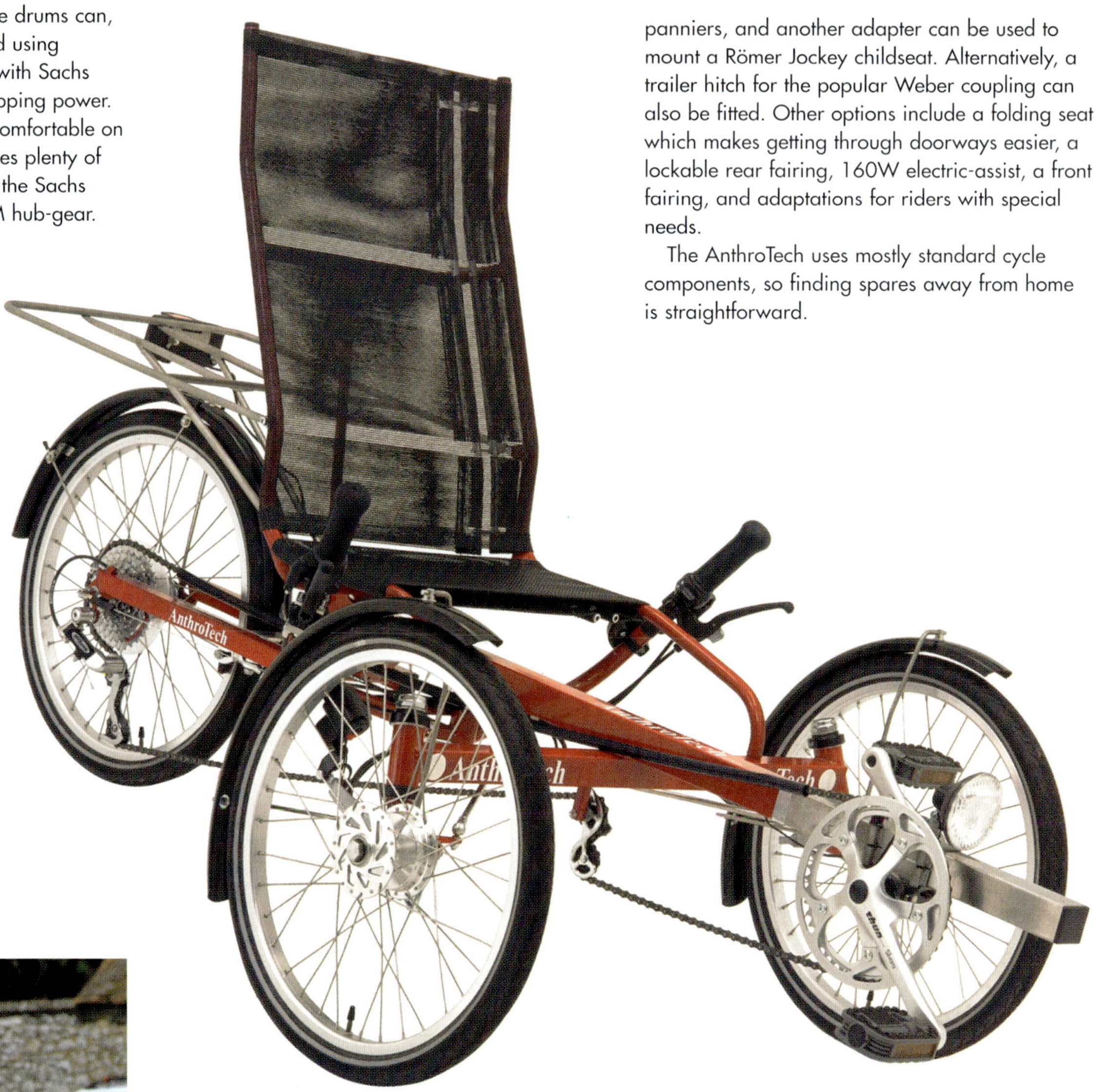

anthroTech leichtfahrzeugtechnik

Anthrotech have been producing trikes since 1993. The founders of the business are Matthias Krauß and Walter Scheidt, who have concentrated in recent years on refining the design, producing a wide range of accessories, and streamlining production. They think it's better to make a single, world-class model, rather than produce a whole range of machines which must share their attention.

Almost all manufacture is done in-house: this gives them full quality control for all processes, and ensures that the local economy benefits from their production activities.

The trikes are available through a large network of dealers in Germany, Austria and Switzerland, and a growing number of dealers in the UK.

AnthroTech Leichtfahrzeugtechnik GmbH , Rothenbergstr. 7, D-90542 Eckental-Frohnhof, Germany.
Tel +44 9126 288 644 Fax +44 9126 288 321
Email anthrotech@anthrotech.de
Website www.anthrotech.de

UK agent: Wheels Within Wheels. Tel +44 161 612 6354

Tarpan & Muli

Practical from the ground up, Bringewald's 'function-bikes' are well-named. These are no-compromise machines, built for load-carrying safely, efficiently and comfortably. Two basic models, the Tarpan and Muli, cater for a wide spectrum of load-carrying needs.

Both models benefit from the '3D' handlebars: adjustable without tools for width, grip position, height and reach. Highly effective two-leg stands support the bikes as they are loaded up, and simultaneously apply a steering lock as the stand is lowered: this prevents the front wheel 'flopping round'. On the Muli, the stand also automatically applies the parking brake for further stability.

Frames are made from heat-treated aluminium, and the unisex frame designs offer adjustability to suit a wide range of riders (1.45-1.95m, 4'9" to 6'5"), and 20" (406) wheels give compact, sturdy designs. All cable runs are neatly arranged in or along the frame tubes, protected from harm. Five- or seven-speed hub gears with back-pedal brakes, and front drum brakes, are standard, with hydraulic drums or disks optional. All function-bikes are thoroughly equipped as standard with full mudguards, spoke-driven dynamo and halogen headlight, rear LED light, two rear-view mirrors, and a very strong folding U-lock. Wherever possible, only non-rusting materials are used.

The Tarpan 'Little Beauty' is the machine for smaller loads, and comes with or without full suspension. Quick-release modular carriers attach to the carrier racks, taking up to 20kg on the front carrier and 35kg on the back, and overall payload rating is 160kg. With the 20" wheels, the luggage has a low centre of gravity, and handling is excellent. On the suspended version, the rear suspension hardness can be adjusted in seconds without tools. The Tarpan weighs between 15 and 18kg – remarkably light for a fully-equipped work-bike.

The Muli series are real heavyweight load carriers – yet the bikes themselves weigh typically at most 20kg, thanks to the aluminium frames. The series runs from the Muli '70', with its three 27x47cm box carriers, through to the Muli 160, with space for 40x60cm boxes. The bikes have lockable ratchet-straps to efficiently secure the boxes, and super-wide two-legged stands – which don't make you jack up the load. The central load platform is incredibly versatile; as well as the standard stacking boxes, any number of modules can be fitted – for example, a seat for two children side-by-side. The Muli 120 'Orange Worker', as another example, fits a full-sized tool cabinet, making it a superb mobile workstation.

bringewald's function-bikes

Horst Bringewald has developed the function-bikes range over several years, testing and developing the range in his home town of Wolfsburg, Germany. He has a strong commitment to pedal-power as a practical alternative to motor vehicles for small and medium-sized loads, and hopes that practical vehicles such as his function-bikes can help persuade big business to replace fleets of vans with more people- and environment-friendly alternatives. Individuals may also be encouraged to use more appropriate mobility devices, such as the function-bikes, rather than the car for an increasing number of journeys.

Bringewald's function-bikes, Wolfsburg, Germany.
Tel.: +49 177 540 74 00
Email bringewald@t-online.de
Website www.bringewald.de

In Germany, the Tarpan costs from Euro 1150 (no suspension) and from Euro 1800 (suspended). Mulis costs from Euro 1350 to over Euro 3000, depending on equipment.

Ten years after the first production Radnabel, two things have happened. First is thorough refinement of the classic design, and second is the development of exciting new versions.

The Radnabel atl-klassik is a supremely practical bike – in German, 'ATL' stands for 'Every day recumbent'. It's very safe, with superb braking, an upright position for a good view in traffic and, in an emergency, the rider's feet can reach the ground in an instant. The pedalling position is excellent, especially on hills, where you can 'crouch' over the bars for extra power.

The atl-klassik is also extremely comfortable. The suspension, using rubber in torsion at the front and an elastomer at the rear, soaks up bumps, and makes high-pressure 20" (406) tyres comfortable. The suspension is zero-maintenance. The seat supports you comfortably in just the right places, without excess area to cause sweating.

Load capacity is excellent. Up to 70kg can be transported on the carriers: 30kg on the front, 20kg on the optional rear carrier, and 10kg in two panniers on a further optional rack below the seat.

Alternatively, childseats could be mounted front and rear, with the load in the two panniers. For weather protection an optional 'Shark' fairing is available. This is a modular system, with sections which can be quickly added together to provide sweat-free protection from the weather for both rider and luggage.

The prototype folding Radnabel, the atl-falter, retains the good qualities of the ATL, and adds a 60-second fold to a 72x84x28cm package. Luggage capacity and comfort are just as impressive, and it's even more agile thanks to the direct steering.

The atl-tandem has a trick up its sleeve: in ten minutes it converts back into a solo bike! In tandem mode, it's a compact, full-suspended vehicle, extremely agile thanks to the direct steering and short wheelbase.

radnabel

Dieter Baumann is a professional musician as well as a bike builder: some say that in both areas of his life he produces works of art. He makes appropriate use of both high-tech and traditional construction methods, hand-brazing tubes and parts, often prepared on sophisticated CNC machines. He is confident in giving a five-year guarantee on all frame components, and generally finishes bikes to order, either as framesets or as complete bikes fitted with whatever components the customer requires. Waiting time is usually just 2-3 weeks.

So far, the atl-tandem is just a one-off, although more can be made to order. Dieter hopes to put the folding bike into production if he receives enough expressions of interest to justify making the complex jigs and tooling required.

Radnabel, Jakobsgasse 19, D-72070 Tübingen, Germany.
Tel/Fax +49 7071 23896

In Germany, a Radnabel ATL Classic costs from around DM 3000 as a frameset, or from around DM 4000 complete, depending on equipment. The folder is expected to cost around DM 5000, and the tandem around DM10,000, with Rohloff hub gear and two disk brakes. The Shark fairing costs around DM 1000.

Clear your mind of all pre-conceived ideas about carrying big loads on a bicycle. Forget about trailers, racks, panniers and unwieldy loads. Think Xtracycle: the bike that hauls.

Imagine stretching your bike by moving the rear wheel back nearly 40 centimetres. Instead of the saddle being closer to the back wheel than to the front, it's now more like halfway between. You've created a load of extra room for cargo behind you, without introducing extra wheels – no sidecar, no trailer and no trike conversion. The FreeRadical is an attachment that does just this: it extends your bike behind the seat tube. With a multitude of places to attach racks, bins and other carrying devices, you can carry everything from timber to tubas, garden tools to groceries, kids to kayaks. And a FreeRadical can be detached easily, so that you get your bike back in its original form. This fold lets the Xtracycle fit in aeroplanes, cars, and bike boxes.

There are advantages galore in the Xtracycle concept. No extra wheels means it's very light. Cargo behind the rider interferes less with the aerodynamics. With no moving parts, it's simple and robust. It carries the bags you already own, whether briefcase, suitcase, rucksack or potato sack. Put it on a road bike and go for a tour. Put in on an MTB and take your gear into the woods for an overnight. Zoom around town and invite a friend to hop on the back. Any competent person with experience of changing cables, and adjusting brakes and gears will be able to install the FreeRadical – it simply bolts in place.

Originally designed for the developing world, Xtracycle is available in several models and is built from TIG-welded chromoly tubing. With a 36-spoke mountain bike wheel, you can carry loads of up to 90kg. The original model, the extrabike, comes with horizontal steel racks that fold out of the way when not in use. The extrabike is available from the company's non-profit partners. It adds 50cm to the length of the bike and enables the machine to be stored on its tail against a wall.

The newer FreeRadical model has a lightweight system of optional plug-in aluminium racks and passenger carrying platforms, and comes with a sturdy top deck of maple. A special edition will be available with a 20" rear wheel. Accessories include extra strong 42-spoke 26" or 20" wheels for even heavier loads, a footplate for increased passenger comfort, and racks that plug in horizontally or fold-down to carry long loads alongside the rider, with accessories to help carry surfboards, windsurfers and kayaks.

xtracycle

The Xtracycle team describe themselves as social and environmental mechanics. They aim to meld the altruism of the charitable enterprise with the efficiency of a market-driven business. They believe that the Xtracycle, with its unique ability to carry cargo but still ride like a regular bike, will forever change the place of the bicycle in the modern transportation mix. They are welders and teachers, who sell Xtracycles to those who can afford them, and teach those who can't how to build their own, through co-operative ventures.

The Xtracycle concept was created by Ross Evans, a graduate in mechanical engineering and Latin American studies. Travelling and working in the developing world, he noted that while bicycles were abundant, they were not as useful as they might be. His response was the Xtracycle.

In 1998 Ross launched the company with Kipchoge Spencer. Based in the foothills of the California Sierras, they are close enough to the mountains to stay tuned into the natural world, yet near enough to the city to stay abreast of urban life.

Xtracycle, LLC, 14618 Tyler Foote Rd., Nevada City, CA 95959, USA
Tel +1 530 470 2388 Fax +1 419 735 1427
Email info@xtracycle.com Website www.xtracycle.com

UK agent: Merlin Matthews: Tel +44 1206 38 2207 Fax +44 1206 38 5729

In the USA, a FreeRadical kit costs $390, including a pair of racks, two Freeloader open-ended saddlebags and the loading deck. Accessory prices are detailed on the Xtracycle website.

In just ten seconds, a full-sized adult tricycle collapses to a tiny package, an ingenious series of pivots, catches and linkages folding neatly together in a tour de force of applied geometry. Those ten seconds represent the pinnacle of over 25 years' design experience. Di Blasi's founder, Mr Rosario Di Blasi, born in 1909, designed this machine with the same skills that have won him numerous patents over decades, and have allowed him and his family to develop one of the largest folding bike companies in the world.

The folding trike weighs just 21.5kg, and the interlocking linkage makes it a simple operation to reach the folded size of 64x62x28.5cm. Just lower the saddle, lower the handlebars, fold in the rear wheel arms, and fold the pedals. Done! Unfolding is just as quick, and results in a full-size seven-speed machine with a wheelbase of 95cm and a track of 70cm, and 16" wheels. A rear carrier takes up to 20kg load.

Di Blasi's bicycle folds even faster – within five seconds. Available either in high-tensile steel or in stainless steel (ideal for marine applications) it folds to 85x22x60cm, and weighs 14.2kg, including five-speed derailleur gearing and full dynamo lighting.

Di Blasi have recently become involved with an exciting initiative to ease traffic congestion. HTM, the company responsible for regional bus services in The Hague, Holland, is working with Di Blasi's importer Plastimo, after HTM conducted a rigorous selection process to find the most suitable folding bike. Bus season-ticket holders receive a free Di Blasi bike, which they can use for the journey between home and bus, and then from bus to their workplace. Over 100 commuters have already taken advantage of this offer.

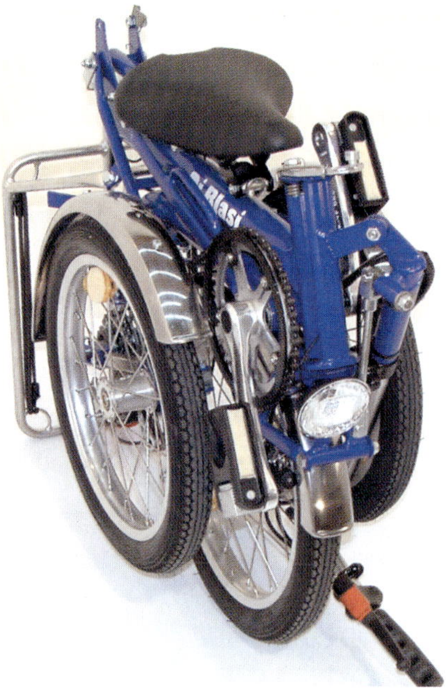

di blasi industriale srl

Di Blasi Industriale has existed for over 25 years. It is based in Sicily, not far from Syracuse. Mr Rosario Di Blasi is an aeronautical engineer by training and former air force pilot officer. His past inventions have included antidecubitus beds and a range of folding mopeds or cyclos, which the Italian air police used for instant mobility on the ground, folding them up to carry them in their helicopters. Both his sons are also trained in aeronautical engineering: Mr Carmelo Di Blasi is responsible for general management and marketing, and Mr Carlo Di Blasi is the manufacturing director. The company now employs around 30 people. To date some 80,000 folding cycles and 25,000 folding auto-cycles have been built. All machines are delivered 100% assembled and about 94% of their value is of European Union origin: this gives several advantages for distributors, including swift delivery, easy and reliable after-sales service, and the chance to reduce stock by up to 75%. Most Di Blasi bikes, trikes and motorised machines go to Europe and the USA, but smaller numbers go to just about every continent.
Di Blasi is represented regularly at all of the major European trade shows. 18 importers share distribution in Europe. Di Blasi bikes are promoted in a variety of markets, including water sports, aviation, business applications, mass-transit operations, and, of course, to cyclists.

Di Blasi Industriale srl, C.da Risicone, Vizzini (CT), Italy.
Tel/Fax +39 095 940 384 Email mail@diblasi.it Website www.diblasi.it

Di Blasi have agents across the world: full contact details and prices are listed on their website.

Nihola Transporter Trike

Load-carriers with the design appeal of the Nihola are rare indeed. It is proof, in metal and plastic, that utility bikes can be anything but utilitarian. But the real quality of the Nihola is the way that the designer appearance hasn't compromised the function: this is one very good load-carrier for shopping, children or business.

The front 'barrel' can carry up to 130kg, and is made from impact-resistant plastic and stainless steel. The round shape noticeably reduces wind resistance. A quickly-fitted raincover with adjustable 'window' keeps children or other payload dry whatever the weather, and doesn't obstruct the rider's view. The frame is powder-coated in a choice of 60 colours, and eight colours are available for the plastic barrel. A removable child bench fits in tidily, with foam cushion and adjustable safety harnesses for two children.

The steering design is particularly sophisticated: unlike many utility trikes, the two front wheels pivot independently. This means you don't have to swivel the whole load as you turn the steering – this makes the Nihola particularly agile. Ackermann geometry means that the wheels don't scrub round the bends. A hydraulic steering damper keeps the handling stable, even at high speeds, and is adjustable to seven levels of 'firmness'.

Other aspects of the design are equally well-specified. Braking is handled by twin drums on the front wheels, and the rear back-pedal (coaster) brake. The drums are activated through a balancing unit, to ensure that left and right brakes act equally. A parking brake on the lever has not been forgotten. Another nice touch is the light-mountings on top of the front mudguards: with front and back lights on either side, the extremities of the trike are clearly marked out for other road users.

The transmission is designed for low maintenance and long life: a five-speed SRAM hub with coaster brake and cartridge bottom bracket. The saddle adjusts over a wide height range, so that the same machine can be used by several members of a family, or several business employees.

Nihola APS

Computer-designed and patented by mechanical engineer Niels Holme Larsen, the first Nihola prototype rolled out in Summer 1998. Several thousand kilometres of testing later, Niels launched the production version. The timing was good: Danish transport policy had swung firmly behind cycling as a practical transport alternative, and the Nihola was just right for the very practical tasks of shopping, child-carrying and deliveries.

Two of Niels' first customers were the Copenhagen Bykological Community Foundation and a green job-sharing scheme. In the meantime, helped by favourable reviews in the Danish press, the Nihola has attracted customers from across Europe.

Nihola APS: Vesterbrogade 137, DK-1620 Kobenhavn V, Denmark. Tel +45 3322 7905 Fax +45 3322 7907 Email nihola@nihola.dk Website www.nihola.dk

In Denmark, the Nihola trike costs from around Dkr 7995, and prices will vary worldwide.

VÉLOS EN VILLE
VÉLOS EN VILLE
VÉLOS EN VILLE

FAMILY CYCLING

FAHRRAD FÜR ALLE
FAHRRAD FÜR ALLE
FAHRRAD FÜR ALLE

KIDS GO FREE!

Cyclists who hang up their trouser clips at the first patter of tiny feet are doing themselves and their children a disservice. They are denying their young family one of the joys of life. In an age where few children under the age of ten are allowed to travel by themselves, cycling as a family can be a liberation just as much as a pleasure. Children love cycling. It allows them to be in touch with their environment, feeling the fresh air on their faces and soaking up the sounds and the scents of the world around them. How much nicer than a day spent hot, bored and cramped, strapped into the back of the family car, or stuck at home in front of the video or the games console.

Children who grow up in the back seat of a car will long for the opportunity to move to the front row and drive for themselves when they're older. By bicycle, children experience individual mobility in a positive way. The mental stimulation and physical exercise inherent in cycling brings self-confidence and awareness to growing minds and bodies. You'll show other would-be cycling families that it can be done, and you'll help increase the demand for streets safe enough for children to cycle in. Streets with reduced traffic volumes, lower traffic speeds and traffic-free sections to create breathing space for the whole community.

Whether simply for pleasure or for purpose, with the right equipment and a bit of planning, most journeys with children can be safely undertaken without the need of a car. Experience shows that, the less you use your car, the less you want to use it, and it'll become more of a burden than the personal freedom enhancer it was once hailed as.

Cycling with your family doesn't begin and end with the childseat. Products are available to suit all ages and sizes of children from newborn onwards. Children grow up fast and their needs will change as they do – so you may find that, once your kids have got the cycling bug, you'll progress through a whole range of solutions for keeping your family a-wheel. In the following pages you'll find all you need to suit your riding style and your pocket. Baby pods, childseats, family tandems, trailer bikes, adult tricycles all the way up to a four-wheeled, four-seater pedal-powered replacement for the family rust bucket.

The range of cycles and equipment for parents to transport their children is better than ever in terms of options and quality. And the choice of lightweight, easy-to-use solo bikes for children has never been so good.

As in any other area of life, you'll need to think carefully about your needs, and those of your children. Trailers and trailer cycles which attach to an adult bike are very practical child carrying solutions for those who do not always cycle as a family. Simply detach them when you need to make a solo journey. Tandem trikes can carry two children and all the luggage, and make for a formidable road presence.

Encycleopedia can't hope to cover the entire range of what is available. But we can showcase some less well-known, high-quality designs that you won't have come across elsewhere – products which will make cycling with your family a practical pleasure.

But, be warned, we can't promise it'll put an end to cries of 'Are we there yet?'

You're never too young. At the age of just nine years old, Alexander Robert Gadd became the youngest person to cycle from Land's End at the southern tip of England to John O'Groats at the north-eastern tip of Scotland on 28 August 1993. Over the 13 days it took him to complete the trip, he averaged 62 miles per day.

Large family? Just how many can you get on a bike? On 30 June 1988, no fewer than 19 members of the Jago sports club at Semarang, Central Java held themselves together on a bicycle for a distance of 200 metres.

A tricycle made for three: David Moore of Rosemead California built the largest tricycle in the world for Arthur Dillon and his family. Called the Dillon Colossal Tricycle, it's 6.7m (22 feet) long, the two back wheels are 3.35m (11ft) high and the front wheel is 1.77m (5ft 10 inch) in diameter. With a set of cranks for Dad only, top speed must be pretty low, and Venice Beach is about the only place you'll see it cruising.

In 1976, Denmark made it mandatory for local authorities to ensure the protection of children from traffic danger on their school journey. Since then, cycling has become the main means of transport for young people. Over 60% of Danish children now cycle to school, compared with less than 2% in the UK.

During the bicycle boom of the 1890s in France, the French President regularly tandemed around the Bois de Boulogne every morning with his wife and children.

In Denmark, using your bike to transport your children is just a natural part of life. The Dolphin child trailer, produced by A Winther A/S, won the prestigious 'ID-Design Award' in 1997. This annual design competition is the most highly regarded in the Danish community. Previous winners include the LEGO construction system.

In India, cycle rickshaws are regularly used for doing the 'school run'. A raised platform with bench seats between the two rear wheels takes up to a dozen children at a time. Quite a load for the driver!

You don't have a choice. Cycling with your children means buying the right gear, for safety, comfort and economy. Quality equipment will last a generation of children – and still be going strong to give pleasure to another family. Burley are one of the few companies that provide quality child-carrying solutions for children of all ages and sizes, from trailers through trailer-bikes to tandems.

The youngest passengers will go by trailer, and Burley are trailer experts: over 20 years of experience and design refinement has informed their present range. The flagship trailer is the two-seater d'Lite, mainstay of many families for decades. It's kept up with the times, and the latest version takes full advantage of new materials and technologies.

Aluminium tubing and dished alloy wheels keep the overall weight down to 20lb (9.1kg), with a maximum carrying capacity of 100lb (45.5kg).

The seats are made of strong mesh to give good ventilation, and are curved back at the top so that child passengers can comfortably wear their safety helmets. This is a trailer where the details have been thought through: soft-edge nylon straps on the five-point safety harness prevent chafing where they contact the skin. An 'anti-dive' seat pad along the front edge of the seat keeps little behinds from sliding forward.

The 'Wide Screen 2-in-1 Cover' uses a clear vinyl window over a mesh screen at the front, and tinted side and rear windows. With the front window rolled up the mesh screen allows plenty of ventilation while keeping out unwanted insect life. A small tab is sewn on at the back for attaching a safety light.

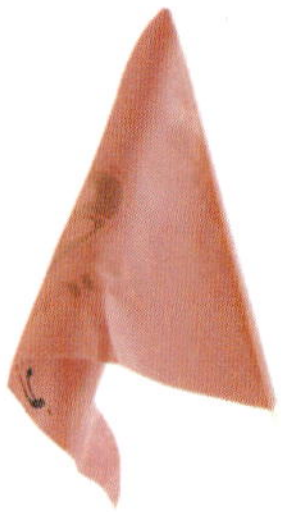

It all folds down into a package measuring 34x32x10".

Families with one young child are catered for with the Burley Solo, a scaled-down and lighter single-passenger version of the Burley D'Lite, with an overall width of 25" and a weight of 16lb (7.3kg).

Accessories for any Burley trailer include the 'Walk 'n Roller' stroller/jogger kit, and an alternative hitch mechanism to fit bikes with non-standard rear ends.

When your child is ready to pull his or her own weight, it's time to move to the next stage: the Piccolo trailer-cycle. Built in powder-coated cro-mo tubing, with plenty of adjustment in the seat and handlebars, it will fit any child up to a weight of around 85lb (38kg). Six-speed twist-shift gearing will get your child used to controlling the transmission, before going solo on two wheels.

The Piccolo hitches to the purpose-built 'Moose' rack, providing a sturdy attachment with the pivot right above the rear axle, so the Piccolo closely follows the line of the lead bike. The hitch pivots on proper adjustable ball bearings, so there's no disconcerting 'play' or shimmy. The Piccolo can be attached or removed from the Moose rack in seconds with no tools, and panniers can be fitted to the rack even with the Piccolo attached. The screw-down attachment mechanism has an additional back-up safety lock to reduce the risk of accidental detachment. The Piccolo is recommended for children approximately four to ten years old, with an ideal captain-to-child weight ratio of 2 to 1 or greater.

Even when your child happily rides his or her own bike, for longer rides it's hard to beat the efficiency of a tandem. Burley's tandem range covers everything from affordable Zydeco family tandems to high-end tourers and racers like the Paso Doble. Both parents can ride the tandem, with offspring on a Piccolo or in a trailer, then as the children grow, they can migrate to the back seat, perhaps, at first, with a kiddy-crank adapter to bring pedals closer to the saddle.

Stoker comfort is a big thing at Burley – almost every model in the range has a 'Softride' option, placing the stoker's saddle on a flexible composite beam that gently absorbs road shocks large and small. Most models can also be equipped with S+S couplings, which allow the frame to split down into sections small enough to pack into a suitcase – a great boon when taking a tandem touring using public transport.

Frames are hand-welded from USA-made True Temper cromoly tubing. Frames and forks are guaranteed for life. Wheels have a hard life on a tandem, so Burley take great care here, too. All models (except the Zydeco) use Wheelsmith stainless steel spokes, and every wheel is trued and tensioned by hand.

burley design cooperative

Burley Design Cooperative was founded in 1975 by cycling enthusiasts who dreamed of a fair and decent workplace, dedicated to environmental protection and human-powered transportation. From these ideals grew Burley Design Cooperative. Burley has been cooperatively owned since 1978.

The 'cooperative' part of the name means that each employee owns an equal share of the business. As worker owners, the employees bring an uncommon degree of pride and attention to their work. They test relentlessly to improve designs, ensuring that every product that rolls out of the Eugene, Oregon facility meets their standards. There is simply no better way to assure quality than to have products made by people with a stake in their business and a passion for what they do.

Wherever possible, Burley use ecological manufacturing methods, such as recycling, and even 'precycling'. They order materials such as tubing in specially-cut lengths to reduce the recycling load, saving both energy and raw materials. Their building, which was designed with the input of the workers, has sunroofs built into the ceiling to bring in natural light. This makes for a nicer workplace, particularly for those doing sewing as they have to do very detailed work – and it also saves energy.

Burley's work environment is structured to promote worker empowerment, decentralisation, and small team focus. These concepts, which are now widely recognised as superior organisational models, have been the foundation of their success for 20 years. Whether assembling a trailer or participating in co-op decision-making, they truly enjoy the challenge of running a business.

Burley Design Cooperative, 4020 Stewart Road, Eugene, OR 97402-5408 USA. Tel +1 541 687 1644 Fax +1 541 687 0436
Email burley@burley.com Website www.burley.com

Prices in the USA are around $399 for the D'Lite, $289 for the Solo and $349 for the Piccolo. Tandems start at around $1099

Tandems are perfect for families: adult and child can ride together in safety and at the same speed. The Two's Company is more versatile than most. With 20" (406) wheels, the rear seat will go low enough for a child to reach the pedals, while the long seatpin adjusts to fit an adult rider.

Saddle height front and rear can be changed instantly with quick-releases, so mum or dad can take it in turns to do the school run. The Two's Company will cope with inside leg lengths of 27.5" to 38" at the front and 24.5" to 33" at the rear. Oversized steel tubing keeps the frame sturdy and stiff, even with two adults aboard. It's shorter than most tandems, however, which means that it will fit across the back of a car on a standard rack.

Drum brakes offer maintenance-free and effective stopping in all weathers, while the five-speed hub gear provides bombproof reliability. It's this ruggedness and versatility that has made the Two's Company popular with bike hire centres.

To introduce younger children to the pleasures of cycling, Brilliant Bicycles have two trailer cycles, the U+1 and the two-seater U+2, each of which will accommodate riders with a leg length as little as 17.5". Both cycles have a 7-speed twistgrip derailleur gear, so as to let your children pedal more effectively. And both can be fitted with a luggage platform for carrying groceries or camping gear. The two-rear-wheel set-up adds stability and eliminates the twisting force on the towing bike's seatpost.

Brilliant Bicycles use the same design for their Add+1, a version of the U+1 aimed at balance-impaired youths or adult riders. As with the other trailers, this is attached with a universal joint and detachable safety wire, so the trailer can't separate accidentally from the towing bike.

brilliant bicycles

Brilliant Bicycles is a division of Pashley Cycles, the Stratford-on-Avon based company with an eclectic range of handbuilt bikes ranging from classic roadsters and Moulton APBs to trials bikes. The Brilliant range itself is made of up of bicycles previously made by Cresswell Engineering, which Pashley acquired in 1997. Models include the Two's Company, U+1, U+2 and Add+1, and also two folding bikes: the lightweight Micro and the robust Foldit. Both of the folders and Two's Company have a long history; they are based on designs licensed from Peter Radnall.
Brilliant Bicycles is also a cycle shop in Berwick-upon-Tweed in Northumberland, and it stocks most of the Brilliant range and many other bikes from Pashley. Test rides can be arranged by appointment, and the Brilliant staff have particular expertise in dealing with bicycles for special needs cyclists.

Pashley Cycles, Stratford-upon-Avon, CV37 9NL, England.
Tel +44 1789 292 263 Fax +44 1789 414 201
Email enquiries@pashley.co.uk Website www.pashley.co.uk

The Two's Company costs £599 in the UK, and prices will vary worldwide.

The school bus doesn't have to be petrol-powered: just mix together a heavy-duty transport trike, a bit of imagination and some sound engineering and there it is – safe, non-polluting and fun! This is just one of the custom 'Gustav W' trikes made by the Fahrradwerkstatt team. Basing their designs on a robust tricycle chassis, they can undertake just about any special adaptation within reason.

There are four basic models and a trailer. All trikes have powder-coated steel frames, with generously-dimensioned taper roller bearings at the central pivot, and height-adjustable handlebars. The 20" (406) front wheels use hydraulically-activated Sachs drum brakes, with a parking brake. The 26" rear wheel usually has a back-pedal brake, built into the Sachs five- or seven-speed hub gears. A rear luggage carrier comes as standard on every model. Maximum load-carrying capacity is rated at 250kg. The machines are all exactly one metre wide – overall length varies between 225 and 245cm. Options available for all models include steering dampers, special colours, Heinzmann electric-assist, and Magura Louise disk brakes.

The boxes and bodywork are made of waterproof birch plywood, and can be custom-designed to order. The Gustav W Shopper has a moderate-sized front box, and is designed as a family vehicle – the flexible front area is perfect for children or shopping. The Transport is the Shopper's big brother: with a huge 120x80cm load area, and optional lockable and waterproof cover, it's ideal for business use – and the box offers a huge advertising area for your livery. The Rikscha is a high-performance people-carrier with striking styling and plenty of advertising space on the bodywork. And the Promotion is a mobile vending unit with a useful fold-out shelf area – configured to customer order.

A very useful trailer rounds off the Gustav W range. With steel frame, alloy 26" wheels and a robust Weber coupling, it carries up to 50kg in its food-grade plastic box.

die fahrradwerkstatt der gustav werner stiftung zum bruderhaus

Die Fahrradwerkstatt der Gustav Werner Stiftung zum Bruderhaus translates as 'The Bicycle Workshop of the Gustav Werner Foundation at the Bruderhaus'. They have employed and trained long-term unemployed workers for over ten years: the challenge of producing high-quality and robust work-trikes and trailers offers excellent opportunities for training in both craftwork and business skills.

Workers are organised into small groups, giving each worker a real sense of achievement and of responsibility, fostering self-confidence. Amongst the supporters of the Bicycle Workshop are the national Employment Office, the Deacon of Württemberg's charity, and regional and local government authorities.

Die Fahrradwerkstatt der Gustav Werner Stiftung zum Bruderhaus: Tübinger Str. 89, D-72762 Reutlingen, Germany. Tel +49 7121 930 7220 Fax +49 7121 930 72218 Email info@die-fahrradwerkstatt.de Website www.die-fahrradwerkstatt.de

In Germany, Gustav W. trikes cost from 1394 Euros, and trailers from 304 Euros. Prices will vary worldwide.

We've found the missing link! The Like-a-bike from Germany is a remarkable play vehicle for children from just two years old – far too young to ride a 'proper' bike, but not too small to enjoy the dynamics of movement and balance.

It's the perfect early introduction to cycling. At first, your child will use it like a hobby-horse, at least one foot firmly on the ground. As confidence develops, they'll begin to lift both feet, scooting forward and balancing, maybe dabbing a foot to the floor occasionally if the bike tips. Soon, they'll be swooping round with panache. They'll also be having a whale of a time, not least because this is no heavy, unresponsive child's bike: it weights just 3.5kg.

As your child grows, the saddle can be adjusted for height. The three settings cover a range of 33 to 39cm saddle height, which suits children up to about five years old. The saddle cover is easily removable and fully washable. A leather cover is available to order.

When your child has out-grown the Like-a-bike, they'll take to riding a full bicycle instantly, as if it's the most natural thing in the world. Balance and steering hold no fears: they can concentrate instead on pedalling and brakes!

The Like-a-bike is built to withstand the worst rough-and-tumble its young riders can dish out. The frame is built from high-grade birch plywood, treated either with high-quality paint or a hard wax coating – all finishes naturally satisfy strict child safety regulations. It can also be delivered with the frame untreated, so that a child could paint his or her own Like-a-bike, before it is wax-sealed.

All the details are child-safe and robust: the steering is damped by felt strips, which also prevent small fingers getting caught between fork and frame. The 31cm wheels run on quality grease-free bronze bearings, and are fitted with solid rubber tyres which won't mark the floor when it's ridden indoors.

Kokua Holzspielzeug GmbH

Like-a-bikes are made by Kokua Holzspielzeug in Aachen, Germany, a small business run by the Mertens family. They realised that the best way to teach a child to cycle is not to use stabilisers, which simply prevent the child developing a proper sense of balance, but rather to remove the cranks entirely. With most children's bikes, that still leaves a heavy steel frame – dead weight can soon kill a child's enthusiasm. The answer is the Like-a-bike.

Learning the Like-a-bike is a great psychological boost: from the very first attempt your child can make independent progress, without adult help, using just their innate ability and co-ordination. They'll be proud of this positive achievement, and will revel in independent mobility, ensuring the Like-a-bike's lasting appeal.

Kokua Holzspielzeug: Wallstr. 15-17, D-52064 Aachen, Germany. Tel +49 241 406 497 Fax +49 241 384 42
Email kokua@t-online.de Website http://home.t-online/home/kokua

In Germany, the Like-a-bike costs around DM 279, and prices will vary worldwide.

Transporting a tandem isn't easy: you may need a special rack to put one on a car, while getting one aboard a train, 'plane or taxi can be difficult or impossible. With the Bike Friday range, of course, all you need is a couple of suitcases.

The entry-level two-seater is the Family Tandem, which has easily adjustable seat tubes and posts to fit riders from 4'10" to 6'5" (1.5m to 2m) up front and from 3' to 6'2" (0.9m to 1.9m) at the rear. An optional child stoker kit accommodates small riders at the back. Once fitted, your child's seat is lowered to reach the pedals, rather than having the pedals raised to reach your child, as on large-wheeled adult tandems. This makes getting on and off easier.

The Traveller is a lighter (sub-40lb), higher specification version of the Family Tandem; it too will accommodate riders of almost any size. If you have two children, or want two adults and one child to ride one bike, the Family Tandem Triple fits the bill. Both centre and rear seats can fit riders as short as 3' (0.9m), while the rear will fit riders up to 6'2" (1.9m). Total load capacity for all three riders is conservatively set at 400lb (181kg). And even though it folds to fit in two cases, the Family Tandem Triple is one of the most affordable triplets around.

Tourists will want the Tandem Two'sday, which will take tyres as wide as 1.75" (45mm) for rough rides or down to 1" (25mm) for smooth surfaces. It can be customised to your requirements, with your choice of racks, gearing, and even an Aria drum brake. The Two'sday ST model, meant for fast road riding or light touring, has larger wheels that will take narrower tyres.

Like tandems, many recumbents are cumbersome to transport. Not the Sat R Day. Like all Bike Fridays it goes into a suitcase and it will quick-fold to go on a train, bus or car boot. It's

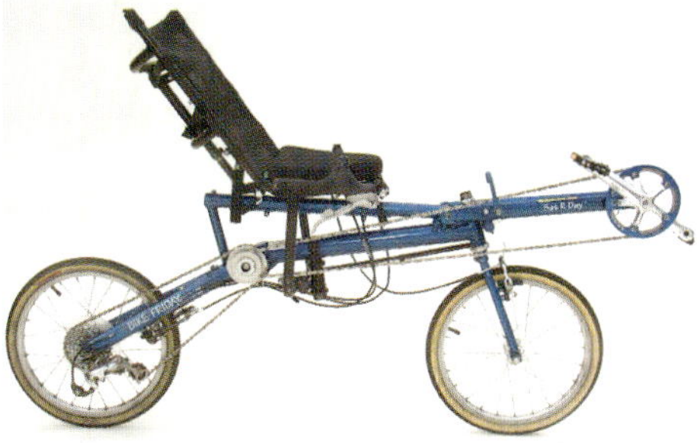

very comfortable, with a padded, web-backed seat, which has an elastomer suspension unit underneath. You have the choice of above- or under-seat steering.

atp green gear cycling

The designer of the Bike Friday, Hans Scholz, was inspired to make a better folder when he took a bike with him on a trip to Europe in 1985. The limitations became quickly apparent, and he determined to make a folder that really did ride like a performance full-size machine. The solo machines are featured elsewhere in this Encycleopedia.

It's a machine that inspired intense customer loyalty, and this is fostered on the Bike Friday website. Bike Friday owners have access to a special section of this site, the Bike Friday Web Club, where they can connect with other owners to organise events, join user groups, arrange home stay exchanges, publish adventure journals and more. Since members list private information inside the Web Club, it is password-protected.

Bike Friday, Green Gear Cycling Inc, 3364 W 11th Ave, Eugene, OR 97402 USA. Tel +1 541 687 0487 Fax +1 541 687 0403 Email info@bikefriday.com Website www.bikefriday.com

In the USA, prices range from $995 for the Family Tandem up to $3195 for a top-of-the-range Tandem Two'sday ST. Prices will vary worldwide.

The Lightfoot Roadrunner is a great do-anything cycle: from touring to trailer-towing, from commuting to child-carrying. The combination of tricycle stability, an large load platform and a weather-protective fairing option make it a truly versatile transport solution.
The Roadrunner is built of aircraft-grade cro-mo steel, and weighs around 58lbs (25kg) complete. The frame can be ordered either modular, which splits into three section for transport, or as a single unit. Turn radius is around 4 feet (1.2m). Single-wheel drive is standard, and the two-stage transmission gives 147 possible gearing combinations, with a low of around 9. This is ideal for pulling heavy trailers, or for cranking easily uphill with a full touring load. The 28 (71cm) square cargo platform can hold touring bags, or could be equipped with a waterproof, lockable box or a child seat. The standard Lightfoot seats are well-padded and comfortable, and are quickly and easily adjustable for leg length and seat recline.
The Roadrunner is one of five standard models in the Lightfoot line. Its nearest relative is the Transporter Trike: slightly longer, and with a larger cargo area, this is a fine machine for everyday urban chores, with all-season stability. The strong shelves over the rear wheels make the load platform even more versatile: long loads can be accommodated either across the width of the rack, or along the length of the trike.
For even more security on corners and poor surfaces, four-wheelers are available. The single-person Cricket is a very stable vehicle which carries up to a gross weight of 500lbs. Its big brother is the Microcar, a side-by-side lightweight quadricycle, designed to reliably transport two people and plenty of luggage efficiently and safely, for recreation, shopping or shuttling children.
A single driver can pedal the Microcar easily. The pilot (captain) controls all braking and steering and each rider has independent shifting and pedalling.
Lightfoots two-wheeler is the Explorer, a very comfortable and stable long-wheelbase recumbent.

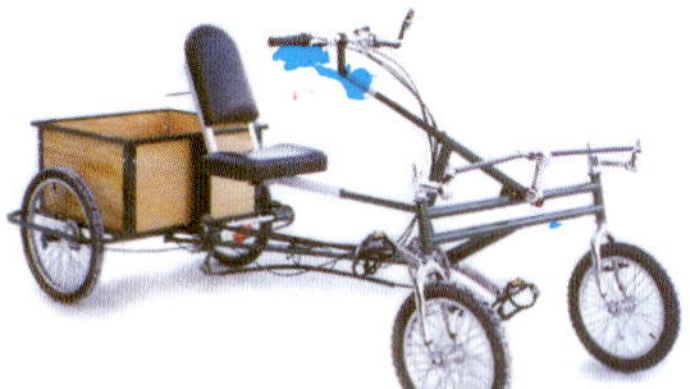

lightfoot cycles

Lightfoot Cycles mission is to create truly useful vehicles. Their machines aim to make a useful contribution to a more sustainable future, providing practical, low-impact family transport. As a consequence, most vehicles use a recumbent position for aerodynamics, comfort and braking safety. The cycles are designed to be affordable through simplicity, rather than by cutting corners on quality which might compromise the usefulness of the machines. Standard components are used wherever possible, simplifying maintenance and upgrades. Multi-track vehicles, for example, all use standard rear wheels rather than special one-sided hubs.
As well as the five standard models, Lightfoot Cycles are happy to build custom machines: these include versions for extremely short or tall riders, arm-powered versions, extra-heavy duty industrial machines, and special trailers. An ongoing project is the PET hand-cranked tricycle, designed to be built from available materials in the developing world.
Lightfoot Cycles: 179 Leavens Road, Darby, Montana 59829 USA.
Tel +1 406 821 4750 Fax +1 406 821 0963
Email info@lightfootcycles.com Website www.lightfootcycles.com

In the USA, Lightfoot cycles cost from $1350 for the Explorer to $2950 for the Microcar. The Roadrunner costs from $1650.

Trailers are a versatile and convenient way of transporting young children by bike. With the Koolite, it couldn't be easier, with some innovative improvements to a tried-and-tested design.

The new hitch puts the pivot point right behind the towing bike's rear wheel, rather than offset to one side, which means that the trailer faithfully follows the path of the bike it's attached to, rather than cutting corners. New users sometimes have trouble clipping kerbs – they won't with the Koolite. Towing is also a little easier, because there are no off-centre forces to cause tyre scrub.

The new hitch and towing arm aren't the only improvements over Kool-Stop's Original trailer, upon which the Koolite is based. Lightweight aluminium and chrome-moly tubing help shave 4lb (1.8kg) from the weight, while aluminium wheel rims aren't just lighter; they'll keep their looks better, too.

Many of the features that continue to make the Original popular have been retained for the Koolite. Children are held securely with five-point safety harnesses, while a single buckle on each harness makes entry and exit quick and easy. The seats are adjustable and can be set facing each other or forward. Visibility from inside the trailer is great: the windows are large, and in hot weather the front and rear windows can be rolled up, leaving a mesh at the front to keep out insects and debris. The trailer itself is very visible on the road: it is bright yellow, with reflective material all around, and has a seven-foot safety flag.

As on the Original, the Koolite's wheels are cambered inwards at 5° to provide better stability. They're not dished, which makes them stronger, but they are quick-release so that the trailer can pack down small. When the side panels are folded down and the towing arm and wheels stowed inside, the package measures just 31x28x10". Since it weighs only 23.5lb (10.7kg), it's not too hard to carry like this. Unfolded its capacity is 100lb and the track of wheels is 30", making it suitable for any cycle path.

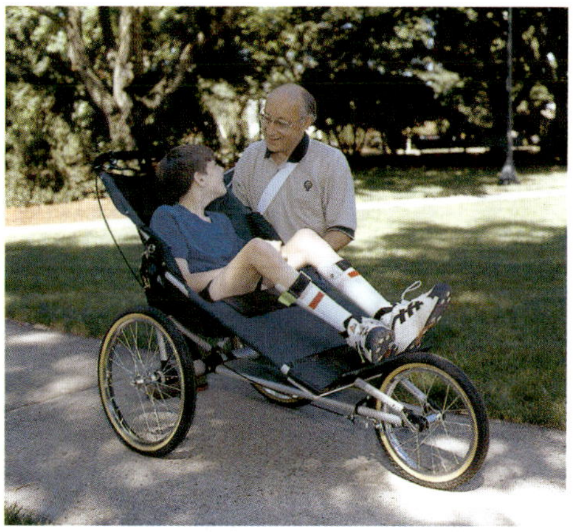

kool stop

Kool-Stop produce a range of trailers for all applications. As well as the Original and Koolite, they offer the Papoose Caboose and the Lil' Trooper, forward-facing child trailers that fold down for storage or transportation like their stablemates.
For luggage, Kool-Stop have three models. The two-wheeled 100lb-capacity Kargo Van is designed for camping gear or groceries. For rugged off-road riding, the one-wheeled Kool-Mule enables a mountain bike without racks to carry up to six panniers. The Wilderbeast is similar to the Kool-Mule but has a large hold-all platform rather than multiple pannier mounts; it will still carry a couple of panniers, however.
Kool-Stop also produce child strollers, and this has resulted in some cross-over with their cycle trailers. Both the Papoose Caboose and Original trailer can be turned into a stroller at a moment's notice with the addition of a Runner kit – a push-handlebar and extra wheel.
Kool-Stop made their name with their brake blocks; these are featured elsewhere in this Encyclopedia.

Kool-Stop International Inc, PO Box 3480, La Habra, CA 90631, USA. Tel +1 714 738 4973 Fax +1 714 992 6191
Website www.koolstop.com

In the USA, the Koolite will cost around $450 and prices will vary worldwide.

Ordinary tandems are great, but they do have drawbacks. The stoker's view is dominated by the pilot's backside, the pilot cannot see the stoker, and the bike is cumbersome to ride solo. The Pino from Hase Spezialräder overcomes all these problems in fine style.

The Pino's pilot sits at the back in a normal riding position while the stoker enjoys a suspended recumbent seat over the small front wheel. Both riders have a clear view of the road ahead, the pilot can see the stoker, and the machine's short wheelbase gives it the nimbleness of a standard bike. Unlike some tandems, either rider can freewheel independently. In fact, the front rider does not have to pedal at all.

At 24kg the Pino is relatively light for a tandem of this type. It's well equipped for town and country riding, with 21-speed derailleur gearing, twin hydraulic brakes and dynamo lighting. And for even greater comfort, there is an optional front suspension fork. It's a great machine for collecting somebody from a station, for physical rehabilitation, or as a family bike that grows with the child. It's also an excellent tourer, capable of carrying standard panniers on the rear rack, plus low-riders under the front seat.

Hase Spezialräder also make a pair of sporty long-wheelbase tricycles. Both trikes are adjustable for riders from 1.3 to 2m in height, have under-seat steering and can carry luggage behind the seat. The KettWiesel (featured in last year's Encycleopedia) is a simple, lightweight trike, designed for three-wheel fun. It has 20" wheels all round, a 7-speed wide-ratio derailleur and twin V-brakes. An optional 30 litre bag can be fitted behind the seat, and the front forks can take a low-rider rack. At a mere 16kg including lighting system and mudguards, it's exceptionally light for a long-wheelbase recumbent trike. For even more fun, two KettWiesels can be converted into a tandem via a special adapter kit.

The Lepus is a more luxurious 21-speed trike with 26" rear wheels and a 20"

front wheel. Frame and seat suspension make this a very comfortable machine, and three hydraulic brakes provide plenty of stopping power. There's a luggage platform behind the seat and an optional childseat adapter. But best of all, the Lepus folds down to a package 120x85x66cm – compact enough to fit into the boot of a small car.

hase spezialräder

Marec Hase, founder of Hase Spezialräder, began creating innovative cycles at the age of 13. He trained as a precision engineer and achieved great success in a government-sponsored youth enterprise competition. Now, still in his mid-twenties, he runs Hase Spezialräder from his factory in Bochum in the heart of the Ruhr.

Hase works closely with organisations for people with disabilities and specialises in adapting machines to suit their needs. In this respect, the Lepus is especially versatile. Options include a lowered bottom bracket, special mounting plates for pedals, suspension fork, crank shortener, safety belts, one-hand operation and electrical assistance.

All Hase cycles are handmade, have powder-coated steel frames and can be customised to your special requirements by the manufacturer.

Hase Spezialräder, Karl Friedrich-Straße 88, D-44795 Bochum.
Tel +49 (02 34) 9 46 90 50 Fax +49 (02 34) 9 46 90 59
E-mail: info@hase-spezialraeder.de
Website: www.hase-spezialraeder.de

A family trailer is a great way to transport kids, and the Danish manufacturer Winther offers a fine example. The Dolphin can carry two youngsters up to about six years old, and converts into a versatile child buggy for walking or jogging. It has plenty of room for extra luggage (60 litres) and can carry a load of up to 45kg. Passenger comfort is assured by elastomer suspension, widely-spaced 20" (406) wheels, shower-proof hood and insect net. The trailer's aerodynamic shape reduces wind noise for those inside while cutting the drag for the cyclist. The rigid base with its low seating position and wide wheel base has been designed to ward off impact, thus affording the children maximum protection. Safety features also include a parking brake, and the Dolphin trailer has been approved by the TÜV test institute in Germany.

Weighing 13kg, the Dolphin is light yet durable, thanks to its aluminium and plastic construction and quality components. For example, the wheels have alloy rims, stainless spokes and sealed-bearing alloy hubs. And when not in use the trailer folds down without tools, forming an easily stored package measuring 101x78x39cm. For protection against the weather if you're storing the trailer assembled, there is a new rain cover, the Dolphin Garage.

Winther also offer a Donkey trailer for shopping or touring. The Donkey trailer is narrow enough to pass through most doorways, up stairways or onto public transport. Its capacious 65 litre box is wipe-clean, being made of frost-resistant plastic. The frame is powder-coated steel and guaranteed for five years. It weighs 11.9kg and has 16" wheels. The Donkey has an additional jockey-wheel so that it can be parked upright. The tow-bar is carefully designed to leave the bike's rear carrier free, so that panniers or a childseat can still be fitted.

a. winther a/s

A. Winther A/S is a Danish family company founded by blacksmith Anders Winther in 1932. In the beginning Winther manufactured toboggans, but soon diversified into children's tricycles and scooters, which established the Winther brand name. In 1947, the production of two-wheeled bicycles for children began. Then, in 1986, the first Winther adult bicycle was introduced. For almost 20 years A. Winther A/S has developed and manufactured trikes especially for institutions such as nursery schools, day-care centres and kindergartens. The newest member of the product line is the aerodynamic Dolphin child trailer, which won the Danish Design Award in 1997.
Production facilities at A. Winther A/S have been environmentally-approved, and the company uses powder coating, the most environmentally-friendly type of lacquering available.

A. Winther A/S, Rygesmindevej 2, DK 8653 Them, Denmark. Tel +45 8684 7288 Fax +45 8684 8528
Email win@a_winther.dk
Websites www.wintherbikes.com, www.a-winther.com, www.winther-cykler.dk

In Denmark, the Dolphin costs from DKK 5.800, and the Donkey from DKK 1700. Prices will vary worldwide.

Family cycling is rarely easier or safer than when your child rides with you on a tandem. Compared to riding on separate bikes, you can ride farther and faster, and you don't need to panic in traffic. The Compagnon tandem has another advantage: your child gets to sit up front.

This gives your child an unobstructed view of the road ahead, rather than a view of your back. And since you sit higher up, you still get a clear view from the rear seat. Your child can even take a hand in the steering – though the adult's bars, which are connected to the forks by a steering arm, are wider, giving you greater leverage and allowing you to guide or override your child.

By sitting in the 'driving seat', your child will feel more involved in the ride. This is more interesting and helps develop an awareness of the road, and of how to behave in traffic. As your child will be steering with you, it can even help develop a sense of balance, which is invaluable for young children when they begin riding their own bikes.

The Compagnon fits children aged from four to ten. Quick-release seatpost bolts mean that the saddle heights are easily adjustable, whether to fit a different-sized child or a different adult at the back. For growing families, the Compagnon is especially useful. With a childseat behind your saddle, and an Add+Bike trailer bicycle fitted to the rear rack, one parent can set off with three children aboard.

The Compagnon is built from steel tubing and has a maintenance-free SRAM Spectro P5 hub

gear. Wheels are 24", and are stopped by V-brakes front and rear. One nice touch is that there's a bell for your child as well as for you.

robert hoening spezialfahrzeuge

Alongside his family cycling products, Robert Hoening specialises in offering pedal-powered solutions for disabled riders or passengers. The Rollfiets (Duet in English-speaking countries) wheelchair tandem is one of the best known. The front half is an ergonomically-designed wheelchair with drum brake hubs, while the rear is a step-through bicycle, forming a tricycle that detaches in the middle to leave the wheelchair free for 'pedestrian' use.

For riders with mobility but some balance problems, Robert Hoening offers T-Bikes, upright 'tadpole' trikes with two wheels at the front. They are available in four different sizes, from pre-school children to adults. An electric assist model is available.

The Twin tandem, and many of the Hoening special-needs machines, are featured elsewhere in this Encyclopedia.

Robert Hoening Spezialfahrzeuge GmbH, Ulmer Strasse 16/2, 71229 Leonberg, Germany.
Tel +49 7152 979490 Fax +49 7152 979499.
Email r.hoening@t-online.de. Website: www.hoening.com

In Germany, the Compagnon costs DM2650, the Copilot costs DM4500 and the Add+Bike DM620. Prices will vary worldwide.

Kinetics is two businesses in one: a fine repair and accessories service for local cyclists, and a specialist service sending unusual machines across the world. If you have a special project in mind but lack the necessary skills and technical resources to build it yourself, Ben Cooper at Kinetics could be the man to call.

Within two days of a customer asking if an electric motor could be fitted to a Brompton, Ben had built a prototype. Special mountings support a standard Zap motor driving the front wheel, with the battery in a modified Brompton front bag. The conversion does not detract from the Brompton's foldability: all you have to do is undo a single connector, lift the battery bag off and the bike folds as usual. Having started as a one-off, this conversion is now available to all, along with several other Kinetics Brompton kits.

Another one-off project, the Trailerbent, was probably the world's first recumbent trailer-bike. Kingcycle rider James Murphy wanted to cycle with his son Liam, who had outgrown a normal childseat or trailer. A trailer-bike attached to the rear carrier (as the Kingcycle has no seat tube), allows Liam to pedal, and gives him the same recumbent position as his dad. Trailerbents can now be made in any size you wish.

Kinetics are also agents for S&S bicycle torque couplings. These can be used to make almost any cycle separable for easy transportation. Ben can silver-braze the couplings into new frames, or retrofit them next time your bike needs a respray. Made in the USA, S&S couplings add no flex, are silent, light and very durable.

Kinetics created the Toucan tandem, shown here, as a showcase for their custom-building skills. Designed for racing, touring or fast day rides, it's a very light machine with a 4130 CrMo main beam and quality tubing from Columbus and Reynolds. It's highly adjustable, and the seats have a foam base, mesh back and aluminium frame. Above-seat steering is standard but under-seat is an option, as are suspension forks, low-rider racks, mudguards and almost anything else you might want.

Although they supply customers anywhere in the world, Kinetics are also pleased to welcome personal visitors to try out their many unusual and innovative products.

kinetics engineering services

Based on the north-western outskirts of Glasgow, near the Kilpatrick Hills, Kinetics was established by Ben Cooper early in 1999. Before that he ran a part-time business building unusual bikes to order, having previously worked for the Harper brothers who ran a shop selling Bromptons and recumbents.

Over the last few years Ben has been pleasantly surprised by the rapidly-growing demand for his services. At the same time he's noticed that bikes are increasingly moving from being purely recreational items to real alternatives to the car. He's expanded his range to reflect this– he now imports, for example, a practical range of Hase Spezialräder and HP Velotechnik recumbents and riese und mueller folding bikes from Germany, and is a Brompton dealer. Want to treat your bike? He's also importing surprisingly affordable titanium cranks from Russia!

If it's a cheap bike you're after, don't bother Ben. But for anything else, whether a custom-built tourer or something completely unorthodox, Kinetics can provide just what you are looking for.

Kinetics, 15 Rannoch Drive, Bearsden, Glasgow G61 2JW, UK.
Tel +44 141 942 2552
Fax +44 141 942 2552
Email ben@kinetics.org.uk
Website www.kinetics.org.uk

The Toucan tandem as shown here would cost roughly £1995 in the UK.

KPH · METRES · YARDS
KILOMETRES · MILES
VELOCITY · POWER
INCHES · FEET
DISTANCE
SPEED
ONCE

SCHNELL UND WEIT

SPEED AND DISTANCE

VITE ET LOIN

THE OPEN ROAD

Riding a bike on the open road gives you a sense of freedom and satisfaction however you do it. On a lightweight road bike or fast recumbent you can hurtle along at high speed, catching an adrenalin rush on the descents, and letting the stress evaporate like sweat on the climbs. On a laden tourer, you can relax as you ride at your own rhythm, absorbing the slowly changing scenery around you. Either way, you win, and the riding itself is its own reward.

When you're racing you get a real sense of speed. Your proximity to rushing tarmac, or to rocks bouncing past beneath your wheels, puts you in the scene in a way that other forms of transport don't. It's a unique thrill, not least because you're travelling under your own power – or the power of gravity – and it's a thrill that you don't have to be a competitive rider to enjoy.

Touring is all about self-sufficiency, carrying all you need on a machine specially built for the task. Long haul comfort is the name of the game. You've got the independence to go where you want, when you want. And your speed – fast enough to go places, slow enough to see things – is just right for getting the most out of any place you travel through.

There is a huge selection of cycles, which between them enable you to travel as far or as fast as you want, in as much comfort and style and with as much luggage as you need. Super-light road bikes will convert the power from your legs into forward motion in the most efficient way imaginable, and they're light enough that you might think twice about attaching a cycle computer to for fear of adding too much weight. Low-profile wind-cheating recumbents – whether for racing or touring – offer the rider a different slant on cycling. Then there's the classic touring bike, a product of years of experience, made all the more practical by inspired design and cleverly applied technology.

Technology moves fast in the world of cycle racing. Races are won or lost by a matter of seconds. Having the best technology is integral to the sport. Riders know this, and so do the designers and the engineers. New materials are tried, frame designs are tweaked or sometimes radically altered to achieve that perfect blend of lightness, stiffness and aerodynamics. Somehow, for the professional road racing scene at least, this all has to be done within the confines of regulations laid down by the UCI (the international governing body of cycle sport). With recumbents, there are no such limitations – the UCI having banned recumbents from racing alongside conventional road bikes in the 1930s. Anyone who has attended an HPV (Human Powered Vehicle) championship will tell you that the diversity of the machines participating is quite breathtaking.

The results of these advances in cycle technology and design are now available to us mere mortals as well as the professionals. In the next few pages you will find the products of the drawing boards and the imaginations of many specialist cycle manufacturers from around the globe. From the exotic to the practical – open your mind to the options and you will find a bike here that is ideally suited to your needs.

The highest speed ever achieved on a bicycle is 268.831 km/h (167.042mph). This was set by Dutchman Fred Rompelberg at Bonneville Salt Flats in 1995. He used a small wheeled, highly geared cycle and, to overcome wind resistance, he followed a pace car fitted with a huge rear fairing that completely enveloped him and his bike.

The first man to circumnavigate the globe on a bicycle was Thomas Stevens. Born in England in 1854 and a 'voracious reader of travel literature, energetic and a realist' Stevens travelled to America at the age of 18. Then on the morning of April 22, 1884, he rolled his newly acquired Columbia high-wheeler along the Oakland Pier in Colorado with the intention of completing the first transcontinental bicycle ride. This he did by early August. He then went on to circle the globe. Stevens' Columbia bicycle was built by the Pope Manufacturing Company, who preserved Stevens' bicycle until a World War II scrap drive took precedence.

The annual Race Across America (RAAM) event follows a course from the Pacific to the Atlantic and covers a distance of approximately 4828km (3000 miles). The current Trans-America solo record holders are: for the men, Rob Kish (1992) completed in 8 days 3 hours 11 mins; and, for the women, Seana Hogan (1995) in 9 days 4 hours 2 mins.

The Tour de France was founded in 1903 by the first world hour-record holder, Henry Desgranges. Desgranges organised le Tour to create interest in the new newspaper L'Auto, of which he was Editor. In the 96 years of the Tour de France, France has won the most times, followed by Belgium, then by Italy and Spain.

Frenchman Eric Barone set the world downhill speed record for bicyclists, clocking 134.782 miles per hour down the snowpacked slopes of KL des Arcs in France on March 17 1999. He beat the former record of fellow Frenchman Christian Taillefer who managed only 131.968 mph.

On August 11 1999, the German Lars Teutenberg set a new HPV world record by travelling a distance of 81.158km (50.42 miles) in one hour, from a standing start. The machine used was a fully-faired, carbon fibre recumbent bicycle known as the 'White Hawk'. During the attempt, Teutenberg achieved a top speed of almost 90 km/h (56 mph).

During the year of 1939 Thomas Edward Godwin, from the UK, cycled a distance of 120,805km (75,065 miles) giving an average distance per day of 330.96 km (205.65 miles). He then rode on until 14 May 1940 when he completed 100,000 miles in 500 days.

Tommy Chambers of Glasgow, Scotland, clocked up 1,286,517 km (799,405 miles) over a period of 51 years. Giving an average annual distance cycled of 25,226 km (15,675 miles). During this time he wore out 10 bicycles, 254 tyres, 64 cyclometers, 39 chainwheels, 76 chains, 33 pedals, 38 lamps and 5 saddles.

Going flat out is what the Prone is all about – and we can prove it. Last year it beat more than 50 competitors to take first and second places in the British Human Power Club championship for unfaired bikes.

The first and only commercially-available prone cycle, the Cool Breeze Prone Low-Profile is a pure speed machine. Its aerodynamics are about as good as they can be for an unfaired machine. Frontal area is minimised and airflow over the body is exceptionally smooth. And with the pedals at the back, the legs don't churn the air before it flows over the body.

Careful design provides enough support for comfort and stability, without affecting the rider's breathing. Shoulders and hips rest on specially-shaped adjustable cushions, and hands fall naturally to the handlebar, which is adjustable for reach and angle. Clipless pedals are recommended to keep the feet secure, and there's plenty of knee clearance.

The Prone's rear end is narrower than last year's version, so that the rider's knees aren't splayed apart to clear the gears. The rear triangle is heavily 'dished', so that the derailleur cassette nestles right inside. The Prone 3 uses carbon-fibre wheels back and front, designed and made by Cool Breeze.

The frame is built from thin-gauge Reynolds 853 tubing. The standard size fits riders over 5' 8" (173cm) tall, but smaller folk can have a bike made to order. The front wheel can be either 20" (406) for ground-hugging speed and efficiency, or 24" (507) for a more open position that some find more comfortable. The rear wheel is the 700C racing size. There's a choice of components, and finished machines typically weigh

approximately 11kg.

A test ride is strongly recommended to overcome any preconceptions about this unusual but wickedly fast machine. With your head out in front and close to the ground, riding the Prone is pure exhilaration – the nearest thing to flying on two wheels!

cool breeze uk ltd

The Prone is the brainchild of Tim Elsdale, who after many years in the British cycle industry, working with conventional upright machines, decided to apply his experience to something very different. Working from first principles, he concluded that the prone position was a more natural way to minimise frontal area than some of the very low-profile 'traditional' recumbents.
Despite the radical nature of his design, Tim feels that traditional skills are still relevant: the qualities of good tubing and carefully-crafted joints are as important as ever. Customers have included some serious racers but there's also interest from everyday riders in search of a real thrill.
Meanwhile, race success continues. A Prone ridden by Thomas Wahl won the hillclimb event at the 1999 European HPV championships and it was Tim Elsdale himself who came first in the BHPC unfaired championship.

Cool Breeze UK Ltd, 194 Upper Street, Islington, London N1 1RQ, UK.
Tel +44 207 704 9273 Fax +44 207 354 9641

In the UK, the Prone costs from £1500. The Prone 3 with carbon-fibre wheels costs over £2000.

It tips the scales at 28.5lb. For a solo bike that would be unremarkable; for a tandem it's unheard of. No surprise, then, that the Tetra Tandem is the lightest in the world. It's constructed from carbon-fibre tubes wrapped with carbon roving at their junctions. The frame alone weighs 6 to 7 lb (2.7 to 3.1kg), depending on rider weights and requirements.

Yet although it's a featherweight, the Tetra Tandem is neither fragile nor flexible. Carbon fibre can be designed with strength and stiffness just where you want it, with no weight penalty. Added to this, the Tetra Tandem frame features a unique carbon fibre gusset. What looks like a fillet of smooth epoxy is actually part of the joint. Look more closely and you can see the carbon fibre weave: the frame is clear-coated. Calfee Design offer a 25 year warranty, but have had no frame failures.

The Tetra Tandem uses titanium for all major metal fittings. Titanium doesn't rust or corrode, and it expands with heat at much same rate as carbon fibre, so the two materials stick together. The geometry and precise frame construction depend on the riders. You get a custom fit, and heavier riders get beefier tubes. If you want all-out speed, you can order an extra-long stoker tube to accommodate aero-bars.

Calfee Design have a growing range of solo bikes. Current models include the Tetra Custom, the Tetra Pro road bike, which has a frame weight of 2.5lb in the 54cm frame size, and the 650C-wheel Tetra Tri for triathlons. In a lower price bracket, the Luna Pro and Luna Tri use aluminium fittings instead of titanium.

What do you buy the cyclist who already has a Calfee Design bike? How about Calfee's 'world's lightest, strongest and most responsive pen holder'. What's it made of? Carbon fibre, of course.

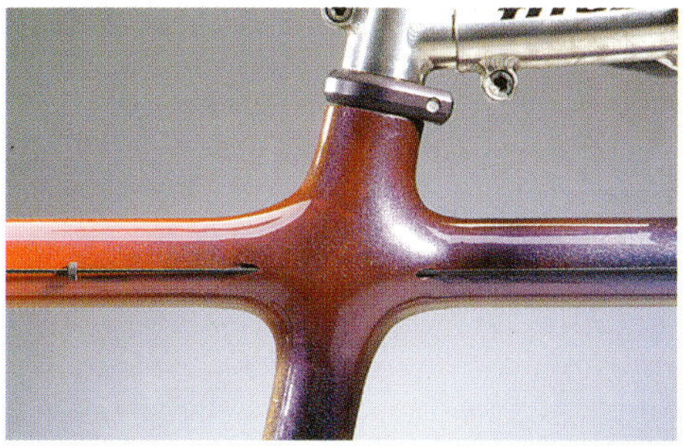

calfee design

When he broke his bike frame in a spectacular head-on collision in 1987, Craig Calfee decided to make something tougher to replace it. He chose carbon fibre. Potentially very light and very tough, it was a material he knew well from his day-job making composite rowing shells. Craig braided the tubes himself then laminated them together with tooling made on a drill press.
Within two years Craig had secured a $10,000 loan, which he used to hire a machinist to make the first production tooling. The Carbonframes Sapphire was introduced at the Interbike show in 1989. Just two years after that, Greg LeMond ordered 18 frames for Team Z. When LeMond wore the Tour de France Yellow Jersey while riding his Carbonframe, the company earned some welcome publicity.
Other famous owners include professional triathlete Dave Scott, who at 40 years of age rode his Carbonframe to second place in the Hawaii Ironman World Championship.

Calfee Design, 2801 Mission St. Suite C, Santa Cruz, CA 95060, USA.
Tel +1 831 466 9041 Fax +1 831 466 9043
E-mail jim@calfeedesign.com (for pricing or sales questions), craig@calfeedesign.com (for technical questions).
Website www.calfeedesign.com

A Tetra Tandem frame costs $5227, with carbon forks an extra $457, and prices will vary worldwide.
A carbon fibre pen holder costs $25.

There's something about the compact, purposeful Tiger that invites speed: it's a bike to let loose on. Yet unlike so many speed machines, you can push yourself to the limit in comfort: that's the advantage of a fast, light recumbent.

The Tiger has a stiff frame and direct, over-seat steering. The seat adjusts for angle, and can be moved along the frame to accommodate riders from 5'6" to 6'2". Three frame sizes mean there's a Tiger for every rider. The relatively high seating position and good manoeuvrability combine to create an effective machine in traffic, and its compact size makes it easy to transport. The front wheel is further forward than on most short-wheelbase recumbents, giving a wheelbase of 42" (105cm) – about the same as a conventional upright bike. This gives good weight distribution – 40% on front wheel, 60% on rear, and helps to keep the 13.2kg (29lb) Tiger stable at high speed, eliminating any tendency to twitchy steering from an overloaded front wheel.

The Tiger's sister model is the Pursuit, a long-wheelbase recumbent aimed at the long-distance cycle tourist. The improved aerodynamics of the longer layout give it a slight advantage over the Tiger when it comes to speed, and shorter riders also find it easier to put a foot on the ground.

Both bicycles have been designed to incorporate 'passive' suspension. A degree of flex is built into the rear stays, and the base of the mesh seat is strung with elastic cord.

The mid-drive transmission gives up to 48 speeds, with a gear range of 20-150". Both bikes are equipped with 20" (406) wheels, front and back. When touring, it is better to have two wheels of the same size to avoid the need to carry more than one spare tube and tyre.

Options include front fairings (made from a combination of Kevlar and carbon fibre), aerospoke composite wheels and a combined tail fairing and luggage box called the 'solar cat'. For the ultimate ride, both Tiger and Pursuit are available in titanium, with frames weighing only 1.45kg (3.2lb). The complete Ti Pursuit weighs in at just 9.5kg (21lb).

rotator recumbent bicycles

Steve Delaire, founder and owner of Rotator, has been building bicycle frames since 1979 and recumbents since 1982. As well as building his own recumbents, he does production work for other manufacturers, including Lightning and Easy Racer, and is based in the recumbent community of Santa Rosa, California. Steve says, "Working with other companies is really good for all of us. It's such a small industry right now and it doesn't hurt to help each other out every now and then."

Delaire believes that the recumbent sector of the market is definitely growing, especially for those people seeking an aerodynamic advantage. "The recumbent bicycle lends itself more easily to a full fairing than an upright bike does. I think that people will eventually start to realise the benefits of streamlining and that market segment will continue to grow."

Rotator Recumbent Bicycles, 4325 Montgomery Drive, Santa Rosa, California 95405, USA. Tel +1 707 539 4203
Fax +1 707 539 5354 Email sales@rotatorrecumbent.com Website www.rotatorrecumbent.com

In the USA, the Tiger and Pursuit both cost from $1,435 for the steel version, and from $4,250 for titanium.

The lower you ride the faster you go! The extra-low Trice XL is fast in a straight line, exhilarating downhill and glides sure-footed through the curves even with the power full on.

Speed need not compromise comfort: every point of contact is adjustable, including the seat fabric tension for lumbar and shoulder support, the seat recline angle, the reach and width of the handlebars and the distance to the pedals. The XL is built with custom-made decorative lugs and smooth fillet-brazing, and dismantles easily into short sections for transport. The frame has full brazed-on bosses for touring and a cycle computer mount. Extender plates near the rear dropouts provide fixing points to fit a full-sized rack over the 20" (406) rear wheel. This keeps the luggage low around the rear axle for stable load-carrying.

The XL is one of ICE's new and expanding range of Trice recumbents. The Classic retains the 26" (559) rear wheel and overall geometry of the original Trice. The Explorer has been designed for touring with a higher and more upright riding position, but with a strong 20" rear wheel to keep the load low and stable. The latest Trice is the X2 Tandem, which can be steered one handed with confidence and has a surprisingly small turning circle. It is almost impossible to lift a wheel even when riding hard.

A wide range of accessories and upgrades are available for all models, including metallic colours, front mudguards that can be fitted or removed in seconds, and racks to take up to four panniers. Hope hydraulic disks can replace the standard Sturmey Archer drum brakes. Other options include a handlebar-mounted mirror, front fairings and electric-assist motors. A narrower track version is also available. Custom Trice, including hand cranked versions, can be made to individual requirements.

inspired cycle engineering

The original Trice was developed in the early 1980s by Peter Ross of Crystal Engineering. One of the first to develop road going recumbent tricycles, he brought the Trice into volume production in 1986 and refined the design over the next decade.
In January 1999 the development and production of the Trice was handed over to Inspired Cycle Engineering, headed by Chris Parker and Neil Selwood. Neil, a keen recumbent cyclist and production engineer of 20 years experience teamed up in the summer of '98 with Chris, a designer, who has been involved with recumbent design and manufacture for the last five years, and together they planned the Trice revolution.
The Trice went through a complete metamorphosis in the following 12 months, and sales more than doubled.

Inspired Cycle Engineering, Unit 9b Spencer Carter Works, Tregoniggie Industrial Estate, Falmouth, Cornwall, TR11 4SN, England.
Tel/Fax +44 (0)1326 378848 Email sales@ice.hpv.co.uk Website www.ice.hpv.co.uk

Prices start from £1,920 for the Classic, £2,100 for the XL, £2,020 for the Explorer and £3,580 for the X2.
Framesets are also available.

"Which way do you go?" Most people react to the Micwic Delta with incredulity and confusion. But get them on board, and the prejudices are swiftly overcome.

Stokers find it a very relaxing ride – just sit back, unwind, and enjoy the panoramic views. Conversation between the riding partners is easy: no shouting is needed with your heads just inches apart. After a few miles, the unusual feeling of travelling backwards becomes quite pleasant: you're freed from the stress of watching the road ahead, and can savour the scenery through which you travel.

The captain has a feeling of complete control: the handling is very stable, and the Hope hydraulic disk brakes authoritative in their stopping power. With the stoker to warn of traffic approaching from behind – and to make eye contact – it's a safe vehicle in traffic, and certainly catches the eye of drivers, who give it plenty of room.

The Delta is a quick machine, thanks to the aerodynamic layout: air flows smoothly over the two riders. The wheel base is short for a recumbent tandem, and it has a tight turning circle. Climbing performance is also good for a recumbent, helped by the very stiff frame of 2" and I 1/8"aerospace grade 4130 tubing. The bike pictured is a race machine, with the 20" (406) wheels built with Mavic rims and Hope hubs. Standard tandem components are used for the transmission, with chainrings stepped up to compensate for the small wheels.

There's plenty of luggage capacity between the two seats, and custom panniers are available to make the most of it – with these in place, the Delta makes a fine tourer.

Plans for the future include a model with quick-adjustment seats and under-seat steering, and a titanium model for those who will not settle for anything less than the ultimate.

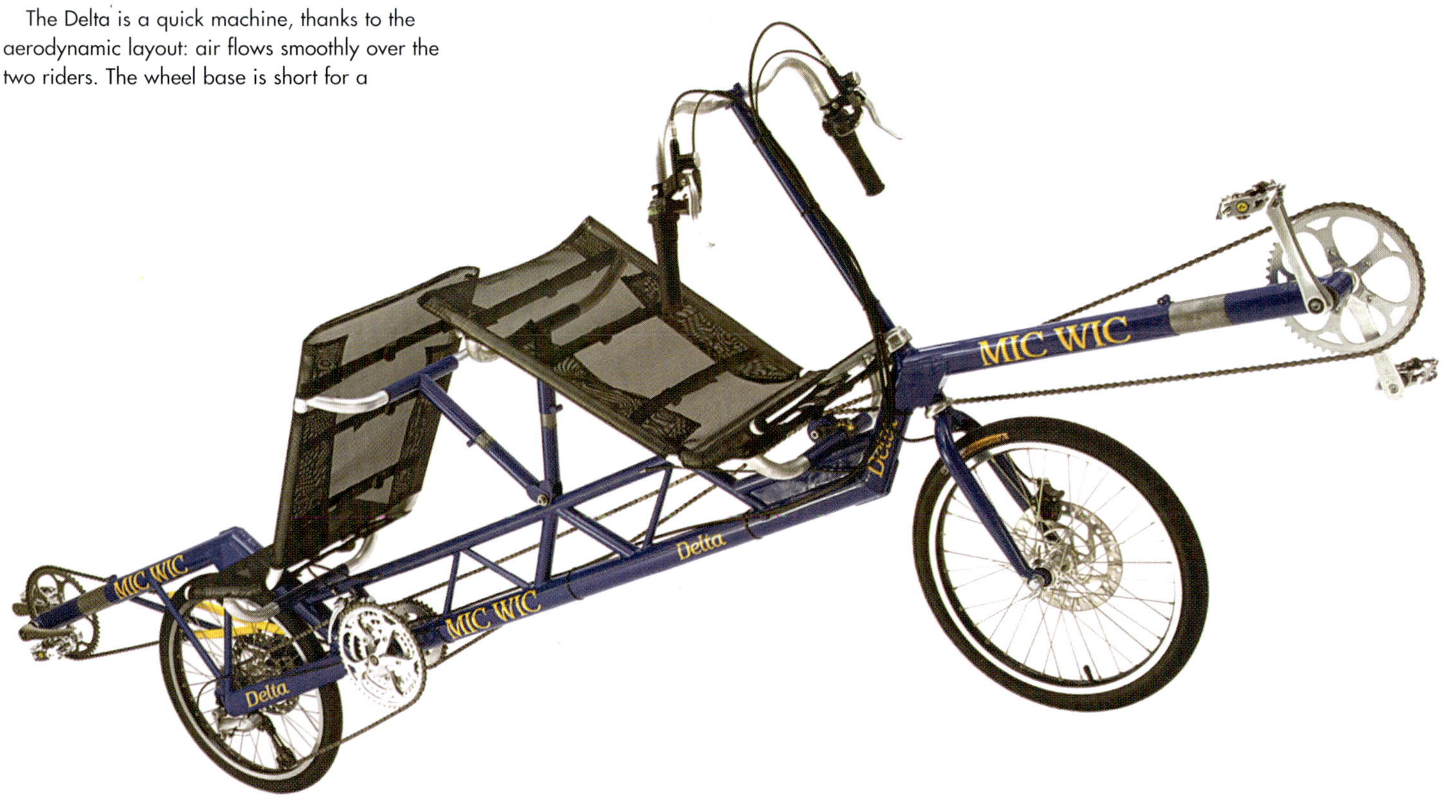

mic wic

Bob Tennant, the founder of Mic Wic, used to be a dedicated conventional cycle tourist and commuted daily by bike, logging over 6,000 miles yearly. Then he rode a recumbent for a weekend and changed his life. He stopped working as a maths teacher, and devoted his time to designing and building recumbents. His wife Alison also has a diamond-frame bike, and neither have seen the light of day since Bob built his first recumbent tandem.

Bob is now working on a more conventional recumbent tandem, called the Mange Two, and is testing a sociable (side by side) tandem called the Suzy. Three solo designs are also available from Mic Wic, the Commuter 7, the Tourister, and the HeirCycle.

Mic Wic are the EU importer and distributor for the full range of recumbent cycles built by Linear in the USA. They also supply recumbents to a company called 'Britain By-Cycle' (+44 1793 770746), a cycle touring company that specialises in introducing people to the joys of recumbent cycling.

Mic Wic Limited, Unit 12, Oaklands industrial Estate, Braydon, Swindon, Wiltshire SN5 0AN Tel: +44 1793 852484 Email Micwic@btinternet.com Website www.MICWIC.com

In the UK, the Delta costs from around £3,500. Other models from Mic Wic cost from around £750. Prices will vary worldwide.

Named after Robinson Crusoe's companion, Bike Fridays have put their tyre prints on the remotest islands on earth. They fit neatly into a suitcase, so travel anywhere in the world, by air, boat, train, or car. Portability isn't their only strength: the Bike Friday was designed from the outset to ride like a 'real' bike, as a training bike or tourer for the air traveller.

The emphasis on performance has been retained as the range of bikes has diversified. Even the entry-level Metro, with components selected for commuting or around-town cruising, uses the same stiff cromoly frame as the more expensive models. The Metro is available off the peg, however, while the rest of the range is custom-built for you: you get an engraved name-plate on your Bike Friday to prove it.

There's a Bike Friday for every purpose. Commuters will want the Metro, the higher-spec Pocket Nomad, or maybe even the Pocket Llama – a Bike Friday MTB. For touring, it's got to be the New World Tourist, which is offered with a wide range of different components; custom front and rear racks are also available. For racing, training, or just riding fast for fun, the Pocket Rocket is a travellers' favourite. Larger 24" wheels with narrower tyres reduce rolling resistance without sacrificing comfort, and it weighs under 25lb. The Dura-Ace equipped Pocket Rocket Pro goes one better, tipping the scales at under 20lb (9.1kg).

Top of the Bike Friday range is the AirFriday series, which was originally designed for world-class triathletes. The titanium suspension beam helps to isolate the rider from road shock, thus reducing fatigue. The AirFriday has alternative geometries for triathlon and road racing, and there is a version for touring, the AirGlide, and for mountain biking, the AirLlama.

All except the AirFriday series quick-fold for easy transport in 15-30 seconds. And all pack into an optional bag or hard-shell suitcase in minutes. If you're touring unsupported, get the TravelTrailer – a hard shell suitcase that converts into a 100lb capacity bicycle trailer.

The options don't stop there – Bike Friday also make tandems, triplets and recumbents, featured elsewhere in this Encyclopeedia.

atp green gear cycling

Ridability is as much a Bike Friday trademark as portability – as owners have proved. Kent Peterson rode the 1300km Paris-Brest-Paris randonnée in under 80 hours on his Bike Friday in 1999.

A world away from the smooth roads of France, Hewes and Susan Agnew took their Tandem Two'sday through Southeast Asia. "One day we had at least 50 miles of deep jarring potholes – 'The road to hell' as one of our compatriots described it. I cannot image a greater test for a touring bicycle and our Two'sday handled it flawlessly."

Such stories regularly reach Bike Friday headquarters in Eugene, Oregon, where they are much appreciated by the workforce.

Bike Friday, Green Gear Cycling Inc, 3364 W 11th Ave, Eugene, OR 97402 USA. Tel +1 541 687 0487 Fax +1 541 687 0403 Email info@bikefriday.com Website www.bikefriday.com

In the USA, Classic Bike Fridays cost from $695 for the Metro to $3,395 for a top-of-the range Pocket Rocket Pro, and from $2,095 to $3,595 for AirFridays.

'Human factors engineering' is how Radius describe what they do: everything is centred about the rider. Comfort is a primary consideration.

The C4, their all-purpose medium-wheelbase recumbent, reflects this philosophy. The padded base and well-ventilated mesh back of the seat give support without pressure-points, and handlebars are adjustable both for position and angle. The pedals are are at a comfortable height, and it's easy to put a foot down as you stop. Handling has been carefully-refined to offer secure handling even at low speeds.

Two versions are available. The C4 Allround has over-seat steering and Sachs Power-Grip twist-shifters, while the C4 Touring has under-seat handlebars and Shimano bar-end shifters. Many riders prefer the low bars for longer journeys, but find above-seat steering more natural for town use. Luckily the C4 makes both possible: with a simple conversion kit and a few hours' work, the steering can be converted from above-seat to below, or vice-versa.

The two models share a TIG-welded cro-mo medium wheelbase frame, V-brakes and Sachs 3x7 transmission. Racks for standard panniers are fitted to every bike (not shown on main image – see the red C4 Allround picture). Mudguards and lighting are also fitted as standard, as is the anti-pogo rear suspension with its Shockworks hydraulic/pneumatic element. There are two frame sizes, to fit riders between 1.62m and 1.98m, and the wheels are 20" (406) front and back.

Prefer blasting along on a sporty short-wheelbase recumbent? The Hornet II is the sports tourer from Radius, and should suit riders who want a lively but comfortable machine with good luggage-carrying capacity. The bike emphasises rider comfort, with a patented seat design allowing easy, stepless adjustment. Similarly, the remote under-seat steering can be shifted forwards or backwards for a perfect fit. Components include Magura Hydraulic Brakes, Shimano bar-end shifters and 27-speed Deore LX transmission. Among the many options are mudguards, mirror, racks for up to four panniers, lighting systems and an unbreakable Lexan front fairing, which both speeds you up and keeps you dry.

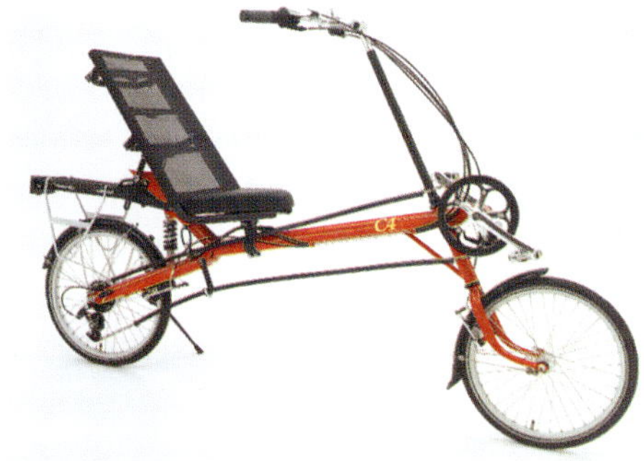

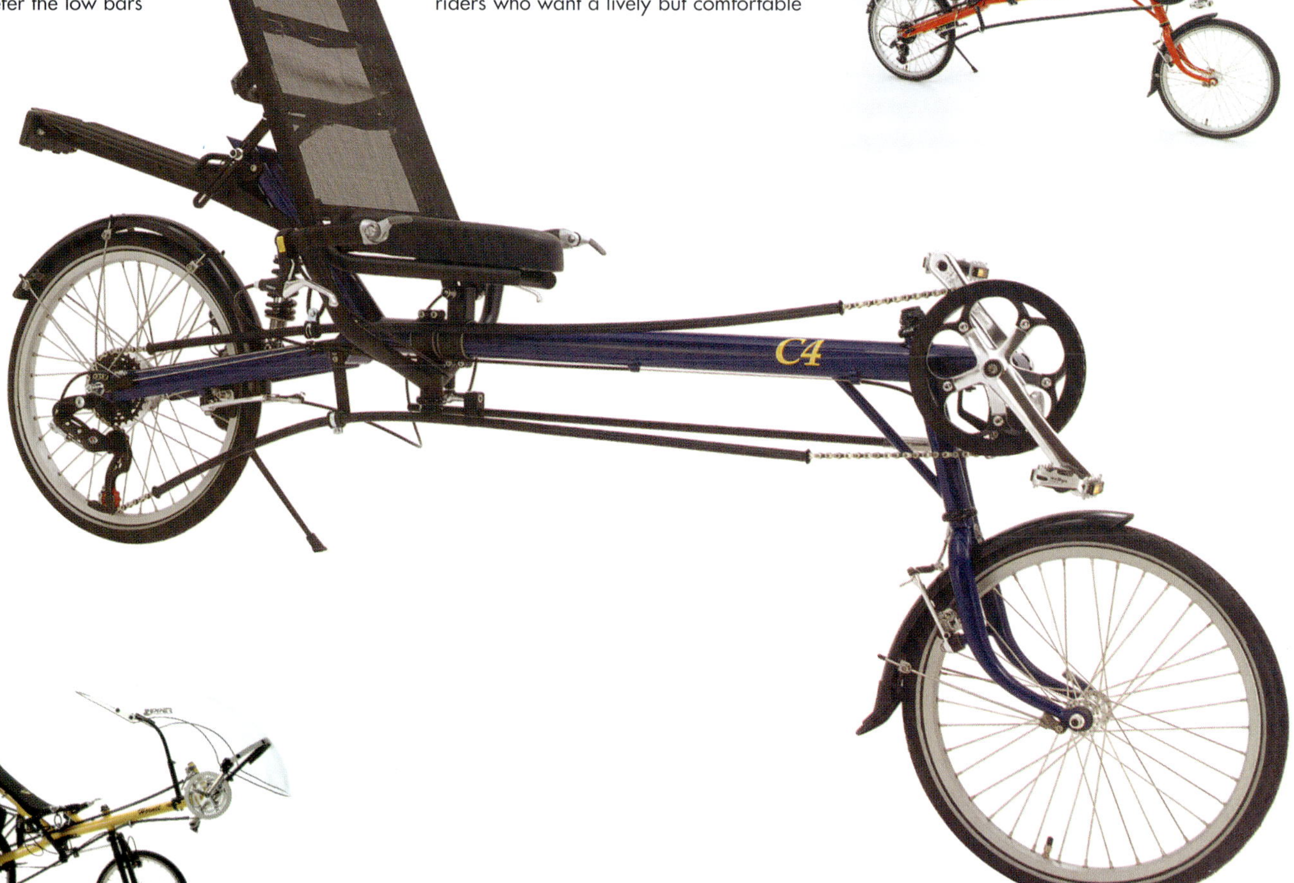

radius liegeräder

Radius have been making recumbents for over 17 years: their Peer Gynt was among the first commercially-available machines – and many are still on the road today. Nils Palm and Frank Tochtrop, who took charge at Radius in 1998, have applied themselves to developing the company's technological base: they use CAD and computer simulation techniques to design the bikes. High-quality TIG welding and precision jigs are employed to assemble the frames, which are phosphate treated before electrostatic powder-coating. Several quality-control stages ensure that both frame manufacture and component assembly are defect-free.

Radius Liegeraeder, Liegerad Münster GmbH: Borkstr. 20, D-48163 Münster, Germany. Tel +49 1805 723 487
Fax +49 215 78 03 58 Email mail@radius-liegeraeder.de Website www.radius-liegeraeder.de or www.radius-recumbents.com
Distribution in the US: Radius Recumbents USA: Buchanan Bikeworks, llc 170 Charles Street, Garfield, NJ 07026, USA.
Tel +1 973 340 9006 Fax +1 973 478 8175 Email RadiusUSA@aol.com

In Germany, the C4 Allround costs from DM 2299, the C4 Tour from DM 2699, and the Hornet II from DM 3510.

Sometimes when you're designing a product, the pieces just fall into place. So it was when Ian Sims put together the Greenspeed GTO. Parts of the jigsaw came from his other models – and assembled, along with some fresh thinking, into a trike which Ian expects will have a very broad appeal.

The Greenspeed GTO combines the best elements of the established GTR touring trike – the popular high-backed seat, and go-anywhere ruggedness, with the stability and speed of the low-slung GTS sports tourer. The GTO's road holding and handling rival the GTS, without compromising ground clearance – in fact, a more compact steering design means that clearance is increased to 4" (10cm).

With his Suitcase Trike, featured in Encycleopedia 99, Ian Sims gave recumbent tricyclists something that had always been missing from their cycling: portability, the freedom to travel with their trike and not just on it. Using S&S torque couplings, the Suitcase Trike disassembles to fit in two suitcases. This technology allows the GTO to do the same vanishing act.

Like all Greenspeed trikes, the GTO uses centrepoint steering, which ensures there's no steering kickback if one wheel hits a pothole. It also means that the brakes can be operated independently without affecting the steering – useful when signalling. You can brake with both hands if you need the extra power, and if you want something with even more bite than the standard Sachs 70mm drum brakes you can specify Hope hydraulic discs.

With 72 gears – a Sachs 3x8 hub, plus a triple chainset – you'll always be able to spin at your preferred cadence, whether climbing in the 15" bottom gear or flying down in the 125" top. Three 20" (406) wheels combine with a 35 or 40° seat angle to keep your riding profile low, reducing wind resistance. The Tioga Comp Pool slick tyres are rated at 90psi.

All Greenspeeds are made to order, so you can select from a wide range of options, including different gears, brakes, accessories, or frame sizes. A 'standard' GTO trike weighs around 18kg (40lb).

greenspeed

Greenspeed take the international market seriously. Most Greenspeeds produced are exported, and Ian Sims often travels long distances to exhibit at international trade shows. He travelled round the world to Britain for the Encycleopedia Try-Out Show in May 2000.
Although they are based in Australia, international ordering from Greenspeed couldn't be easier: you can even do it over the internet. Greenspeed will normally arrange for the trikes to be delivered by courier to your door, and will take care of all customs formalities for you. They also have agents dealers in several countries, so that local test-rides can be arranged.

Greenspeed, 69 Mountain Gate Drive, Ferntree Gully, VIC 3156, Australia. Tel +61 3 9758 5541 Fax +61 3 9752 4115
Email info@greenspeed.com.au Website www.greenspeed.com.au
Dealers in Germany, UK and USA: see page 144-145

In Australia, the GTO costs A$4650, and prices will vary worldwide.

"Like a prop for a sci-fi movie" was how one American customer described the Toxy ZR. It was a sincere compliment: the ZR is a space-age bicycle in more than looks. It's made from aerospace materials, and has a rocket-like turn of speed.

This is largely due to the aerodynamics: low-riders are always fast, and the ZR is no exception. Frontal area is under 0.25 square metres with a typical rider, compared to around 0.5 for an upright cyclist. With the optional rear fairing it's even faster – and has about 70 litres of lockable, waterproof luggage space as well. The seat adjusts from around a 30° laid-back angle, for even more speed, to a more upright 45° for those who prefer a little more height.

The front-wheel drive system is a tried-and-tested way to avoid a long flapping chain to the rear wheel, and the large rollers guide the chain efficiently to the SRAM 3x7 hub – other transmissions are also possible, including the Rohloff 14-speed hub. The turning circle is surprisingly tight.

The aluminium frame weighs around 2.7kg, and with fork and damper about 3.7kg. The mono-arm rear suspension is a particularly elegant detail, and the hydraulically-damped suspension significantly increases comfort. Disk brakes at the back, and a V-brake on the front give superlative braking for the 20" (406) wheels.

The ZR is the fastest Toxy; others in the range have other strengths. The original Toxy is the versatile SWB machine, with steering either above or below the seat, and for 2000 it is available in a special touring version, the 'miles & more', with racks for four panniers, mudguards, and lights.

For smaller riders Toxy offer a special treat – the Toxy S. This is especially designed for riders between roughly 1.45 and 1.6m tall (4' 8" to 5' 3"). Even smaller riders can go for the Toxylinchen, or 'sweet little Toxy', which suits most riders up to a height of around 1.40m (4'6") – with a choice of either under- or over-seat steering.

arved klütz spezialräder

When Arved Klütz was asked at primary school what he wanted to be when he grew up, he had his answer ready: an inventor. He was already in training, playing with Lego late into the night. As he grew, he soon moved on to bicycles, cycle-touring from the age of just 13. At 16, he started making his first tandems and recumbents from 'recycled' bicycles. Alongside these experiments, he founded a company making fine metal furniture for restaurants, shops and trade show displays. Some of the machines he needed for these creations are still used for the bicycles today. Others were sold, as Arved would up the business and began studying engineering at Hamburg University. An interest in motorbikes brought him to the big two-wheeler trade show in Cologne in 1993 – but it was the possibilities of the cycling market that grabbed his attention. Within a year he had designed, made and sold the first Quantum recumbent. Ever since, the company has grown, and Arved just keeps inventing.

Quantum Liegeraeder, Steinstr. 5, 25364 Hörnerkirchen, Germany. Tel +49 4127 92283 Fax +49 4127 92284
Email info@quantum-toxy.de Website www.toxy.de

In Germany, the Toxy ZR costs around DM 4500, and prices will vary worldwide.

Extreme conditions, on many continents, have proved a tough testing-ground for Optima recumbents. These machines excel on the long haul.

The Lynx, shown here, is a fast and comfortable all-round recumbent, which nicely combines an aerodynamic riding position with plenty of practicality. Panniers are no problem: like all Optima recumbents, it has a superb rear carrier, which fits either conventional cycle panniers or special recumbent models. Carrying capacity is a hefty 50kg – a nice safety margin, especially when using a childseat, for which Optima can provide an adapter.

The ergonomically-formed fibreglass seat shell can be fine-adjusted for height and angle, and seat covers come in a choice of covers, all easily removable and washable. The Lynx shown uses open-weave 'air filter' material for a resilient, well-ventilated ride. Comfort is further increased with the adjustable suspension element.

There's quite a range of Optimas, to suit most tastes. Tourers will appreciate the the 26"-wheeled Condor and Orca, or go for the Dragon with a 20" front wheel. The nimble Dolphin and the low-rider Baron racer both use dual 20" wheels – the Baron is a real speed machine, highly aerodynamic and weighing from just 9.8kg. The Duett tandem doubles the fun – it is one of the lightest and most rigid recumbent tandems around. There's also a trike, the Rider.

With reliability high on the priorities, there's no compromise anywhere in the specification of any Optima recumbent. Wheels are top-quality alloy, with stainless spokes and good-quality high pressure tyres. All machines (except the Baron racer) come complete with chainguard, mudguards, computer mount and bell. Standard colours include traffic red, yellow, silver, ice red and ice blue – naturally, custom colours can be created on request.

optima cycles

Optima Cycles are one of Holland's longest-established recumbent manufacturers, and they build reliability into their bikes from the very beginning. They make their machines entirely from non-rusting metal: most of the touring frames are stainless steel, while more sporty models use aluminium. The frames are then epoxy powdercoated with a clear overcoat. Every nut and bolt is also stainless steel. All frame parts are made on CNC laser or water-jet cutting machines for tight tolerances and perfect fit between parts, and there is a full five-year frame guarantee. Optima bikes are manufactured completely in the Netherlands.
Optima bikes and trikes are sold exclusively through dealers: in case of difficulty contact Optima in the Netherlands, or visit their website.
Optima Cycles, Industriestraat 3A, 1976 CS Ijmuiiden, Netherlands. Tel 0031 255 514 215 Email info@optima-cycles.nl Website www.optima-cycles.nl

In the Netherlands, the Lynx costs from f 2995 (around 1360 Euros), and prices will vary worldwide.

An exhilarating mixture of recumbent efficiency and comfort, mixed with racing bike dynamics and light tourer versatility – that's the brief HP Velotechnik set themselves for their stunning new Speedmachine. In the mountains of Majorca, where they took the prototype for final testing and photography, the Speedmachine exceeded expectations, with a fun-factor 'off the scale'.

The Speedmachine's rider leans back in a comfortable yet aerodynamic position, ergonomically supported by an adjustable glass-fibre seat. This is slightly higher than in a racing HPV, allowing good visibility in traffic without unduly compromising performance. Steering is direct for maximum control.

Key to the Speedmachine's success is its adjustable suspension system. A new steering tube suspension de-shocks the front, the back end being cosseted by their 'No-Squat' system. This, by clever positioning of the pivot point, minimises energy losses. And if you want adjustable damping, an optional spring element provides it at the turn of a knob. Transmission uses Shimano XT derailleurs, and when it's time to stop, hydraulic disc brakes provide plenty of power. The rear carrier is fully suspended and big enough to carry a pair of panniers for light touring.

For grander tours, HP Velotechnik offer the Street Machine Gran Tourismo (GT). This is the latest evolution of the original Street Machine, building on nine years of experience. The Street Machine GT has new hydraulically-damped suspension for both wheels, the rear system incorporating No-Squat technology. The seat has 10 degrees of angle adjustment and there's a choice of under-seat or above-seat steering.

The Street Machine GT's standard specification includes Shimano Deore 9-speed derailleur, Swallow City Marathon Reflex tyres and Alesa rims with DT Swiss stainless steel spokes. If you prefer to use components of your own choice, HP can supply frame kits. Accessories include the Streamer aerodynamic fairing, guaranteed to improve riding comfort and efficiency. Constructed from clear polycarbonate on a lightweight frame, it's quick to fit and detachable in seconds. Better yet, it can even be rolled up for storage.

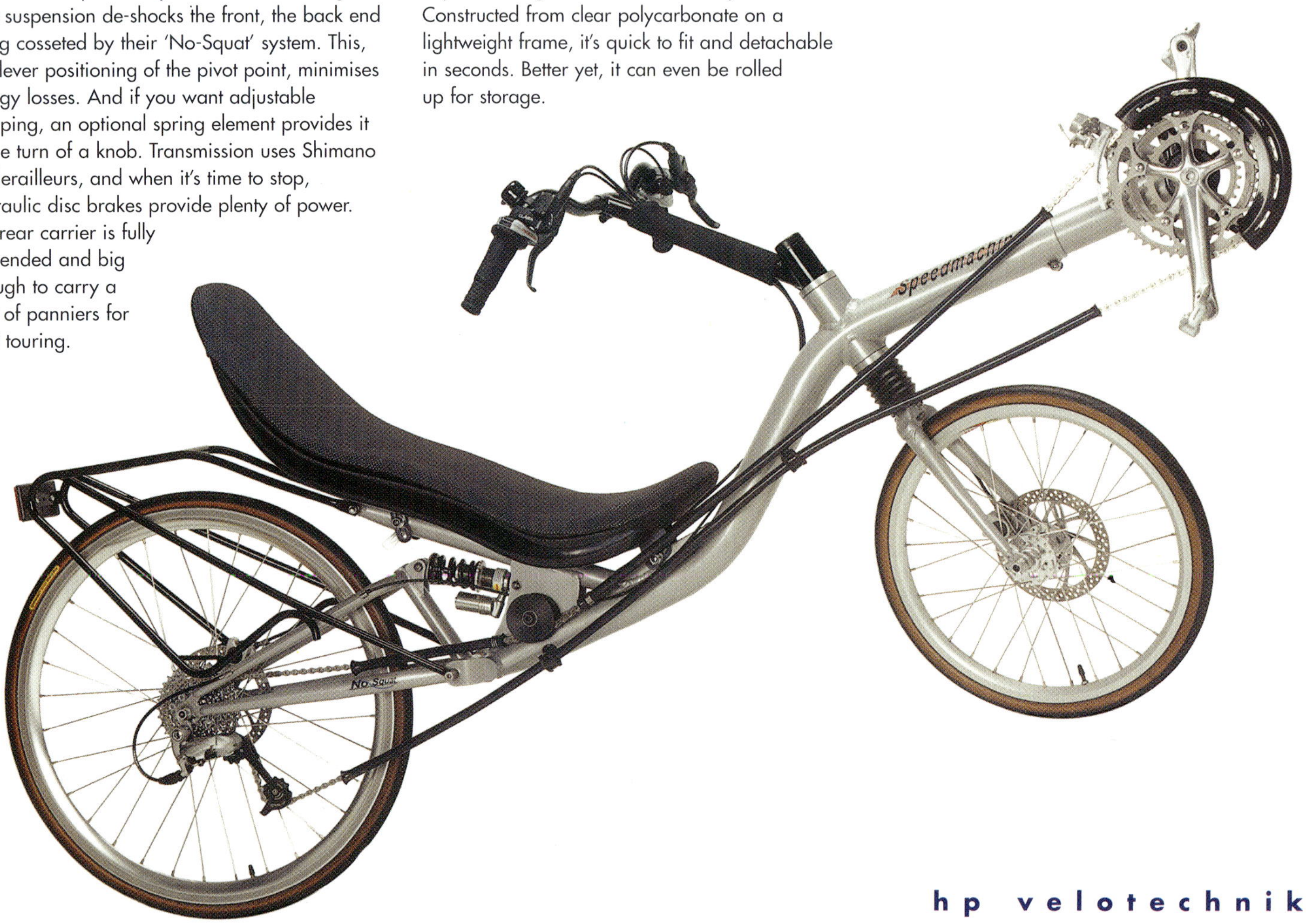

hp velotechnik

Paul Hollants and Daniel Pulvermüller were young students with a passion for cycle technology when they founded HP Velotechnik in 1993. Their aim was to produce a bicycle that fulfilled their vision of an ideal HPV more than anything previously available. The resulting Street Machine became an HPV classic.

HP listen carefully to feedback from customers, testers and the cycle trade, and act on what they learn. A product of this approach is the Wavey, a simple but effective short-wheelbase machine for cyclists new to recumbents.

The firm has its production facilities, warehouse and office in an old farmhouse in Kriftel, a small town near Frankfurt. There they concentrate on development and assembly, out-sourcing specialised work such as laser cutting, welding and powder coating to suitably-qualified partner companies. With the launch of the Speedmachine, HP Velotechnik look set to move into a new and exciting phase.

HP Velotechnik, Paul J. W. Hollants und Dipl.-Ing. Daniel Pulvermüller GbR, Goethestraße 5, D-65830 Kriftel, Germany.
Tel +49 6192 41010 Fax+46 6192 910218
E-mail mail@hpvelotechnik.com
Website www.hpvelotechnik.com

Cross-country mountain bikes don't have full suspension: that used to be the received wisdom. Full suspension was fine when you had gravity on your side on a downhill course, but if you wanted to ride up hills, full suspension made pedalling equal pogoing. No longer!

Giant have introduced the world's first no-power-loss rear suspension: the NRS design, which stands for No Resonance System. Sounds like hype? Even Mike Burrows, Giant's design consultant, acknowledges that the system really works – despite his chagrin at not inventing it himself!

Previous attempts at rear suspension had often been modelled on the motorcycle, ignoring – and as a result exaggerating – the disruptive effect of the cyclist's enormous, very slow moving pistons (or legs). To compensate, the suspension had to be 'locked out' to prevent bobbing and bump absorption, or left 'soft' to absorb both bumps and energy. The NRS design is very different, though it may not look it. It uses the rider's pedalling input to its advantage. It's a bit like a see-saw – on one side the wheel is pushing up to compress the spring, on the other the rider is pushing down trying to extend the spring. The result: equilibrium.

The system is set up with no 'sag', which is to say that the shock is not pre-compressed by the rider's weight. Bumps compress the rear shock, while pedalling input tries to extends the shock – but there's no movement available, because there's no sag. So the shock can't extend any further when the rider pedals out of the saddle: it climbs like a hard-tail, and descends like any other dual suspension bike.

"I'm definitely faster against the clock," notes Giant XC racer Rune Hoydahl, lending support to Giant's claim that, on average, the NRS adds 2-4 km/h to maximum XC speeds.

The NRS design is fitted to all of Giant's cross-country dual suspension bikes. Top of the range is the XtC Team, based on sub-2kg 6013 aluminium frame. The NRS suspension unit offers 3.5" travel at the rear axle, while up front there's an 80mm-travel Rock Shox SID SL Hydracoil fork. Other components include 27-speed SRAM ESP gearing and Hope Hydraulic disc brakes.

giant

The NRS design is the result of a collaboration between Giant and Renault Sport, better know for their successes on the Formula 1 circuit. One of Renault's suspension engineers, Pascal Tribotte, happened to be an MTB enthusiast. He talked over his ideas during a chance meeting with a salesman in a Giant dealer's shop. The management of both companies saw the opportunities, and the NRS design was born.

Giant have been building bikes since 1972, and since 1981 have been producing them under their own brand name. They are now the world's biggest bicycle manufacturer, and in 1998 they sold 1.5 million Giant bicycles worldwide.

Giant Europe, Pascallaan 66, 8218 NJ Lelystad, The Netherlands, Tel +31 320 296 296 Fax + 31 320 296 200.
Website www.giant-bicycles.com

NRS bikes are available over a wide price range, and can be found at Giant dealers worldwide.

The ultimate touring cycle needs two things above all else: comfort and carrying capacity. The foldable Mako, featured in Encycleopedia 4, was a superb tourer, but pannier space was somewhat limited. Building on the successful design elements of the Mako and adding space for six panniers, the Mako Grand Tour prototype was a step closer to the perfect touring machine, but designer Richard Thorpe was still not satisfied with one aspect of this comfortable recumbent – the unwieldy nature of a fully-laden, two wheeled recumbent. A trike was the logical conclusion, and the Mako tr was born.

The extra wheel on the Mako tr adds security and peace of mind. Stopping and starting a two-wheeled recumbent that's heavily loaded with gear can be tricky, especially on hills, as can riding in traffic. Three wheels provide stability while carrying loads, and hill starts are a breeze. The Mako tr has a high seat, which puts your eye-level as high as a motorist's and gives you a better field of view. As a bonus, it is possible to look over hedges while touring, something that can be difficult to do on many touring trikes. Physical comfort comes from an adjustable and breathable seat, and also from a Formula-One-style push-rod rear suspension unit. The riding position is relaxed but not extremely laid-back. The fairing improves performance by reducing drag, and improves safety by lending the whole cycle enormous road presence. It provides weather protection too, but as you're not enclosed by the fairing, you're not isolated from the wind-in-your-face experience of cycling. You won't overheat either.

Luggage capacity, the other primary concern for tourists, is excellent on a two-wheels-at-the-back trike. The large load platform behind the seat for luggage is easily accessible, a convenient shape, and the load won't adversely affect the handling.

The Mako tr is built from carbon fibre tubing, and each tube has a different fibre lay-up and material depending on the mechanical loads that it's exposed to. The fairing is also carbon fibre. It doesn't rattle or shake, as the Mako tr is equipped with a proprietary TFS anti-vibration system. Overall weight is just 36lb. The Mako's rear wheels have camber adjustment for angled road surfaces. Drive goes to both rear wheels through a limited-slip adjustable differential. Two independent disc brakes for the rear wheels offer huge stopping power. An optional electric-assist model is available.

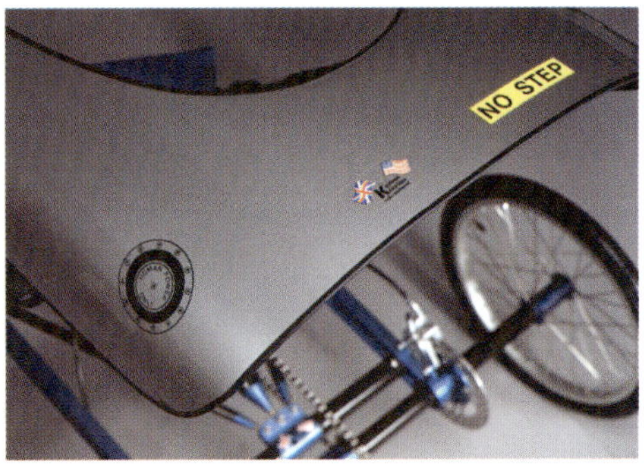

karbon kinetics international

For the past three years, Richard Thorpe has been the CAD Manager for a major composite manufacturer in London. He has been involved in the design and manufacture of Formula 1 crash structures and wings, automotive monocoques, wing assemblies, engine components, and many other composites structures – including designing a full-suspension all-composite mountain bike for Formula 1 Cycles. By using sophisticated CAD software and stress analysis tools, he's found that composites and other high tech materials can be designed to be competitive on price.
The Mako tr is currently available, KKI's folding bike will be released in late 2000, and the fully-sealed drivetrain MTB is planned for late 2001.

Karbon Kinetics International, Monument, CO, USA
Tel: +1 719-487-9882
Website: www.karbonkinetics.com Email: richard@karbonkinetics.com

Prices start at $3800 and will vary worldwide, and also depending on the individual's requirements.

Two decades of recumbent design stand behind the latest Linear. With this model, the CLWB, they've made a machine short enough to be sporty, yet with all the comfort of a long-wheelbase recumbent.

CLWB stands for Compact Long Wheel Base, and it's a layout with many advantages. There are no storage problems: the CLWB is much the same length and weight as a conventional lightweight bike. It has an exceptionally comfortable seat with quick-release adjustment for almost any leg length. There's lumbar support for the lower back and a generous foam seat pad. The steering lets your hands hang loose in a relaxed position yet with full control.

When you ride the CLWB, your whole weight is within the wheelbase, keeping handling well-balanced: there's plenty of weight on the front wheel for a sure grip. The chain drive is simple, direct and efficient, with no idler pulleys or plastic tubes to run through. SRAM 3x7 gearing gives the CLWB a very wide range. High pressure tyres are fitted to both rear 20" (406) and front 16" (349) wheels. Brakes are FSE dual pivot callipers. The front fork is cro-mo steel, and the anodised aluminium box section frame is produced using Linear's proprietary extrusion process. There's a choice of paint finish – smoke, polished, black or red.

For relaxed long distance cycling, it's hard to beat a long wheelbase recumbent with under-seat steering. Linear's version overcomes the transport and storage problems in style: front and rear wheel quick-release and fold under, while the seat folds forwards. It comes in five frame sizes and a tandem version is available as a frameset only. Both the LWB and their Sonic SWB machine have under-seat steering, a 26" rear wheel, 20" front

and SRAM 3x7 gearing. Frames are anodised in silver or black.

A wide range of accessories is available for all Linears, including rear rack adapters and mounts for bottle cages, lamps and computers.

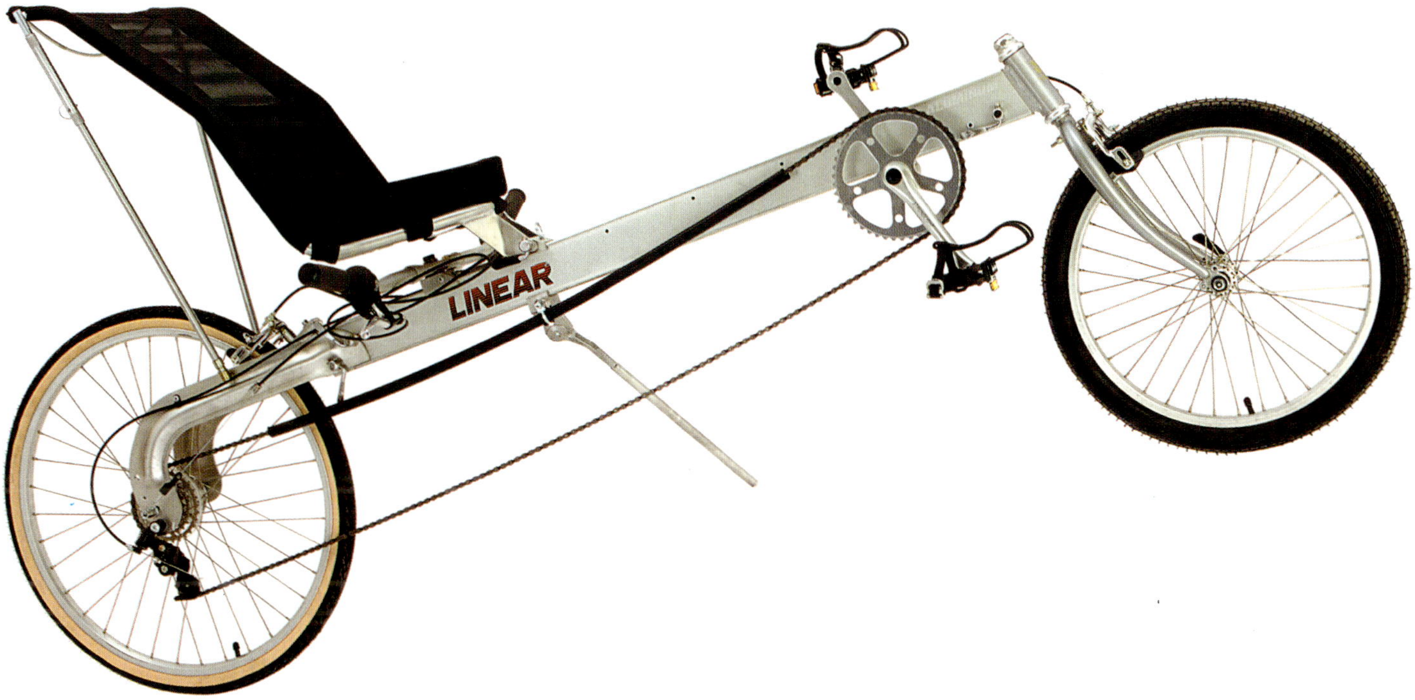

linear manufacturing inc

Based near the Mississippi River at Guttenberg, Iowa, Linear was founded in the early 1980s. Dirk Kann, a specialist aluminium product manufacturer, designed the original machine. Dirk adopted an extruded aluminium box section as the main beam, to which the sub-assemblies and components were bolted, clamped or riveted. Bicycle enthusiast Steve Hansel joined Linear in 1986 and five years later bought the company from Dirk Kann.
Linears are among the most widely available recumbents in the USA, and Linear is one of the largest and longest established manufacturers – a tribute both to the soundness of the original design and the company's ability to develop the product. A thriving mailing list is maintained for Linear owners, and instructions for joining are at the Linear website.

Linear Manufacturing Inc, 32744-MK Kestrel Ave, Guttenberg IA 52052, USA.
Tel +1 319 252 1637 Fax +1 319 252 9030
Email linear@netins.net
Website www.netins.net/showcase/linear or www.linearrecumbents.com

UK agent: Mic Wic, Tel: +44 1793 852484 Email Micwic@btinternet.com Website www.micwic.com

In the USA, the Compact costs from $1099, and the LWB from $1350.

Economies of scale mean many cycle manufacturers mass-produce – and as most purchasers are average-sized males, that's the market they focus on. But what if you are short, female or both? You could easily end up with a badly-fitting bike, an MTB when you wanted a tourer, or a poorly-equipped copy designed for kids. Not only will such compromises take the pleasure out of cycling, but strain on the lower back could cause serious damage. The solution may be a custom-built bike from Chas Roberts.

Roberts is one of the most famous names in handbuilt cycles. Chas builds all sizes of racing and audax bikes, tandems, MTBs and tourers, but specialises in smaller frames. He understands that it's not enough simply to scale down the frame dimensions, especially when building bikes for women, who have shorter arms and bodies but longer legs than men of the same height.

Shorter cyclists need a lower stand-over height and a shorter top tube. But frame angles change with smaller bikes, so a careful balance of head tube angle and fork rake is vital for good handling. Component choice is also critical: bars need to be narrower and have shallower drops for smaller shoulders, arms and hands.

It's particularly important not to shorten the head tube too much, as this reduces frame rigidity and steering predictability. In some cases a move to the smaller 26" wheel may be the answer, but with the Clubman Compact, Chas Roberts offers a frame as small as 18" while retaining full-size 700C x 32 wheels. The Clubman Compact is an excellent lightweight tourer developed over several years, which offers good stand-over clearance, shorter reach and stable handling. Importantly, the pedals don't overlap the front wheel – a potential danger with badly-designed small bikes.

Apart from the Clubman Compact, the Roberts range includes the Cumbria, a heavy duty tour and commute bike with robust 26" wheels; the Bonita, a lightweight audax and touring cycle built especially for women; and the Transcontinental, Chas's flagship tourer, ideal for long distance comfort. Or if you want something totally bespoke, particularly with a smaller frame, Chas Roberts is the man.

roberts

With a world-wide reputation as a master framebuilder, Chas Roberts has been custom-building bikes for a third of a century. When other young lads had part-time jobs in the local butchers or delivering newspapers, 11-year old Chas was brazing cycle racks in the cellar of the family home. That's because cycle building runs in the family: Chas's father was works manager for the famous Holdsworth and Claud Butler lightweight cycle factories before setting up on his own in the early 1960s.
Croydon-based Chas has accumulated considerable expertise in the design and building of small, custom-built bikes. Although initially more expensive than a typical mass-produced machine, a Roberts special has many advantages, including perfect fit, top quality construction, and whatever braze-ons and colour scheme you want. It's also likely to keep its value better than an off-the-peg product.
Although Chas specialises in smaller frames, he will of course build for any size of rider – he once made a bike for Britain's tallest man!

Roberts, 89 Gloucester Rd, Croydon, Surrey CR0 2DN, UK. Tel +44 208 684 3370 Fax +44 208 665 9763

Speed isn't only for racers: everyday riders appreciate just as keenly the ability to travel further and in greater comfort. This is the thinking behind the new Quest, a practical street and touring recumbent with the aerodynamics of an all-out racer.

The designers of the Quest came up with an innovative new take on the problem of aerodynamics. They were convinced that benefits were achievable, particularly in sidewinds, by paying particular atrtention to the trike's cross-section – and they found that the optimum shape was loosely-ovoid, similar to a Darius windmill (which can operate in winds from any direction). A 1:5 scale model was built, then tested at Delft's Technical University. The results suggested that wind resistance could be reduced by 38% over comparable faired trikes, and that sidewinds would actually help forward motion through the 'sail' effect, which is well-known to disc-wheel users.

The Quest uses the traditional tadpole format, with two steering wheels at the front and one driving wheel at the rear. All three wheels are suspended. The fairing provides weather protection as well as improved aerodynamics. It's made of glass-fibre with epoxy, and is coloured with a strong polyester coating, which is applied in the mould. The fairing is partly structural, but has some support from an aluminium sub-frame. It doesn't enclose the rider's head, however: having the head free is better for cooling, avoids the problem of fogged windshields, and gives that essential 'on a bike' feeling.

The Quest is designed for practical, everyday use. Although it's only 76cm wide, in order to fit better through doorways and cyclepath obstructions, there's still plenty of luggage room. Drum brakes on both front wheels are low-maintenance and work equally well in all weathers. Crucially, the 27-speed drivetrain is enclosed within

the shell of the full fairing, so the chain does not pick up water, dirt or salt from the road. It makes the drivetrain last much longer; a machine of Allert's did 50,000km with the same chain and sprockets.

j & s fietsdiensten

J&S Fietsdiensten are a new company founded by Dutch cyclists Allert Jacobs and Ymte Sijbrandij, both of whom spent five years working for Flevobike. Allert is a bike designer who worked on the aluminium Alleweder and designed the Carbon Alleweder, which we featured in Encycleopedia 4. Ymte Sijbrandij is the Dutch champion recumbent racer.

For day to day use, both Allert and Ymte always rode the Alleweder, then later the Carbon Alleweder. Ymte even rode his over the Alps to Italy to visit friends in Turin. After over 180,000km of road experience between them, Allert and Ymte decided to set up a separate company to build a faired tricycle that better suited their ideals. The Quest is the result.

J&S Fietsdiensten, De Vecht 28, NL-8253PH Dronten, Netherlands.
Tel +31 321 332717.
E-mail ymte@ligfiets.net
Website www.ligfiets.net/j-en-s

The Quest costs f 12,500 in the Netherlands, and prices will vary worldwide.

Top-end technology is not for everyone – few need uncompromising race-ready machinery – but it's a vital weapon in any bike manufacturer's armoury. If you're aiming for quality throughout your range, pushing the limits at the top is essential. Batavus and Be One, two Netherlands-based Accell-group companies, embody this philosophy perfectly.

Batavus are one of the Netherlands' largest cycle manufacturers. They make everything from children's bikes to shoppers, folders to touring bikes – and at the top of the range, they make mountain bikes, racers and suspension town bikes to match the best in the world. By keeping up with the cutting edge, the whole range benefits, taking advantage early of new technologies in materials, design and manufacture.

On the road, Batavus make everything from top-end racers like the Team Pro to high-specification roadsters and touring bikes. The traditional, quality Dutch roadster remains the mainstay of the range: these are machines of huge reliability, offering life-long quality. Batavus have also taken this classic design and developed it for today's technology, and the high comfort expectations of consumers. The Jakima FLX is a good example, with discreet rear suspension to further enhance the comfort of the upright riding position.

Where others might cut corners on equipment, Batavus insist on quality: mudguards, chainguard, carrier rack, toolkit and lock all come as standard, ensuring that the owner isn't bothered by the need to add to or upgrade the machine when all they want to do is ride in style.

Be One's emphasis is more on off-road excellence, and the Team DH is the top of their downhill range, engineered for extreme conditions and loading. Flying at high speed down a mountainside, the stresses on the bike can be huge: long-travel suspension soaks up the bumps, but the frame must also be strong enough to provide a rock-steady steering platform, and to survive the inevitable impacts. Be One engineers achieved this through innovative combinations of sheet and tubular materials.

batavus and be one

Both Batavus and Be One bikes are part of the Accell Group, an international group of companies based in Heerenveen, Holland, with strong bicycle brands such as Batavus, Koga-Miyata, Sparta Holland, Cool!-Loekie, E-go, Hercules, Lapierre and Mercier. With annual production of more than 700,000 bicycles, the Accell Group is one of the three largest in Europe.

Batavus are one of the Netherlands' largest cycle manufacturers, making everything from children's bikes to top-of-the-range racers. They've made a conscious effort in recent years to move towards 'comfort' as the guiding philosophy: not just riding comfort, but making the whole experience of owning a bike as easy as possible.

Be One are a separate pan-European brand: through professional marketing and racing success they've achieved excellent brand awareness throughout Europe and beyond. Be One enthusiastically scout out and develop their team riders: in each country where Be One Bikes are sold, the importers and local distributors spot new talent and sponsor young riders. High-performing riders are then nominated for the Be One Europe Team. The Be One World Team draws its riders from this European Team. This policy has bred success: in the 1999 race series, the World Team reached the victory platform no fewer than 90 times, and the Be One team is consistently one of the top three MTB teams worldwide.

Both Batavus and Be One bikes are available through specialist dealers, listed on their web sites:
Batavus: www.batavus.nl
Be One Bikes: www.beone-bikes.com

Telelever suspension, disk brakes… haven't we seen this somewhere before? Indeed we have. BMW are not the first, and won't be the last, to borrow some good ideas from motorcycle technology and apply them to the bicycle.

While many car manufacturers who offer bicycles simply re-badge an existing design, BMW have made the effort to apply their considerable resources and engineering expertise to their 'own-brand' bicycles. The result is a bike that stands on its own merits, with performance to match the best.

The BMW bike range spans everything from weekend cruisers to city bikes, all folding. Most of the range fold in half: move a few quick-release levers, and the whole rear end of the bicycle swings round, leaving a package not much larger than the two wheels. Careful design ensures that it locks completely solid when it's in the riding position.

It's the top-end mountain bikes that offer the best showcase for BMW's engineering. The telelever suspension, originally developed for their motorbike range, consists of a frame-mounted shock absorber linked to simple sliding suspension forks. Without the need to fit suspension units into the fork legs, these can be made lighter, making for a more responsive front end. Maintenance is also much simplified.

The BMW mountain bikes have other tricks up their sleeve. There are two folding stages: remove the front wheel, and the rear triangle folds up and under in seconds. Remove the rear wheel as well, and you have a very compact package indeed.

bmw ag

Why does a car manufacturer make bicycles? Because they have come to the conclusion that their market is not just about cars, it is about providing their customers with mobility. There are times when a car is not an appropriate form of transport, and by providing a bike for these occasions, BMW extend their service. By taking the bike business seriously, they also ensure that the brand attributes of quality and reliability are maintained.

There is also a strong element of lifestyle marketing going on here – purists may frown, but anything that gets non-cyclists onto bikes can only be a good thing. If it's the cachet of the BMW badge that makes them take that first ride, so be it. By providing quality bikes for everyday users, and innovative high-tech bikes for enthusiasts, BMW have made a significant move to become one of the more forward-thinking car manufacturers.

BMW Mountain Bikes are distributed through BMW dealers worldwide.
Websites: www.bmw.com or www.bmw.de

High-speed thrills are second nature to the people at Rans. Their business started with sailtrikes – wind and pedal-powered trikes, one of which once covered 60 miles in 66 minutes. They moved on to light aircraft – and recumbent bikes for those who want to do their flying on terra firma.

Top of the range is their Signature model, the Velocity², pronounced Velocity Squared. Launched in April 2000, this is a low-riding, long-wheelbase recumbent built for speed, with a light TIG-welded CrMo frame and an optional fairing for optimal aerodynamics. The 27-speed derailleur gearing, 100psi (6.8atm) Primo tyres (26" rear and 20" front). Overall weight is 33lb (14.7kg), including fairing and mounting hardware.

All Rans recumbents use their own-design seat, with reflective safety strips and water bottle fittings built into the frame. Steering is laid-back, direct and above-seat for comfort, simplicity and positive control. In the short-wheelbase models and tandems, the steering flips forward, making it easier to get into the seat.

The entry-level Sport series includes the long-wheelbase Wave and Tailwind models, and the short-wheelbase Rocket. The Classic series includes Rans first-ever model, the by now much-refined Stratus, and its shorter counterpart, the V-Rex. The Suspension series includes the long-wheelbase Gliss and short-wheelbase Vivo, both with a pivoted rear triangle acting on a Cane Creek AD-5 Air Shock.

The Screamer is Rans' tandem: by placing the stoker's chainset under the pilot's seat, and the pilot's chainset over the front wheel, Rans have created a particularly compact, light and stiff frame. The Screamer TR version uses S&S couplings, which let you split the frame for portability.

Accessories for Rans recumbents include fairings, mudguards, a new range of powder-coated aluminium front and rear carrier racks, and luggage bags that slide onto the top of the seat. Suspension forks are an optional extra for the Rocket, V-Rex and Screamer.

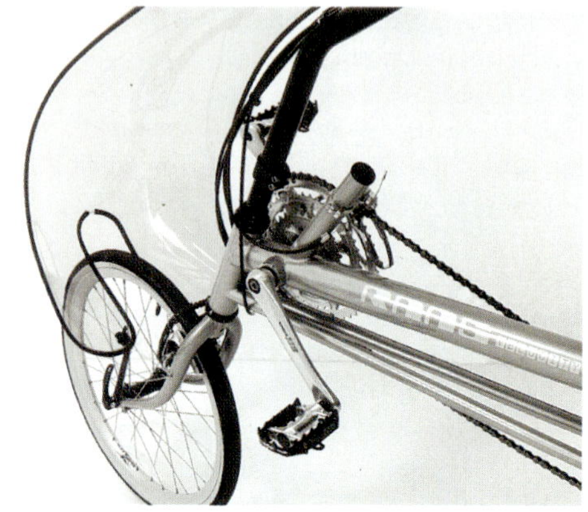

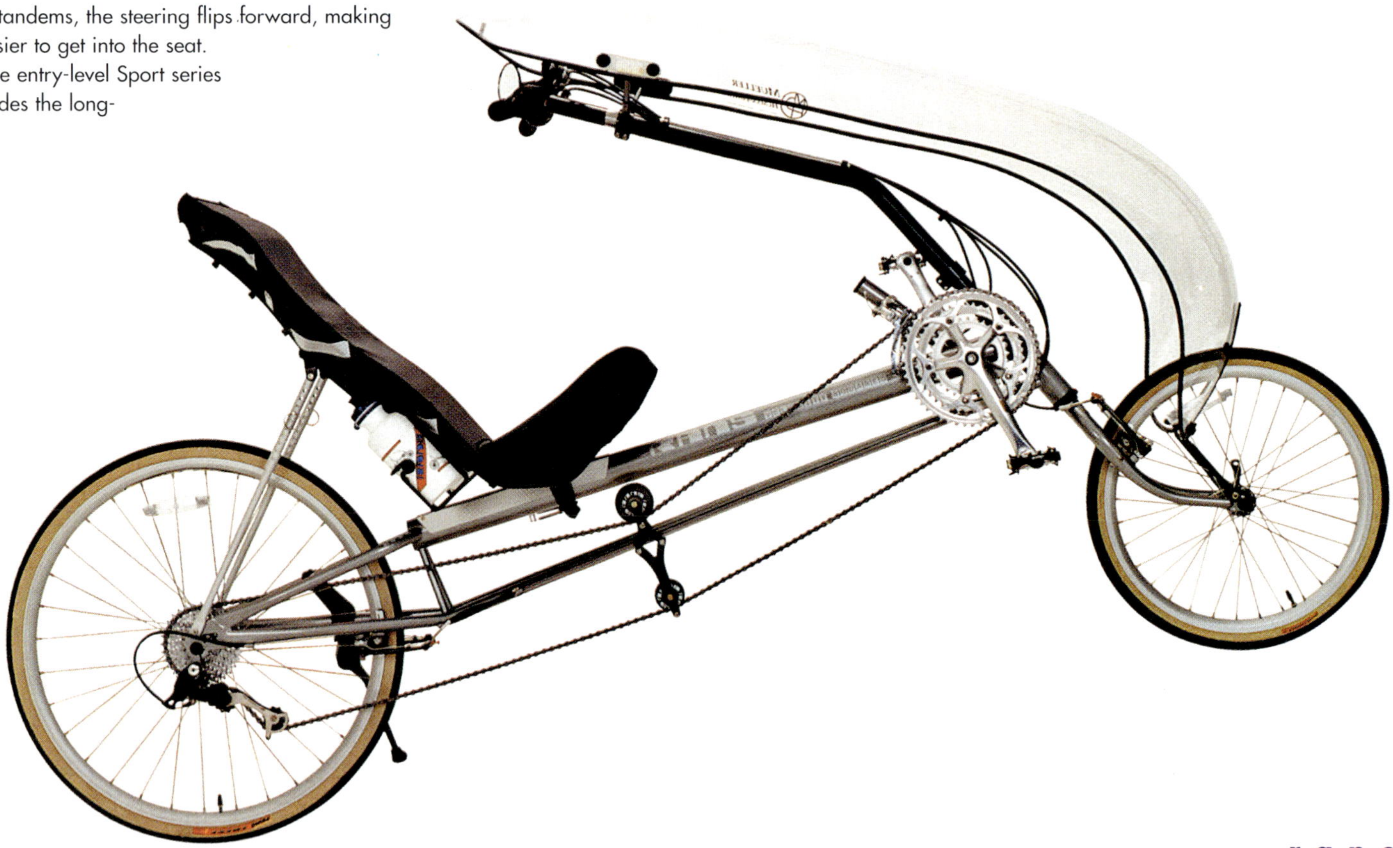

rans

Rans was established in 1974 to build sailtrikes – three-wheeled wind- and human-powered land yachts. Despite a period of commercial success, by the early 1980s production of Sailtrikes had ceased. Rans then turned to lightweight kit planes and recumbents, and continue to expand. The Stratus was their first production recumbent and, after 18 years of refinement, still has pride of place in the Rans Classic series.

Based on the plains of western Kansas, Rans now market 10 recumbents and 13 lightweight aircraft kits. At their newly constructed factory, they use cutting edge CNC technology to produce safe, high quality aircraft and bicycles.

Rans Inc., 4600 Highway 183 Alternate, Hays, Kansas 67601, USA.
Tel +1 785 625 6346 Fax +1 785 625 2795
Email bikes@rans.com
Website www.rans.com

In the USA, Rans bikes cost from $ 795 to over $ 2000. The Velocity² costs from around $1950.

Most folding bikes put portability high on the agenda, with the ability to ride far and fast taking second place. Airnimal Designs have taken the opposite approach. With their Chameleon they've aimed to design a bike that rides like a high-quality road bike, yet folds quickly for transport.

The frame is crafted from 7005 aluminium tubing, a high quality aircraft-grade alloy with exceptional fatigue characteristics. The 24" wheels (bead seat diameter 520mm on the Chameleon, 507mm for trail use) are an unusual choice, but, say the designers, combine the superior gyroscopic effect of big wheels – hands-free riding stability – with the light weight and responsiveness of small wheels. There are a number of high-performance tyres made in these sizes. The unified rear triangle suspension brings comfort with no 'biopacing' and minimal rider-induced vibration. Frame, wheels, suspension, and carefully-designed steering geometry combine to make an unusually fast machine with a smooth and stable ride, even on demanding road surfaces.

The Airnimal has a three-level fold. The fastest and easiest makes the machine small enough to fit two of the bikes into the boot of a small car. The second stage, which requires the removal of both wheels, fits the entire bike and wheels into a case measuring 23x23x11.5" (58x58x29cm). Finally, without the wheels, the Airnimal can be folded so compactly that it will fit into an aircraft hand-luggage case (56x36x20cm). This means that the frame can be kept with you, and it's just the robust wheels and touring accessories which you'll have to entrust to the baggage-handlers.

The basic bike, with a 27-speed Shimano 105 groupset and the standard carbon fibre fork, weighs around 10kg. In addition to the case and bag, a range of accessories to adapt the bike for touring, commuting or light trail use is available

airnimal designs

While Yap Fook Fah was studying Engineering at Cambridge University he met Richard Loke, a keen ultra-distance rider and co-editor of the British recumbent magazine, Recumbent UK, and soon became fascinated by many aspects of cycling. With his engineering background, that fascination quickly developed into a desire to improve and develop aspects of bicycle design, and the two spent several years experimenting with ideas and prototypes to form the design philosophy behind Airnimal Bikes. Fellow cycling enthusiast and CAD specialist Ong Jyh Jian soon joined the team, and they worked together to bring their vision of high performance, easily-transportable cycles to production. The first Airnimal Bikes were born in 1998.

Airnimal Designs: Tel +44 1223 523973 Email info@airnimal.com Website http://www.airnimal.com

Recumbent UK: Website http://btinternet.com/~laidback/recumbentuk

Why follow tradition when it doesn't make sense? Thorn have confounded the old truism that all serious road bikes need 700C wheels. They've made a superlative range of 26"-wheeled touring bikes, taking full advantage of the world's most popular tyre size. Only for certain racing applications, they say, do the relatively fragile larger wheels offer an advantage: for general use, the robust and easy-rolling 26" is supreme.

As well as simply making taller frames for taller riders, Thorn offer different top tube lengths, too – many bikes come in an impressive 18 sizes, each size with its own proportional geometry, to fit riders with a wide range of leg, arm and back lengths. Thorn now specify individually-commissioned heat-treated Reynolds 725 taper-gauge (conical) tubesets for each of the EXP, XTC and Nemesis bikes. Details such as a bottom-bracket drain plug and thoughtful component selection make a big difference to reliability in the long haul. All Thorn bikes use brazed fork crowns rather than the welded unicrown MTB design, for a more supple ride.

The EXP expedition tourer is a true workhorse, perfectly balanced even with a full load of luggage. Its frame is painstakingly constructed: it has extremely heavy-duty dropouts, the lugless-brazed frame tubes are completely sealed – even the bottle bosses are closed off. This frame will never corrode from inside. Thorn's own extremely robust tubular steel carrier racks are the ideal accompaniment.

The Thorn XTC is a light all-round tourer, suitable for long day-rides, moderate off-road use and lightweight cycle camping. The tubes are low-temperature brazed into cast lugs, joints are carefully filed, and the frames are treated internally with Waxoyl preservative.

The Nemesis is an ultra-lightweight sports tourer for those who want a quick-handling, multi-function machine. With a short wheelbase lugless sealed-tube frame, it responds with lightning-quick, road-racer handling – yet it's tough enough to perform manoeuvres you'd never think of attempting on a racer. Couriers, apparently, love it!

Other models in Thorn's range include the Nomad, Audax, Brevet, the Club Tour, no fewer than six tandems, and a pair of triplets.

st john street cycles

In the 17 years since St John Street Cycles opened, it's grown from a small town cycle shop into a large specialist business. Via mail order, telephone and the web, St John Street offer an unusually wide range of components, accessories, clothing and cycles. Robin Thorn is co-owner of the company and puts his success down to hard work, ethical trading and a talented workforce of nearly 30 dedicated cyclists. It's their experience, together with feedback from thousands of customers, that goes into the design of the Thorn range of touring cycles, tandems and frames. Top end models are manufactured in St John Street's own frameshop on their large site at Bridgwater, Somerset. The workshop can also add S+S couplings to almost any frame, new or old. They advise that this operation be performed on existing frames in the off-season – rather than waste riding time in the summer!
Full details of the bikes are on the SJSC website – there are 18 pages on the solo bikes alone! There's also online shopping, full details of paint finishes available, and more.

St John Street Cycles, 91-93 St John Street, Bridgwater, Somerset TA6 5HX, UK
Tel +44 1278 441500 Fax +44 1278 431107
Email sales@sjscycles.com
Website www.sjscycles.com

In the UK, framesets for the new solo range cost from £349 to £899, and complete bikes from £599 (ClubTour), through £1099 (XTC) to around £1349 (EXP) – prices will vary according to specification. See the SJSC website for more details.

How fast is a Windcheetah? It's the most common question that AVD, manufacturers of the Windcheetah, are asked. The whole machine oozes speed – the Windcheetah has a remarkably small frontal area. Yet some owners wanted even more speed, so AVD (Advanced Vehicle Design) designed the beautifully-styled Airflow fairings.

The front and rear carbon-fibre bodywork gives the Windcheetah about a 12% speed advantage, say AVD, and don't have any of the heat or noise penalties of a fully-enclosed bodyshell. The weight is minimal, and the fairings have other benefits too: they protect you and your luggage from the weather, and together with a set of specially-commissioned Windcheetah rechargeable lights, enhance the all-round practicality of the vehicle.

Speed is not always a priority. Recent years have seen the Windcheetah profit from a new range of specialised touring accessories, and the latest products are extra-large Supercube panniers for expeditions. These fit low down and forwards under the seat, and are supported by a lightweight sub-frame. Smaller Weekender panniers for short tours or commuting fit to the standard rear rack.

Assembled from some 60 specially-made components, and involving 140 precision machining operations, the Windcheetah retains a certain cachet as one of the most sophisticated recumbents on the market today. The engineers behind the trike have a simple brief: to produce the best performance possible. Windcheetahs may not be cheap, but AVD like to quote Henry Royce: "Quality is remembered long after the price is forgotten."

advanced vehicle design

Bob Dixon of AVD first met Mike Burrows in 1992. Soon afterwards, when Mike joined Giant as a senior design consultant, he licensed Bob to build Windcheetahs. Bob has been producing the machines ever since and carefully refining the design at the Cheshire factory, six miles from Manchester airport.

Bob welcomes factory visitors, and out of hours visits can be arranged by prior appointment. He's always happy to arrange a full tour of the production facilities and a test ride in the countryside nearby, especially for the many customers who travel long distances to collect their machines in person. AVD export over 90% of their machines.

AVD also produce a very different machine, a load-carrying quadricycle. There are two models: the Taxi, for driver and two adult passengers with luggage, and the Truk, with a tough aluminium pickup body. Both have articulated chassis for a smooth ride on rough ground, without the complexity and weight of suspension.

Advanced Vehicle Design, L&M Business Park, Norman Road, Altrincham, Cheshire WA14 4ES, UK
Tel +44 161 928 5575 Fax +44 161 928 5585

Email bob@windcheetah.co.uk
Website www.windcheetah.co.uk

What do ex-Olympic rowers ride? Bicycles? Of course not! They ride the Thys 222 Rowbike. It's a machine designed by a top-class athlete for serious use, and there's even a European Championship to test yourself against other rowing cyclists.

The rowing action rivals the efficiency of pedalling – some would say surpasses it – and certainly uses most major muscle groups In the body, providing an excellent work-out. Unlike a rowing boat, the seat stays still on the row-bike, keeping handling predictable, while the leg and arm motions, linked by the cable, provide the motive force. The leg-side runs on a hardened chromium-steel bowsprit using sealed-bearing runners, mounted on eccentrics to take up wear.

The transmission is carefully designed to cope with the large forces generated during the power stroke. The chainless bike is propelled by a 3mm stainless steel cable that runs over the patented 'Snek', which replaces the sprockets on a conventional bike. The Snek is an conical aluminium drum with a spiral groove, around which the cable is wrapped.

As the groove is much longer than the stroke, it's possible to shift the propulsion cable to another part of the Snek with the modified derailleur, giving a useful gear range of 230%.

To ensure a good fit, the Rowingbike has adjustable arm-stroke cable and handlebar height. A special steering damper helps minimise any handling input from the rowing action. Designed for reliability and low maintenance, the bike has a demountable bowsprit, cro-mo frame and V-brakes. The 26" rear wheel and 20" front both use deep-section aero rims and high-pressure tyres. A rechargeable lighting system is available as an optional extra. The machine weighs about 14.5 kg.

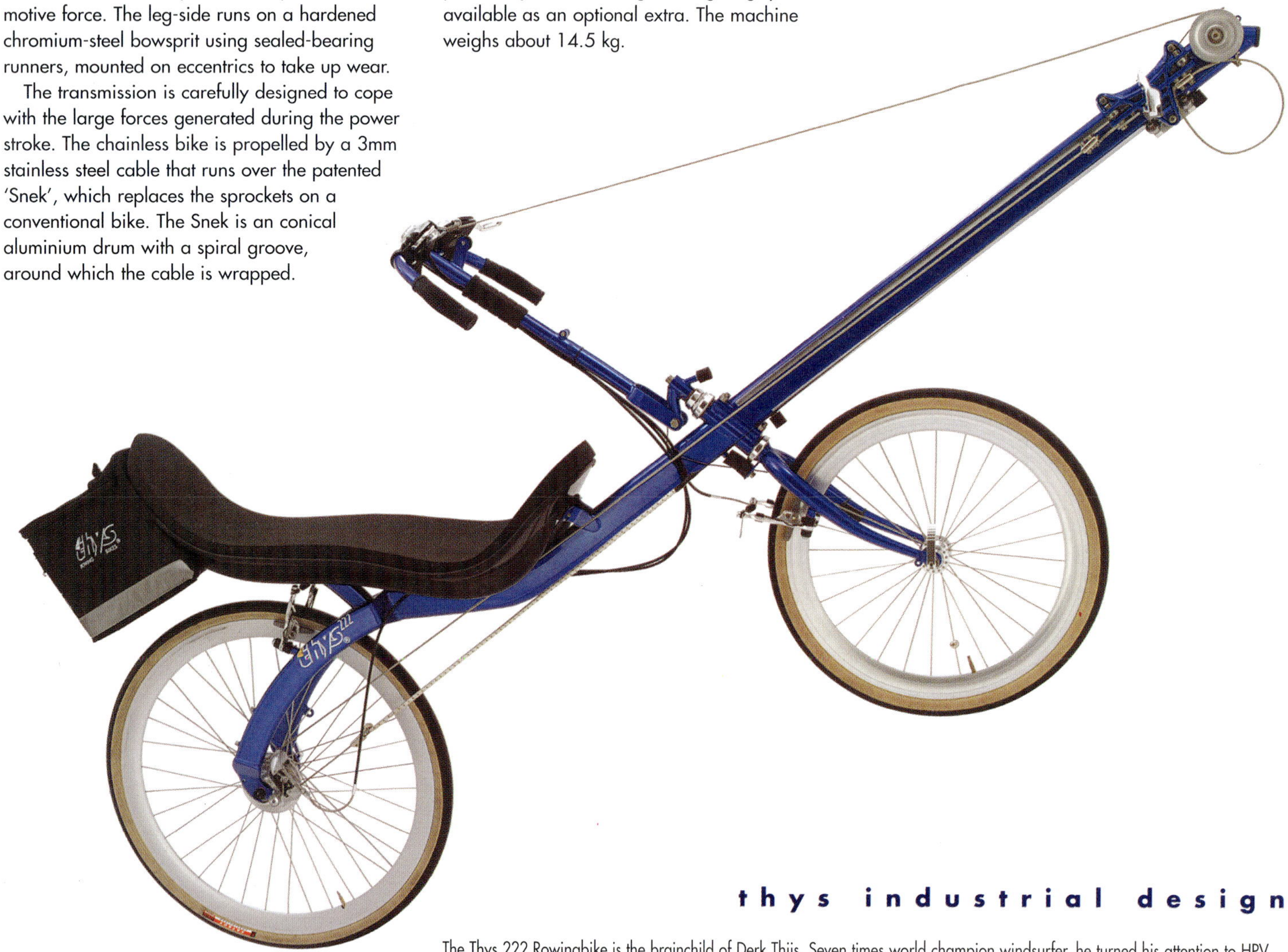

thys industrial design

The Thys 222 Rowingbike is the brainchild of Derk Thijs. Seven times world champion windsurfer, he turned his attention to HPV design in 1983. Working extensively with fellow Dutchman Bram Moens, creator of M5 recumbents, together they produced two record-breaking HPVs. As befits a windsurfer, Derk is based just a few miles from the sea at Middelburg, capital of the south-western Dutch province of Zeeland.

Inspired by the use of muscle power in a rowing skiff, Derk started developing rowing bikes in 1985. Since then he's gained 110,000 km of experience with this mode of propulsion. A major breakthrough came when, with his brother Bert, he designed the Snek variable transmission. They patented it in 1998 and it's now a key element of the latest Rowingbike, the Thys 222.

The annual single-class European Championships for the Thys 222 is held in Zeeland, on the island of Neeltje Jans. The 1999 event attracted more than 40 competitors, including several ex-Olympic and world champion rowers. If you don't yet own a Thys 222 Rowingbike but would like to enter, you can hire one for the race, and for a few months beforehand for training.

Thijs Industrial Designs, Koorkerkstraat 10, 4331 AW Middelburg, Netherlands.
Tel +31 118 634166 Fax +31 118 612511
Email thys@zeelandnet.nl
Website www.rowingbike.com

In the Netherlands, the Thys 222 Rowingbike costs 2090 Euros, including 17.5% Dutch VAT. Prices will vary worldwide.

'Coming a cropper' was, to the young daredevils of the high-wheeler's heyday, all part of the fun of riding those magnificent machines. Other riders, who enjoyed the freedom and thrill of cycling, but not the danger, had to wait until the inventors came up with a safer sort of cycling.

The solution was the design which came to be known as the 'Dwarf Safety'. By making the front wheel smaller, and moving the rider back and down, weight was shifted to the rear wheel, significantly reducing the chance of the rider flying over the handlebars. To compensate for the smaller wheel, a chain drive was used to increase the distance travelled with each turn of the pedals.

It is this design which Mike West, a York engineer with twelve years' experience of building high-wheelers, has re-created. Modern technology ensures that the chains on Mike's machines are much more reliable than those on nineteenth century originals. Mike also offers concealed modern ball-bearings for the axles, in place of the plain bearings often used on original machines.

The rims are made by another York craftsman, Len Clucas, to be built by Mike into wheels with the old-fashioned but very effective 'V' double spokes, with two ends at the rim. It takes three days to build a wheel: such long spokes need to 'settle in' overnight between truing sessions to allow the wire to stretch. 40" wheels are standard, but this can be reduced to 38" for shorter riders. The tyres are made of three-quarter inch thick rubber moulded around a 'helicoil' wire.

Ride this bicycle and you'll combine the exhilaration of high-wheeling without the terror: you'll also recapture a very special moment in history. The most famous model with this layout, the 'Kangaroo' of 1884, enjoyed just a few years of success before being superseded by a new generation of bicycles with chain-drive to the rear wheel.

Mike stresses that the machine shown here is his prototype, and further machines will be equipped with more highly-refined handlebars with extra knee clearance. He has also made numerous detail improvements to tidy the appearance, including a radically-altered hub and fork layout.

mike west

Mike West has been building high bicycles for twelve years. His original product, the 'Challenge' high bicycle, is built to a variety of specifications, and with choices of handlebar shape, handle grips style, crank and pedal type.

Wheel sizes are from 50" to 54". The bigger the wheel you can comfortably ride on, the faster you can go, since every turn of the pedals takes you the same distance as the circumference of the wheel. Yet the larger the wheel, the further there is to fall! A rider 6' (183 cm) tall can ride a 50" (127cm) wheel, but 53" (135cm) is recommended.

Mike strongly recommends that if you are going to ride one of his bikes on a regular basis you should choose the modern and cheaper crank and pedal option; they make for a more enjoyable ride and don't look particularly out of place.

Mike West, Bishopthorpe Bikes, 35 Keble Park North, Bishopthorpe, York YO23 2SX, UK.
Tel +44 1904 703 413

In the UK, a cycle from Mike West costs £1500, although this will vary according to specification.

SOMETHING SPECIAL · SOMETHING SPECIAL · SOMETHING SPECIAL
alpinestars usa
SOMETHING
SPECIAL

ATTRAKTIONEN

ATTRAKTIONEN
ATTRAKTIONEN

SOMETHING SPECIAL

VÉLOS GÉNIAUX

VÉLOS GÉNIAUX
VÉLOS GÉNIAUX

ALL RIDERS WELCOME

Bicycles are a great common denominator. Whatever your requirements, bikes can be adapted to suit them. Hand-cranked trikes and wheelchair tandems are just two ways of opening up cycling to a wider audience – and there are plenty more to cater for other special needs.

Cycling gives you independence, and that's doubly true if you're disabled. The able-bodied have an easier choice of recreational pastimes, and access to a public transport system that doesn't discriminate against them. For the locomotor-disabled, 'wheeling' is one of the best forms of exercise available. And the usefulness of being able to get where you want to go when you want to get there can't be overstated.

Cycling combines the benefits of exercise with mobility, pleasure and practicality. You can have a great time travelling under your own steam, and keep fit in the process. Once you discover the benefits of pedal-power, you may be surprised by what you can achieve. The fact that you walk with crutches is no barrier to being able to move just as freely as any able-bodied person once in the saddle.

The purpose of pedal power is to enhance and extend the incredible power of the human body. If your body's not conventional, cycle technology can adapt to suit your special needs. There are as many disabilities as there are disabled people, so the diversity of bikes for disabled people covers a vast range of needs. They are made all over the world by inspired designers and engineers, many of whom are disabled themselves. The range goes from extra user-friendly standard bikes, via easy-to-balance trikes, side-by-side tandems and detachable wheelchair tandems, to ultra-light racing recumbent trikes with hand-cranked transmission.

The machines are often made in small production runs and may require considerable individual adaptation and the construction of special parts. So bikes for disabled riders are often not cheap. But their potential for changing the quality of the owner's life makes a well-chosen machine more than good value for money.

The astonishing diversity of pedal-power is one of its main charms. All over the world simple human-powered machines still perform a host of vital public functions: the knife grinders of Africa and India, the classic 'Stop me and buy one' ice cream trikes of Europe and the pedaleros of South America with their cycle-taxis. Alongside these are machines which are made for no other purpose than fun and entertainment, like the seven-seater conference bike – every business board room should have one!

Theme parks with attractions based on the humble bicycle are springing up all over the world. And it's surprising that, despite all the tremendous high-tech thrills and spills available, the human-powered rides are often the most popular, with adults and children alike.

The annual 'Kinetic Sculpture' race in Northern California has now been running for over twenty years. Fantastic locally built contraptions take to the streets, beaches, rivers and bay for this very popular three-day race. The entries get more and more outlandish and the resourcefulness of their designers never fails to amaze.

Pedal-power has always attracted the most inventive minds. Bike-trains, boats, planes, mini-airships, lawnmowers and even farmyard diggers have been built to harness the output of human muscles. Now we're starting to see a new breed of fun bikes: small-framed machines with huge balloon-tyres, four-seater family cruisers, and four-wheeled off-road recumbents with independent suspension and hydraulic disk brakes. The world of recreational cycling just gets better and better.

Disability no barrier: Hugh Culverstone, from the UK, completed the Trans-America race (RAAM) in 1986, recording a time of 13 days, 11 hours and 1 minute. He did this despite having lost one leg at the age of 18 as the result of an unusual stress fracture at the neck of the femur. He also completed a distance of 635.199 km (394.705 miles) in a 24-hour unpaced road ride in 1983 – he was only marginally behind the winner who had the advantage of two working legs.

In September 1997, Karen Darke and Pete Allison, from Scotland, completed the first hand-cycled crossing of the Himalayas from Bishkek, in northern Kyrgyzstan, to Gilgit in Pakistan. They used a specially built Greenspeed tandem recumbent trike to complete the 1400 km ride in 26 days, crossing the Karakoram range at a maximum altitude of 4733m.

Steve Ackerman of the US National Handcycling team has not only ridden around the world on his handcycle but has, for the past nine years, taken groups of disabled cyclists across the rocky mountains in the gruelling 'Ride the Rockies' tour, 450 mile ride through Colorado's rocky Mountains.

Kevin Doran of Huddersfield, England set a new World Arm-powered Hour Record at Manchester Velodrome on Saturday 19th June 1999. Kevin's previously held record for the hour was raised to 33.10561 km (approx. 20.575 miles) with his record times for 4,000 metres and 10km also being broken.

In October 1980, Steve McPeak rode a unicycle that was 31.0m (101ft 9 in) tall in Las Vegas, Nevada. This is the tallest unicycle ever mastered. He rode it a distance of 114.6m (376ft) and used a safety wire suspended from a crane.

The longest tandem bicycle ever built is one of 20.4 m (66 ft 11 in). Built by the Pedaalstompers Westmalle of Belgium for no fewer than 35 riders. They rode approximately 60 m (195 ft) in practice on 20 April 1979. The machine weighs over one tonne.

French endurance rider, Gerard Laurent crossed the English Channel by pedal-power in September 1999. He set off from the Isle of Wight on a conventional bicycle fixed to a Shuttle Bike conversion kit. The kit consists of two inflatable pontoons either side of the bike and a propeller, driven by the rear wheel, attached below the front wheel for steerage. The crossing to St Vaast Le Horgue, on the Cherbourg peninsula, took him just over 30 hours.

Own the road – it's standard advice for cycling safety. On the ZEM you can claim your space without trying, because a four-wheeled sociable has the one attribute most cycles lack: width.

Side-by-side cycles aren't new. Experiments were made with them at the end of the 19th century. They didn't catch on because they were too heavy. Nowadays, great strides have been made with materials, and the aluminium ZEM weighs around 70kg, and can be pedalled by just one person – or powered along by four! At the 1999 HPV Championships in Interlaken, a ZEM took third place in a 5km hill climb up 17% slopes, in a 50m sprint, and in the 20km circuit race. Four adults can get up to 50 km/h (31mph) on a flat road. The safe load limit is 400kg, so it's reassuring to know that the ZEM uses motorcycle disc brakes – these are the only non-standard components.

Despite its performance, the ZEM is first and foremost a practical vehicle. With seats that adjust to fit anyone from a five-year-old child to a tall adult, the whole family can get aboard and cycle in safety. There's an optional childseat that fits between the seats for anyone who can't reach the pedals, and all seats have seatbelts.

The ZEM has other roles, too. It turns heads when used for advertising (each ZEM is powder-coated to the customer's requirements – if ordered in advance), and one was used as a wedding vehicle for two Swiss newlyweds.

The ZEM is 2.70m long – not much longer than a tandem – and 1.23m wide, which is narrow enough for most cyclepaths. Storage isn't the problem it would seem to be, as the ZEM can be parked vertically on its rear end. Gearing comes from two seven-speed Sachs hub gears at the front, and two 21-speed Sachs derailleur systems (using front and rear derailleurs) at the rear. Each rider has an independent freewheel.

Options include an auxiliary electric motor, a front baggage rack, a rain cover, an additional child-seat, and a computer. Future developments include a super-light version, a sail, and a two-person ZEM. If you were wondering about the name, it stands for 'Zero Emission Machine'.

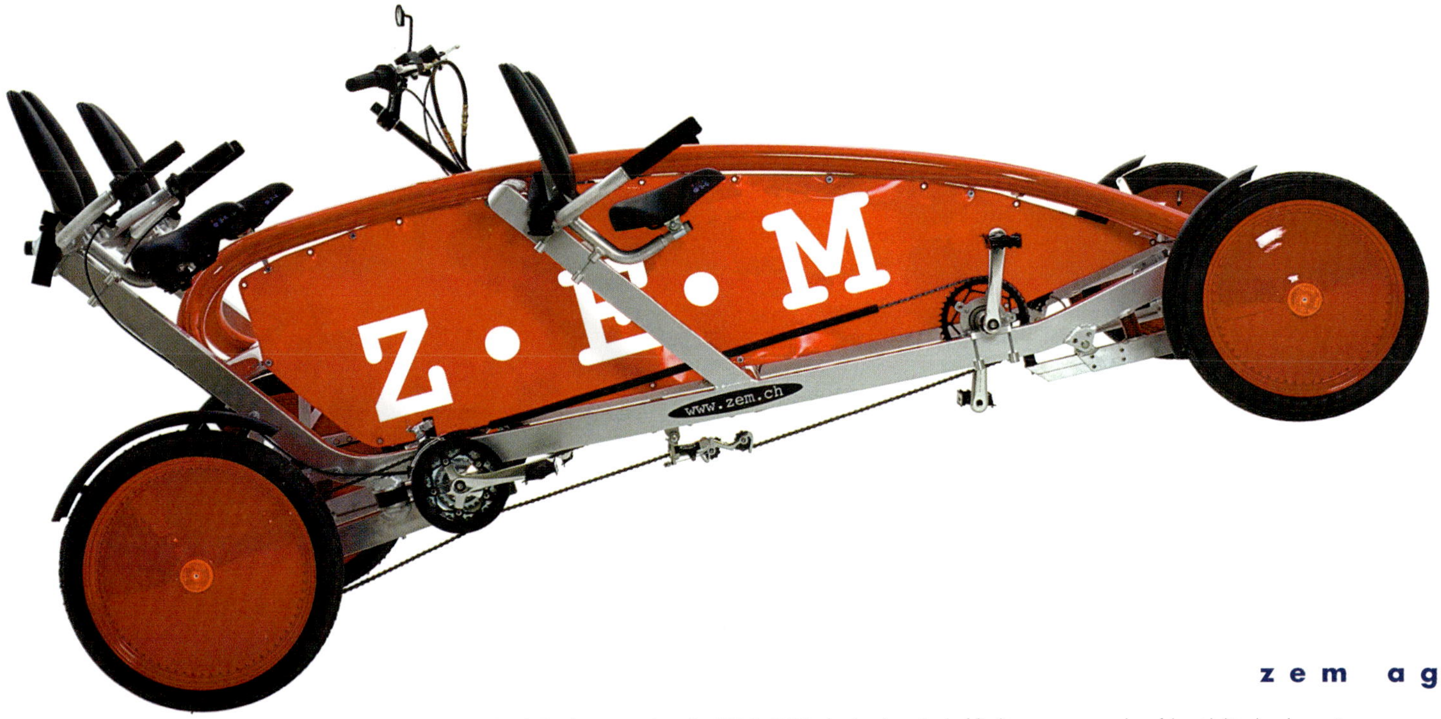

zem ag

Ruedi Frey began work on the ZEM in 1995 after he despaired of finding a way to cycle safely with his daughters. 'I was horrified,' he says. 'My daughters would wobble on their bikes, and cars just pushed past. I wanted a cycle that gave our family more room in traffic.'

After numerous sketches, and discussions with friends who shared the same worries, Ruedi set up a company with friends to design the ZEM. Computer modelling indicated that the hoped-for width of 1.00m – the legal limit for a bicycle in Switzerland, though not elsewhere – would have to be increased to 1.23m for stability. Undeterred, Z.E.M. AG employed an engineering firm that had experience of electric vehicles, Martin Kyburz AG, to develop and produce the ZEM.

The first prototype was ready in February 1999, and the bike went on display at IFMA Cologne in September that year, where it was singled out as one of the stars of the show. An electric-assist model has since been launched. ZEM would be interested to hear from potential agents worldwide.

ZEM: Postfach, CH-8034 Zurich, Switzerland. Tel +41 1 383 6363 Fax +41 1 383 6362
Email zem@zem.ch Website www.zem.ch

In Switzerland, the ZEM costs from SFr 9800, and prices will vary worldwide.

Wherever it goes people turn, stare and talk. Is it a bike? Is it a fairground ride? In a sense, it's both. ConferenceBike is the world's most sociable tricycle. Its riders sit in a circle chatting. One steers and operates the brakes, and everyone pedals or freewheels as they please. This isn't a bike, it's a party on wheels!

"It's somewhere between art and industrial design," says inventor Eric Staller. "It's practical-ridiculous. It's a twist on other multi-person bikes. All riders contribute to the forward motion while sitting elbow to elbow in a two metre-diameter circle. The feet of the riders can be seen pedalling up and down in the middle, as if mixing an invisible substance. I find it interesting to dream up a confection like this and then work with an engineer on the give-and-take process of marrying aesthetics to physics."

ConferenceBike's unusual appearance lowers inhibitions, and gets people talking. It's a hit at cycling events and festivals, for cultural tours, team building, board meetings, school seminars, staff training, advertising and marketing Eric even suggests it can be used to promote world peace. When summit talks are deadlocked, just put the heads of state on board and take them for a ride!

Since its invention in 1991, the ConferenceBike, formerly the Octos, has been continually improved. It now weighs only 70-85kg, depending on the model. This equates to around 12kg per rider. It is 2.50 metres long and almost 2 metres wide, but can turn within its own length.

ConferenceBikes are made from quality steel tubing and are powder coated. Strong motorcycle wheels and disc brakes are used. Saddle height is adjustable to suit a wide range of riders. New for 2000 is a compact 6-seater. This model is just 1.50 metre wide, making it the perfect ConferenceBike for inner city use. A heart-shaped 5-seater Love Bike is available for special performances.

Photo courtesy of York Evening Press

staller studios nederland

Eric Staller is a American artist and designer living in Amsterdam. He became disillusioned with the art world in the 1980s, feeling that he was preaching to the converted. He wanted to take art out into the streets. His first project was the Lightmobile, a Volkswagen Beetle covered with over 1600 computerised lights. He has since focused on pedal power, being interested in devices that stimulate community, which cars don't. "People are driving to and from work alone," he says. "They go to a fitness facility after work and ride a stationary bike to nowhere while talking to no one. Yet we can have social lives, fit bodies, shared experiences, while going places, and without poisoning the air."

Staller Studio, Netherlands. Tel/Fax +31 20 624 9198 Email info@conferencebike.com Website www.conferencebike.com
A ConferenceBike costs 9500 Euro plus tax and delivery costs.

Why climb onto a bike when you can climb in? The Heintz-Bike Velocross makes life so much easier, especially for those with limited limb mobility or other disabilities, thanks to an extremely low step-through height and well-thought out, considerate design. It's also great for the able-bodied.

The foot-plate and unobstructed frame design make a huge difference for those in early stages of physiotherapy or for frail riders: instead of the abrupt, large-angle limb movements needed to mount a bike, the whole action of steeping on and gliding off is gentle and elegant. Simply step on and push lightly off, sit down, and move the feet to the pedals. With its low centre of gravity and stable handling, the Velocross has a particularly secure ride.

All ages can benefit – from six or eight-year-olds who can scoot along, to the very elderly – from the very short to the very tall, up to around 1.9m (6'3"). It has been used successfully by those with limited growth, limited limb movements, balance problems, age-related frailty, amputated limbs, and artificial implants (such as hip joints or back stiffening).

To ensure that the low, 14cm (5.5") step-through doesn't compromise frame stiffness, the Velocross uses several innovative manufacturing techniques. The main frame members are 70x45mm aluminium square-section tubes, bent to a 520mm radius – in fact, a whole circle is formed, then the sections for two machines are cut out. These sections then slot precisely into a strong aluminium casting which forms the foot-plate, and it's welded top and bottom. The casting is so precise a fit that no jigs are needed – except for final inspection. The construction is extremely strong and stiff.

Saddle height is adjustable to give a frame size of 43 to 56cm (around 17 to 22"), and the curve of the rear tube ensures that reach to the handlebars varies according to the height of rider. An adjustable stem takes care of fine-tuning.

Interchangeable rear suspension swing-arms allow the use of either 24" or 26" wheels, giving a choice of ground-clearance and step-over heights. The suspension can also be adjusted to change frame height, and also for hardness.

heintz-bike

Steffen Heintz, the inventor of the Velocross range, comes from a medical background, and saw the need for a more friendly design of bicycle. Several prototypes showed that to fit a 46-sized (size 12 English) shoe on the footplate, the curved structure was the best solution. It's also a highly competent styling feature.

Several versions of the Velocross are available: mountain-bike models with full suspension, city/touring versions with capacity for luggage and childseats, and a range of therapy-bikes, which can be fitted with special adaptations if required. There's a stationary ergometer attachment, for when a totally stable platform is needed.

All bikes are also available with electric-assist motor systems.

Heintz-Bike, Winterleitenweg 80, 97204 Höchberg, Germany.
Tel +49 931 4070534 or 4070535 Fax +49 931 4070536

In Germany, prices start at DM 1995.

Side-by-side tandems are sociable by name and sociable by nature. Sitting shoulder to shoulder makes conversation easy and unforced, whether or not the riders are of equal fitness. The Twin is even more egalitarian than most tandems: it can take a wheelchair seat between the front wheels for a disabled participant. Or, in addition to its two riders, it can transport up to six children!

The Twin's adaptability is largely due to its innovative front platform. This will take the wheelchair seat or one or two childseats. It can also be used as a load-carrying platform, and in this format it will carry up to 100kg. A childseat will fit behind each of the rider's saddles – and then an Add+Bike trailer bike can be fitted to each rear rack. The Twin's two riders don't have to be adults; with 20" (406) wheels and a step-through frame, the Twin will accommodate riders of very different sizes.

Both riders can pedal or not, as they choose, and the left-hand rider operates the steering. A right-hand drive version is under development. There are two back-pedal hub brakes in the rear wheels, and drum brakes up front. Each rider has an independent 7-speed hub gear. If you need more help, the E-Bike-Twin option provides auxiliary electric power.

The Twin has a large presence on the road, making it relaxing to ride in traffic: motor vehicles can't just squeeze past. Nevertheless, at 105cm wide and 185cm long it's small enough to fit on most European cyclepaths. It's also easier to transport or store than it appears, as the two drive units separate without heavy tools from the front platform unit. The assembled Twin weighs 54kg.

robert hoening spezialfahrzeuge

Robert Hoening specialises in making the world of cycling accessible to those who might otherwise not get to enjoy it: specifically, families and disabled riders. His growing range of specialist family machines includes the Compagnon and Add+Bike for families, featured elsewhere in this Encycleopedia.

For disabled riders he offers the Rollfiets wheelchair tandem, also known as the Duet, and trikes: the upright T-bikes. There's also a similar machine to the Compagnon called the Co-Pilot, which can accommodate disabled children with a back-support, seatbelt or many other appropriate accessories. His machines are distributed through agencies in individual countries, as he believes special needs are best understood at the local level.

Robert Hoening Spezialfahrzeuge GmbH, Ulmer Strasse 16/2, 71229 Leonberg, Germany. Tel +49 7152 979490
Fax +49 7152 979499. Email r.hoening@t-online.de. Website: www.hoening.com
Agents: see page 145

In Germany, the Twin costs DM7000, the Rollfiets costs DM8000 and the T-Bike (for an adult) from DM4000.

Gliding around on the water under human power can be supremely tranquil and relaxing, as rowing boats and punts have proved for centuries. Yet these boats neglect the strongest source of human power – the legs. Some leisure park pedalos do use foot power, but are usually let down by poor design and construction. Nauticraft's Escapade is a different breed entirely – a proper, seaworthy boat that uses pedal power to the fullest.

The Escapade has supportive, recumbent-type seating, and traditional bicycle pedals and cranks. The drive unit uses a non-corroding timing belt to turn a large, relatively slow-turning propeller. Since the propeller can 'slip', only one gear speed is required – a 1:4 ratio. Because of direct connection between the drive and propeller, to reverse you just pedal backwards.

A large rudder gives effective steering, controlled by fore-and-aft lever-handles mounted on either side of the cockpit. The hull shape is refined to move effectively through the water, and the sleek windshield contributes good aerodynamics, particularly in windy conditions. There is enough space, shelves, and compartments around the operator to hold ample gear. A 'jump' seat in the back will accommodate a friend or two – whether two or four-legged. A designed-in platform and hand-holds in the transom allow a swimmer to climb back aboard.

The Escapade is 3.7m (12'2") long, 1.22m (4') wide, and has a draft of 0.5m (20"). It weighs 147kg (325lb) and has a maximum loading capacity of 238kg (525lb). The keel is ballast-filled, which makes the boat very seaworthy, and gives the operator a feeling of stability and security. Durability is assured through an impact-resistant, rotationally moulded hull. For long life,

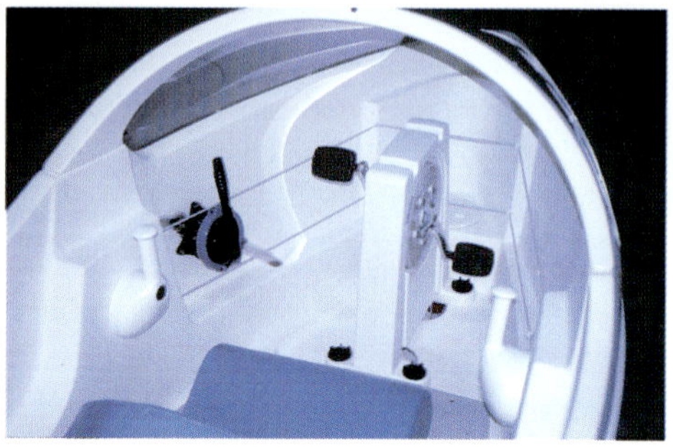

ultra-violet stabilisers are incorporated into the polyethylene material, and all bearings, fittings, and fasteners are corrosion-proof.

A variety of options are available for the Escapade – including a bimini top, transport/storage cradle, and canvas covers.

nauticraft inc

Nauticraft Corporation was set up in 1995 by Curtis Chambers, an injection moulder from Michigan, USA. Chambers, a pedal boat collector and aficionado, discovered the Waterbug and Mallard, two pedal boats designed in the 1980s by renowned yacht designer Garry Hoyt. These two boats had seen only limited production and had been mothballed by their makers, the Harken brothers of yacht hardware fame.

Chambers subsequently obtained a license to build the Mallard, re-named it the Escapade, and engaged Tom Parker of Parker Designs to develop a rotational moulding manufacturing process. As this was being completed, the new drive unit (using a roto-moulded frame) was designed and developed. The Escapade has been in production since 1997. Parker Designs is now developing two new pedalos for Nauticraft – a single person pedal boat and a side-by-side model. Both will be available within the next year.

Nauticraft Corporation, 5980 Grand Haven Road, Muskegon, MI 49441, USA
Tel +1 231 798 8440 Fax +1 231 798 7739 Toll Free +1 888 709 7097
Email info@nauticraft.com
Website www.nauticraft.com

The Escapade costs from US$2950 plus shipping. Prices will vary worldwide.

Herr Friedmann is completely blind – and his wife is so affected by rheumatism that she can only get around in a wheelchair. Draisin, a cycle mobility company from Germany, were proud to be able to give this couple independent mobility, in total safety and comfort, on one of their special bikes, the Capitän Duo.

The Capitän Duo is a tandem trike – perfect for those with limited agility who need a stable riding platform. The Capitän also has double steering – both riders participate in guiding the vehicle, though the leverage can be arranged so that one rider dominates. In the Friedmann's case, Herr Friedmann occupies the rear seat, providing the motive power, while his wife sits on the front, with a support plate for her legs, as she's unable to pedal. She can, however, perfectly well provide steering and braking for the tandem, and communicates closely with her husband to control the 'engine'. An adapter attaches Frau Friedmann's wheelchair to the back of the trike.

Draisin gain deep satisfaction from such outcomes: they believe in enhancing quality of life through freedom of movement. They have been able to help many people who had given up hope of riding a bicycle again to re-discover the pleasure of cycling, and have developed a wide range of special-needs cycles to achieve this. They also have many years' experience of creating special adaptations, fitting cycles precisely to riders of whatever age and ability.

Draisin have made successful therapy-bikes for children, stroke survivors (hemiplegia), those with muscle wastage, epileptics, prosthesis users, the visually impaired, those with balance problems, and many other complaints. The elderly can benefit particularly from Draisin bikes, and most models can be equipped with electric-assist systems.

The engineering which makes these marvellous solutions possible is rigorous: the single-tube chassis designs are extremely simple, stiff and strong, yet have low step-over height. Modular drive systems are reliable, versatile, and low-maintenance. Trikes use differential drives for predictable handling. Hydraulic brakes are often used for balanced braking, and to ensure that plenty of stopping power is available with minimum hand pressure. Thorough in-house testing and quality control ensures safety and reliability.

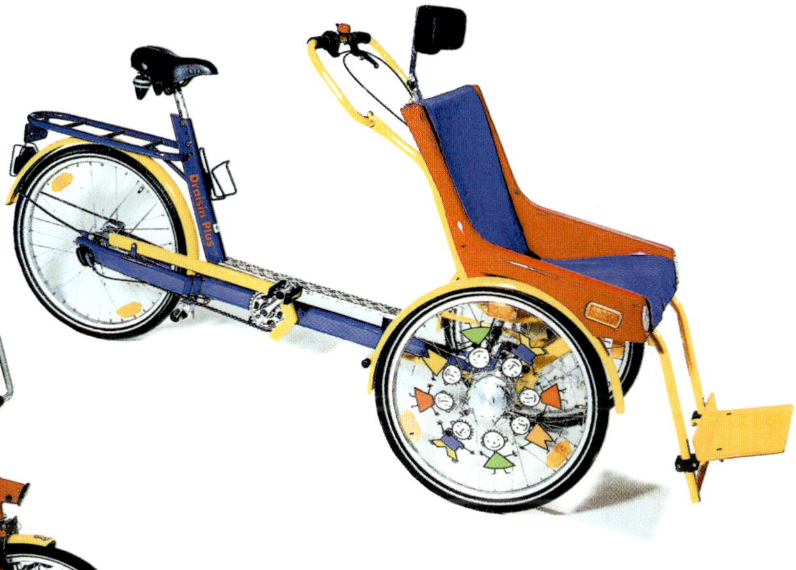

draisin

Draisin offer personal service from the beginning: free demonstrations of the machines are provided, and they offer extensive test runs so that you can be sure a bike is right for you. They can also supply a 30-minute video or CD about their services for a small fee. In many European countries, the cost of special-needs bikes may be met by health service funding, and Draisin are delighted to be able to advise on this.

In their publicity, Draisin use a nice phrase: "Give us a call – even if you think that what you want is impossible!"

Draisin GmbH, Risisee 1, 77855 Achern Gamshurst, Germany.
Tel. +49 7841-260 51
Fax +49 7841-260 81
Website www.draisin.com
Email info@draisin.de

EXTRA ENERGY
DESIGNED IN THE U.S.A.
LOOK

extra
energy

More power to you

Gone are the days when the pleasure of cycling was inextricably linked with the not-so-pleasurable strain of hill-climbing or the tiresome grind in the teeth of a headwind. Today we can choose how hard we work, thanks to a new genre of vehicle, the pedelec. This ExtraEnergy section of this year's Encycleopedia gives just a brief glimpse into what may become a new renaissance for pedal-power in urban transport. The new technology offers the opportunity for whole new sectors of society to rediscover human-powered mobility, thanks to pedelecs which bring the comfort level of cycling up to the level expected by today's consumers. That this is a reality, rather than some optimistic fiction, is proved by a look at the sales figures for 1999.

Worldwide, 500,000 pedelecs and e-bikes were sold: 200,000 pedelecs in Japan, 200,000 e-bikes in China, 40,000 pedelecs and e-bikes in Europe, 40,000 pedelecs and e-bikes in the USA and 20,000 pedelecs and e-bikes in the rest of the World. In this Encycleopedia we show a few examples, which fall more or less into the various categories proposed by ExtraEnergy. SRAM are the first to launch into the easy-pedelec category with their Sparc. The Lafree fulfils many of the comfort-pedelec criteria admirably. The Flyer exemplifies the potential of a sports pedelec. The Heinzmann Estelle embodies the properties of an e-bike – but is also available as a pedelec. The Heinzmann drive is also very suitable for the practical creation of load-carrying pedelecs. The Rabbit Tool folding e-bike is an excellent example of a vehicle to be used in conjunction with other modes of transport. The Rabbit Tool hub motor is also particularly suitable for use in multi-track load-carriers and special bikes. The Lynch motor system also opens up interesting new possibilities for the evolution of load-carrying e-bikes and pedelecs.

ExtraEnergy, the German-based international organisation which promotes human/electric vehicles, divide electric bikes into two categories:

Pedelec: THE POWER COMES ON WHEN YOU PEDAL

It's like cycling with a tailwind. The power of the motor assist is coupled to the effort of the rider using a force or motion sensor. Because the motor is only active when you're pedalling, the human power element is always dominant. Pedelecs, which Yamaha first brought to market in 1994, have the potential to create a new generation of personal transport, which rides like a bicycle, yet is as comfortable as a motorbike.

E-bike: HAND-CONTROL OF THE THROTTLE

On an e-bike the motor power is regulated using a twistgrip or knob, as on a moped. Muscle and electric power are completely independent. E-Bikes can be ridden both in purely electric or muscle/electric modes. E-bikes tend to be more like electric mopeds than bicycles. The trend is to ever-increasing motor power, and this tends to dominate the human power element.

Pick a pedelec

Pedelecs for all

Car buyers can choose from a wide range of types: limousine, van, sportscar, cabriolet, pick-up. In the future you will be able to choose a pedelec to suit your exact needs in just the same way. Here we show five examples of how pedelecs might develop in the future.

Easy pedelec

If you find walking hard going, and cycling is too strenuous, then easy pedelecs offer a new chance at mobility and recreation. Speed and range are suited to shopping trips or convivial day-trips of 20 to 30km. Weight should not exceed 18 to 20kg. The easy pedelec rides like a normal bike, but much easier – it's like a built-in tailwind!

Comfort pedelec

The comfort pedelec is the vehicle for business users, everyday commuters or occasional riders, and also for day rides. Comfort and riding fun, and no traffic jams or parking problems, are guaranteed with a comfortable saddle, full suspension, lockable luggage box and other features. An infrared security system protects from theft. The extra weight of this comfort equipment, which would otherwise make hill-climbing hard, is compensated for by the electric motor. A partial or full fairing could also be added. You can start your working day fresh, not sweaty. After work you'll pedal away happily instead of going to the gym.

Sport pedelec

Sport-oriented and trend-conscious young people will embrace the sport pedelec as a new fashion, which is also most suitable for everyday use. Speeds of 35km/h and more in combination with individual, dynamic design and corresponding branding bring image, fun and fitness.

Load-carrying pedelec

The load-carrying pedelec is equipped to carry loads of all sorts. The vehicle is highly powered, so that steep sections can be overcome even with a full load.

Race Pedelec

The race pedelec is designed for high speeds, with an aerodynamic shape for low wind resistance, low weight and exclusive design. Its attractive racing image makes this an important showcase for pedelec technology.

The Extra Energy section of Encycleopedia was compiled and written by Hannes Neupert of Extra Energy, a non-profit organisation dedicated to promoting muscle-electrically powered vehicles.

Extra Energy, Koskauer Straße 98,
D- 07922 Tanna, Germany,
Tel +49 36646 27094 Fax +49 36646 27095
Email Info@extraenergy.org
Website www.extraenergy.org

With load-carrying and pedicab services springing up the world over, demand is booming for practical electric-assist. When the load becomes heavy, or the terrain hilly, 100 watts of human power can struggle to cope – at least at realistic speeds.

To the rescue come Lynch Motor Company, long-term builders of ultra-lightweight electric vehicles, and manufacturing specialists Garmendale Engineering. Together, they have developed a kit to add electric-assist to pedal-powered vehicles, especially those carrying heavy loads.

The heart of the system is the '190' Lynch motor, a 12V 'pancake' motor which offers excellent torque at low speeds, and has a high power-to-weight ratio. Combined with mounting and drive systems from Garmendale Engineering, the kit offers substantial power-assist for hills, or to extend operating range, at vehicle speeds of up to 15mph. The 12kg battery pack either charges overnight or fast-charges in just 30 minutes, and can be changed in seconds. So with a spare battery back at base, or a rapid-charger, units can operate continuously through the working day, without carrying too much extra weight in batteries.

As we go to press, the system is being evaluated by several manufacturers of load-carrying cycles worldwide, and is in use on Cycles Maximus vehicles (see elsewhere in this Encycleopedia). One of the most exciting applications is a new pedal/solar/electric cyclecar being developed by Lynch and Garmendale for Collinda, a company specialising in electric/solar boats. This machine will carry four adults or $4m^3$ of load in a compact, lightweight vehicle with a minimal footprint (1m x 2m). The low step-on height gives easy access, even for elderly or less able passengers. It should be available in late 2000.

Illustration: Geoff Apps

lynch motor company

Lynch motors are much more than just another boring industrial motor company who've turned their beady eyes on the cycle scene. Ever since 1985, Cedric Lynch, who invented the Lynch motor, has been winning events in electric cycle racing, and experimenting with electric power for lightweight vehicles – all driven by the desire for fuel-efficiency.

Garmendale Engineering is a general manufacturing and prototyping company whose other projects have included trams and narrow-gauge railways, theme park and fairground vehicles, electric scooters and industrial plant.

Collinda is a chemical company which contributes 5% of its profits to their 'Responsible Care Scheme', sponsoring projects to reduce CO_2 emissions. They have developed solar powered boats in India, and the SB Collinda which was the first boat to cross the English Channel under solar power. There are now over 200 solar boats in Europe. Using technology developed in the boats and electric rickshaws, Collinda have sponsored the lightweight city vehicle shown here.

Lynch Motor Co, Richard Fletcher, PO Box 919, London N1 1XL. Tel +44 20 7607 8141 Fax +44 20 7609 3625
Email lynch_motor@compuserve.com Website www.lynchmotor.com
Garmendale Engineering, Roy Shelmerdine. Tel +44 115 932 7082 Fax +44 115 930 9391 Email g.e.l@dial.pipex.com
Website www.garmendale.co.uk
Collinda Ltd, Malcolm Moss. Tel +44 1372 278 416 Fax +44 1372 278 559 Email malcolm@collinda.co.uk Website
www.collinda.com

At just 16kg, the Rabbit Tool EX-Bike from the USA sets new standards for an e-bike. Using an aluminium frame from Dahon and their very compact alternating-current motor/generator, Rabbit Tool have developed this bike as a showcase for their motor technology. It's a commuter vehicle for short distances, to be used in conjunction with other modes of transport – hence the focus on a minimum-weight design. A backpack bag from Dahon makes trips by bus, air or train hassle-free.

The motor is a gear-reduced brushless AC design with a continuous rating of 300W. The range goes from the standard front and rear wheel versions to an ultra-compact design which, including the tyre, gives an 8" wheel, suitable for, for example, wheelchairs, lawnmowers, handcarts or industrial applications. The variant with one-sided wheel support and integrated disk brake is unique world-wide, and is ideal for multi-track recumbents, transport bikes or trailers. The motors are up to 95% efficient in a wide range of conditions – Rabbit Tool are delighted to provide technical details. Different windings are available to suit the torque required.

The motor also offers the possibility of electric braking, and regenerative braking at very high efficiencies – feeding current back to the batteries when going downhill or reducing speed. This patented technology opens up exciting new possibilities for the manufacturers of e-bikes and pedelecs: regenerative braking is powerful enough to make normal braking a rarity, only needed in emergencies, and it has the potential to greatly extend the range of electric vehicles. It also confers independence: prop the rear wheel off the ground, and pedalling will re-charge the batteries. It could also be used to generate stationary power – ideal for camping.

The 7 or 13 Ah nickel metal hydride batteries are contained in close-fitting aluminium tubes, for optimal dispersal of the heat generated during the charging process. The standard charger takes two hours, and is designed to sense the state of the batteries, using smart charging to greatly extend battery life. It is contained in a metal casing the size and shape of a drinks bottle, so can be easily transported. A one-hour charger is under development. The batteries can also, of course, be solar-recharged.

rabbit tool

O.J.Birkestrand heads a mechanical engineering firm making small machine tools in Illinois, USA, and has been developing the electric wheel's hub motor assembly for several years. Motor, throttle, controller and battery pack are designed to be fitted to existing vehicles with minimum modification. Birkestrand is keen to emphasise that Rabbit Tool are not vehicle developers: the Dahon machine is a technology demonstrator, designed to show manufacturers of existing lightweight vehicles the potential of their new motor and battery technologies. Rabbit are in the process of tooling up for high-volume production of the system, allowing for wider distribution.

Rabbit Tool USA, 105 9th Street, Rock Island, Illinois 61201, USA.
Tel +1 309 793 43 75
Fax +1 309 793 4632
Email rabbittool@revealed.net
Website www.rabbittool.com

In the USA, complete systems (motor, battery, throttle, controller) cost from $500.

SRAM's Sparc system is the first product to qualify for ExtraEnergy's Easy Pedelec classification. A pedelec with the Sparc drive switched off rides very much like a standard bicycle, thanks to the low overall weight of 5.5kg, and because a switched-off Sparc has no excess mechanical losses.

The Sparc System consists of the following elements: first, the powered hub in the rear wheel, which contains the well-proven Spectro five-speed Internal gear hub as well as the electric drive. Then, the Sparc Remote Control Unit on the left-hand side of the handlebar, the twist-shifter for the five-speed hub on the right-hand side, the battery box fitted between saddle and carrier rack, and the compact charger, which is small enough to take with you.

At any time the rider can activate the unit and check the power resources using the remote control unit and switch on the handlebar. You can choose between two assist modes. The standard mode offers assistance with starting off, for acceleration, and for hill-climbing, up to a speed of 18 km/h. The Speed mode reinforces the riders efforts up to 24.5km/h. The riding range offers up to 40km depending on riding mode and style, according to ExtraEnergy measurements.

The Sparc system will be used by several cycle manufacturers in 2001.

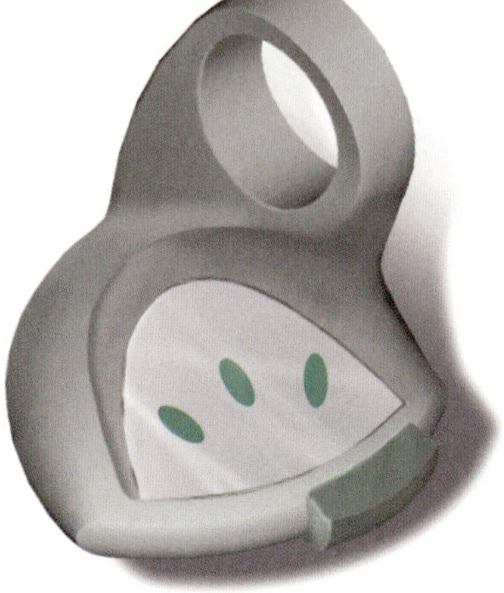

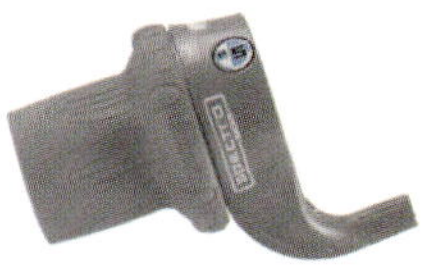

sram

SRAM was founded in Chicago in 1987 by Stan Day. The total staff was six. Today, SRAM is the second-biggest component manufacturer in the cycling world.

The product that made SRAM's name was Grip Shift. By 1992 SRAM had produced one million shifter sets, and in 1995 every bike in the Men's World Cup Cross Country and NORBA National Championships Cross Country was equipped with Grip Shift shifters.

In 1997 SRAM acquired Sachs Bicycle Components, a European company dating from 1895 and famous for its hub gears. A year later, SRAM sold their 34 millionth shifter set, and in 1999 they opened their Internal Hub Factory in Germany. Today they sponsor Team Cannondale, Giant, Rocky Mountain and Tomac.

SRAM's name, incidentally, belies their big company status. It's simply an acronym of Scott, Ray and Sam, the names of three of the company founders; Ray is Stan Day's middle name, while Sam designed Grip Shift. They decided on an acronym for a simple reason: 'All the cool names were trademarked.'

SRAM Corporation, 361 West Chestnut Street, Chicago, Illinois 60610, USA.
Tel +1 312 664 8800. Fax +1 312 664 8826
Website: www.sram.com

SRAM Europe, Basicweg 12-05, 3821 BR Amersfoort.
E-mail srameurope@sram.com

SRAM products are available through dealers worldwide.

The Flyer is, as its name suggests, an urban airline: it's like taking a private plane through town. Even the Flyer Classique, described in the last Encycleopedia, gave an effortless gliding-along sensation – but the new Flyer puts all previous models in the shade!

The technical revolution, which gives this exhilarating riding feeling, lies in the drive unit integrated into the Flyer's bottom bracket. The bottom bracket axle is, at the same time, the axle of an extremely slow-turning motor. This turns at exactly the same speed as the rider pedals, and reinforces the efforts of the rider. Because the motor is gearless, the Flyer is silent, like no other pedelec. This is particularly pleasant when riding in the countryside, when any noise is intrusive.

Both muscle and motor power are transmitted via the chain to the SRAM Spectro 3x7 transmission at the rear wheel. The motor assists progress up to a speed of 35km/h, with a range of around 30km. The energy for the motor is provided by the battery box, which is contained within the aluminium frame. In the battery box are nicad battery cells (5 Ah) and the charger with cable. The battery box is easily removable and can be recharged in any standard plug socket in three hours. After one hour, half of the battery capacity is already re-charged. This opens up the opportunity to fill up your batteries even in short pauses on long journeys. As with all pedelecs, the range depends on the gradients during the ride, and on the riding style. A display on the Flyer shows how much energy is going to the motor at any time, so you can optimise your riding style to suit.

The Flyer is available in four versions: F2, F4, F6 and F8. You can also choose between three frame sizes and various optional equipment specifications. The Flyer F4, F6 and F8 models are permitted for use in Switzerland as mopeds without any speed restriction, and can be ridden without insurance numbers or compulsory helmet use. In most other countries of the world they are not currently permitted for

such use because of their speed potential. The Flyer F2 model is restricted to 24 km/h, and so is accepted as a bicycle in most countries worldwide.

bk tech ag

Visit BKTech AG in Kirchberg, Switzerland today, and you can hardly believe that this company was founded only in 1995 by Reto Böhlen, Philippe Kohlbrenner and Christian Häuselmann. It's particularly impressive that the second-generation Flyers – being delivered since early 2000 – compare favourably with products launched onto the pedelec market by multinational companies. In technical terms and in riding quality, the Flyer team admit no equal worldwide for their new version. BKTech shows that with plenty of enthusiasm, strong determination, a little luck and the right team, visions can indeed become real.
The Flyer is distributed in Switzerland in Flyer Centres, and international distribution is being finalised as we go to press. On the Flyer website www.swiss-flyer.com, Flyers can be reserved and individually configured to the buyer's requirements.

BKTech AG, Industrie Neuhof 9, CH 3422 Kirchberg, Switzerland.
Tel +41 34 448 60 60 Fax +41 34 448 60 61 Email info@swiss-flyer.com Web www.swiss-flyer.com
Prices vary according to model and specification, and range between around 3300 and 6000 Swiss Francs.

The Lafree pedelec range has created a distinctive, hi-tech look, to appeal to today's younger consumer. Lafree are supporting this with an appropriately enthusiastic presence on the internet – at www.lafree.com you can get a taste of the Lafree fun-factor. You can test it for yourself, with a downloadable game, Lafree fun, which helps you get the hang of the power-assist controls.

The Extra Energy test team experienced the Lafree fun-factor first-hand: in their 1999 tests, they awarded the Lafree the highest overall points of any pedelec. Particularly in town traffic, which demands regular, repeated acceleration after traffic lights, pinch points and junctions, the Lafree's fast acceleration speeds your progress. In the Extra Energy 1999 city test, in the hilly old town in Modena, Italy, the Lafree clocked up the highest average speed of any pedelec on test.

The Lafree promotes a very sporty image, and is distinguished by many clever details. For example, the rock-solid two-legged stand has an operating lever for easy parking, and the charger is built into the battery box, with a spring-loaded cable dispenser roll – as often used on vacuum cleaners.

The riding position, the particularly wide saddle and the VPC (Variable Power Control) twist-grip, with which the power-assist from the motor is controlled, give high riding comfort and fun-factor.

The Lafree is available in Europe in three basic models. The E-race in bright yellow with suspension forks, the E-trans in brilliant blue, and the E-world in silver or dark red. The E-race and E-trans models are delivered with short mudguards and without light or rear carrier – but they can easy be upgraded with these accessories if required. The E-world is available in two size, one with 24" wheels, the other with 26" wheels, and is equipped as standard with luggage carrier and long mudguards. A lighting set and front basket are available as accessories.

giant europe, lafree

Lafree is a daughter company of Giant, and produces exclusively muscle/electric hybrid vehicles. The Lafree Race was originally developed for the American market. Since 2000, it has been available in the European market in a modified form, together with the E-Trans and E-World. With the Lafree, Giant is well-placed to become one of the world's leading pedelec manufacturers. Alongside its own-brand Lafree bikes Giant also produce pedelecs for the Ford subsidiary Th!nk, and further co-operative arrangements with other manufacturers are expected.

Lafree Europe is a division of Giant Europe bv.
Lafree Europe BV, Pascallan 66, NL-8218 NJ Lelystad, Holland. Tel +31 320 296 333 Fax +31 320 296 363

For more information, please email to info-usa@lafree.com for the United States, and info-europe@lafree.com for Europe.
Website www.lafree.com

The Lafree is, to date, available in the USA and Europe. Prices in Europe are between 926 and 1004 Euros, excluding tax.

Heinzmann hub motors are highly-rated in the electric bike scene, especially for special-purpose applications. The standard range includes around fifty variants: Heinzmann believe that this range is unrivalled world-wide, and there should be a motor for every requirement, from a special version in a 12" rim, for a maximum speed of 17 km/h, to a 28" wheel with top speed of 54 km/h.

Motor power ranges from 155 watts to 900 watts, and working voltages range from 24 to 36 volts; built-in gearboxes offer further variety. There are two gearbox versions, using steel or plastic gears. By combining these possibilities with the various nicad battery packs and electronic controllers available, and with the choice between an e-bike setup with twistgrip throttle or pedelec mode with pedalling sensor, there should be a suitable variant for every purpose. If there's no solution available off the shelf, then Heinzmann have a reputation for swiftly responding to customer needs with made-to-measure variants.

Several well-known cycle manufacturers are now using Heinzmann motors as standard equipment on their bikes. Alongside the motors themselves, a range of kits to retro-fit are also available, including all cables, throttle, sensor, charger, batteries and the corresponding special rear carrier.

As well as components and retro-fittable kits, Heinzmann also offer complete e-bikes and pedelecs. There are three estelle models available: the estelle Classic D e-bike with twist-grip control on the handlebar, the estelle Classic S pedelec with sensor, and the estelle City with a particularly low step-through frame.

fritz heinzmann gmbH and co

Over the last five years, Heinzmann have made quite a name for themselves when it comes to bicycle hub motors. Fritz Heinzmann GmbH is a traditional, medium-sized company with about 200 employees worldwide, and it can look back on a company history stretching over more than a century. Heinzmann was founded near Dresden in 1897. Their first products included steam engines, lathes, turret-head machine tools and even soap-making equipment. From the 1920s, mechanical speed governers for combustion engines became the dominant product. After the War, the company moved to Albershausen, near Göppingen. Speed governers were still their mainstay, but Heinzmann took new technology on board and went from purely mechanical governers to hydraulic systems. Analogue electronic governers were first produced in 1980, and were for the most part replaced in 1991 by a digital range. Since 1985 Heinzmann have also manufactured electric motors. A particular speciality is D.C. motors, in all sizes for a very wide range of applications. One important product area is bicycle motors, which they've made since 1993. In the picture Markus Gromer, who runs the company together with his father Anton Gromer, presents one of the largest D.C. motors produced by Heinzmann.

Fritz Heinzmann GmbH & Co., Am Haselbach 1, D-79677 Sch^nau, Germany.
Tel +49 76 73 82 08 122 Fax +49 76 73 82 08 194
Email info@heinzmann de Web www.estelle.de

Estelle bikes are available either through dealers or direct from Heinzmann. Full information on specifications and prices can be found on their website.

ZUBEHÖR
ACCESSORIES
ACCESSOIRES
MUDGUARDS · PANNIERS · SECURITY
LIGHTS · MUDGUARDS · PANNIERS
Campagnolo

Change for the better

Owning a bike is an evolutionary process. You don't just walk into the shop, buy one in the correct size then forget about it, like you do with an off-the-peg suit. After you've bought a bike you tailor it to your own requirements. Maybe you change the saddle height a bit here, adjust the handlebars there, add this light or that rack. Your bike grows with you and is adapted to suit your changing needs and riding style. It takes time until the machine you handed over your hard-earned cash for becomes truly yours – until you are at one with it.

Custom-built machines don't come cheap and few of us will ever own one. But the good news is, any bike can be fine-tuned until it rides right for you. Tinkering with bicycles isn't rocket science – anyone with a bit of common sense and a basic toolkit can make changes to the components attached to their frame. Keen cyclists can while away hours poring over the latest accessories catalogues, drooling over pictures of the newest groupsets and gadgets, the brightest lights and the most comfortable saddles.

Selecting the right components for you is a challenge. Learn to see through the vagaries of fashion and choose what it is you truly need to give you that bit more comfort, speed or practicality. Some of the cheapest and most mundane pieces of equipment can transform the way your bike feels and give your cycling enjoyment a whole new boost. But choose with care: everything you attach to your bike will have to be propelled forwards using your own precious muscle power.

There is a bewildering array of accessories for every type of bike and every type of rider. Within this collection are some real gems, and in the next few pages we have tried to bring together a few of these – products that caught our eye because of their quality, their practicality or their sheer inventiveness.

Essential extras

A disc wheel first appeared in 1892 in Britain's annual Stanley Show. The Cyclists' Touring Club Monthly Gazette reported: 'Whether the avoidance of the resistance of the air to the moving spokes is an appreciable advantage can only be proved on extended trial, but on the subject of cross windage that rider can testify to the fact that it is unsafe…'

In the USA in 1896, 60,000 people were employed in producing cycle accessories by 600 different manufacturers. It was estimated that there were between two and four million active cyclists in the USA at the time, compared to one million each in Britain and France.

Throughout history, dogs and cyclists have never got on well. At the turn of the 20th century there were several devices available to deal with offending canines. Gunpowder-filled anti-dog pellets for use in a handlebar mounted revolver were marketed in the Netherlands, and in the United States there was a patented ammonia squirter called the Dog-Scare.

In 1895 the USA had two patent offices, one for bicycles and bike components, and one for everything else. That same year saw the introduction of clipless pedal systems. In April 1895 Charles Hanson of Peacedale, Rhode Island invented the first clipless pedal, featuring a twist to lock, twist to unlock device and having a measure of rotational float. In July 1895 Elijah Harris invented a suction cup clipless pedal, where suction cups on pedal stuck it to the shoe. And in October 1895 Canadian Marmaduke Matthews invented the first recessed-cleat, dual-sided, spring-actuated clipless pedal, the like of which we still see today.

Winters don't get much more serious than in Finland: long, harsh and very, very cold. For serious winter cyclists, Nokian are the people who make serious tyres, and they haven't stopped innovating for over 60 years.

Studded winter tyres are Nokian's trademark product, and they are still the only bicycle tyre manufacturer to offer such tyres. Using either aluminium or tungsten carbide steel studs fixed securely to the tyre tread, these make ice-riding a practical reality for thousands of winter cyclists – be they racers, downhillers or commuters.

The latest downhilling tyre is the Freddie's Revenz, an 2.3" wide MTB tyre for winter competition on the hardest courses, with 4mm carbide-tipped aluminum studs and double-skinwall construction. For more general mountain biking and cross-country racing, there's the Extreme 296 (with 296 studs): a winter mountain bike tyre which functions well on several different surfaces, and has a tread pattern deep enough for snow riding, too.

Cycle commuters have not been forgotten: the Hakkapeliitta W106 is a 106-stud tyre for any winter cyclist, with reflective sidewalls, and available in both mountain-bike (26") and town-bike (700C) sizes.

Nokian were also the first company to make really wide tyres for downhill racing, and they have been much-imitated after bringing out the Gazzaloddi 3.0, with its motocross-like pattern and a very durable double-skinwall construction. This tyre soon became a legend in the downhill world. Mounting it on the front is usually no problem, but you need a special rear frame design.

Nokian is still leading from the front, designing the new generation of 24" downhill tyres. The 3-section Gazzaloddi 24 has about the same outer diameter as normal 26" MTB tyres, so it fits most downhill forks.

Alongside these speciality tyres, Nokian offer a complete range of road and MTB tyres.

nokian tyres

The story of Nokian Tyres began in 1898 with the founding of Suomen Gummitehdas Oy (The Finnish Rubber Works Ltd) in Helsinki. The company moved in 1904 to the township of Nokia on the Nokianvirta river, where the main factory is still sited. At first, they made footwear and industrial rubber products, and their first tyres in 1925 were for bicycles.

In 1967 the rubber factory merged with a paper mill and the Pohjolan Kaapeli cable factory in Nokia to form Oy Nokia Ab, and a new bicycle tyre factory at Lieksa in Northern Carelia started work in 1974. Then, after the Nokia group began to concentrate on telecommunications, the company was listed in 1995 on the Helsinki Stock Exchange as Nokian Tyres plc.

In 1998 Nokian Tyres produced about 11,000 tyres per day – and rising. Altogether, they make over 1000 different products, specialising since the start in tyres for northern conditions.

Nokian Tyres plc, Pirkkalaistie 7, Box 20, FIN-37101 NOKIA, Tel +358 3 340 7111, Fax +358 3 342 0677.
Website www.nokiantyres.com Email info@nokiantyres.fi
Nokian have agents in many countries: see their website or pages 144-145 for details.

The Rohloff Speedhub is like no hub gear you've ever seen before. At a stroke, it overcomes the problems of efficiency, range, weight and maintenance which have relegated hub gears to utility bikes for half a century.

The overall gearing range is 526%, equivalent to a 27-speed derailleur system, evenly spread over 14 speeds, and all controlled by a single twistgrip. You can change gear while pedalling, and shifting happens almost instantaneously – no need to pause or back-pedal, and no painful gaps between the gears. Instead of the indexing being in the twistgrip, it's in the hub, so cannot go out of adjustment. And whereas 5- and 7-speed hub gears have efficiency losses in the order of 3-15%, Rohloff claim a mere 2-4% for the Speedhub – about the same as a well-maintained derailleur.

Inside its well-sealed silver, red or black shell, the Speedhub's multiple epicyclic mechanism is safely protected from mechanical damage and the weather. The control cable linkage has no protruding toggle chain, roller or clickbox to get smashed. The Speedhub is only some 300g heavier than a top-end derailleur system, and is lighter than many mid-range derailleur set-ups.

No wheel dishing is needed, so 32 spokes are more than adequate, even for MTBs, for which there are specially-made DT Swiss spokes. A Speedhub rear wheel built with 32 symmetrical spokes is as strong as a regular 48-spoked 8- or 9-speed dished rear wheel. Two-cross spoking can safely be used with 26" and 700C wheels, and single-cross for smaller wheels down to 18" diameter.

All versions have 32 spoke holes, but tandem versions are available with larger holes for stronger 2.35mm spokes.

Unlike other hub gears, the Speedhub is available with a quick-release or solid axle, and has the standard 135mm over-locknut dimension, making it easy to fit to a frame built for derailleurs.

Mountings for disc brakes are optional and can be retrofitted. The latest Speedhub DB (disc brake) version has a quick-release shifter cable system outboard of the disc, with a 'black box' coupling, detachable from the hub without tools. The disk is supplied with the hub, and is compatible with brake callipers from Hope, Magura, Shimano and Hayes.

rohloff

Bernhard and Barbara Rohloff's family company first achieved fame for its high quality chains. The 1990 Tour de France and World Championships were both won by riders using Rohloff chains. Rohloff's latest S-L-T 99 high performance derailleur chain incorporates their patented Super-Link-Technology and promises high efficiency combined with reduced drivetrain wear. Indicative of their concern for the whole life-cycle of transmission systems, the Rohloffs make a series of high quality tools – the Revolver 2 chain riveter, the Caliber 2 chain wear indicator and the HG-IG-Check, a wear indicator for Shimano Hyperglide sprockets. They also produce an automatic chain lubrication system for derailleurs, the Lubmatic, and a special bio-degradable chain lubricant, Oil of Rohloff.

Rohloff GmbH, Mönchebergstr 30, D-34125 Kassel, Germany.
Tel +49 561 875 615 Fax +49 561 875 338
Email service@rohloff.de Website www.rohloff.de

It's a perennial problem: how do you make a standard bicycle into a practical family load-carrier? Solutions don't come much more comprehensive than the KHW Allround Set 2000, a modular system for family cycling that even includes the family pet.

The basis of the system is a lockable and waterproof carrier box, which attaches securely to the seat-tube of almost any 26"- or 28"–wheeled bike, with or without a rear carrier rack. The box has an easily-accessible opening on each side, unlocked via the central flap. There's plenty of room inside for food, children's toys, spare waterproofs or other essentials. Two water bottles (not included) rest snugly in front, secured by quick-release straps, and there's plenty of heel clearance. The sides and rear of the box are decorated with large reflective patches for safety. Total capacity is 30 litres, and weight is a reasonable 1900g.

Onto this base you can mount a variety of modules. The most complex unit is the childseat: complete with adjustable headrest and foot supports, for children up to seven years old (22kg). A comfortable plastic armrest keeps the child gently yet securely in position – and is moulded into a child-friendly animal shape. Adjustable shoulder straps keep the upper body stable. The weather-protection hood pivots up and over for easy access, and keeps both sun and rain off the child. It also has a protective 'roll-cage' effect. The seat-tube mounting has a particular advantage when carrying children: there's a slight suspension effect, so that road shocks are absorbed and the child gets an easier ride.

When it's loads not children you're carrying, then you can mount a simple basket, perfect for bags of shopping or the like. The basket moulding offers plenty of useful strap-down points.

Need to take the cat to the vet – or would you just like to take your pet with you on a ride? The Allround Set basket complete with pet cage could be the answer. As with all elements of the system, the plastic base can simply be wiped clean in seconds.

khw geschwenda ltd

KHW stands for 'Kunststoff -und Holzverarbeitungswerk' or 'Plastic and Wood Processing Company'. The company celebrated their 50th birthday in 1998, and they have been using and refining their plastics expertise for over 25 years. A long history of successful innovation in the areas of children's winter sports equipment has been recognised by a series of national and international design awards, and has resulted in numerous patents. Their fine range of toboggans and sledges is particularly impressive. The Allround Set 2000 is a showcase for their advanced moulding technology: such a high quality finish and dimensional accuracy is not easy to achieve with such large, thin-walled mouldings.

Kunststoff- und Holzverarbeitungswerk GmbH, Alte Lage, 98716 Geschwenda, Germany.
Tel +49 36205 7490
Fax +49 36205 74934
Email KHW-Geschwenda@t-online.de
Website www.khw-geschwenda.de

When you apply your brakes to scrub off speed, the kinetic energy has to go somewhere – into your rims and brake blocks. It gets turned into heat, and on long descents rim and block temperatures can ride alarmingly – brake blocks may even melt, as veteran Alpine tourists will attest. Kool-Stop made their name – literally – by addressing this problem with an air-cooled 'fin' design.

Back in the 1970s, Kool-Stop also pioneered a high-friction brake block compound that worked well in wet conditions. Today, they offer different grades of brake block for different conditions. Their black pads are designed to perform best in dry conditions, while their salmon pink ones are designed for all other environments. The green pads? They're for ceramic rims, which cause other pads to wear rapidly. All the brake pads use Kool-Stop's 'Rim Friendly' compound, which maximises friction and pad life but minimises rim abrasion. A warning line prompts you to replace the blocks before you wear them down to the metal and grind your rims.

As well as three different grades of pad, Kool-Stop offer specific blocks for different kinds of cycling. Whether you want brake blocks for your road bike's sidepulls, or blocks for your mountain bike's V-brakes, Kool-Stop will have a model to suit. And their block will likely be superior to the factory-fitted pad.

Kool-Stop's latest brake block is the Eagle 2, an innovative design suitable for all cantilever systems. It features an aluminium stem, which saves weight, a larger, lighter pad, and an angled tip to plough mud and rain away from rims. The angled tip also provides correct 'toe in' when you fit the brakes.

For the fashion-conscious, Kool-Stop even manufacture a Vans tennis shoe design of brake block, giving new meaning to the term 'brake shoe'.

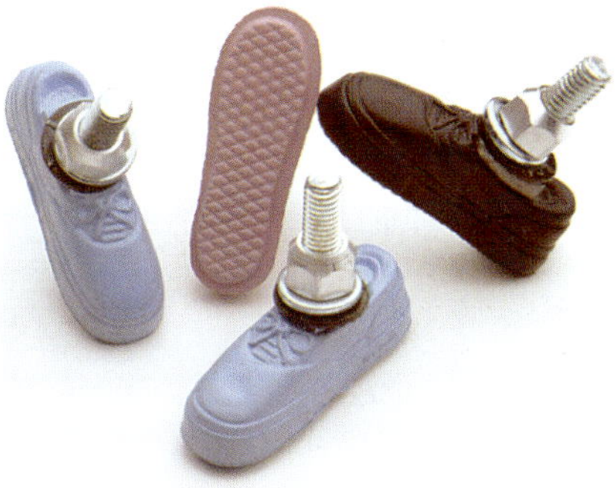

kool stop

Richard Everett began making friction products in 1970, after coming out of the US military. He started the Everett Manufacturing Company with his father Harry, who had previously run a company developing and producing brake pads for automotive and industrial use. Gene Smith of Kool-Stop became a partner in 1974. Kool-Stop have gone on to produce a whole range of innovative accessories and family cycling products, some of which are featured elsewhere in this Encycleopedia.

One of Kool-Stop's early innovations was to mould the friction material around an internal metal frame rather than crimping a pad into a metal shoe. Richard believed this would be a better product, removing the danger of brake pad and brake shoe parting company. Now, of course, this design is the cycling industry standard.

Kool-Stop International Inc, PO Box 3480, La Habra, CA 90631, United States. Tel +1 714 738 4973. Fax +1 714 992 6191. Website www.koolstop.com

In the USA, a pair of Eagle 2 pads will cost around $8, and prices will vary worldwide.

Bicycles are consumer goods – so why don't they meet the design expectations of today's consumer in the way that, for example, even the cheapest portable CD player or radio does? A new generation of materials and computer-assisted design have made possible shapes and forms with attractive, organic qualities far removed from the utilitarian low-tech of traditional cycle parts. SRAM's components for 2001 exploit new technology to the full, and aim to spark a new wave of creativity in cycle design, retaining high functionality while broadening the appeal of cycling through design excellence.

The most dramatic component in the range is the Smartbar, which brings together all of the 'handlebar functions' into one co-ordinated unit. The confusing mass of often-conflicting design signals from gears, brakes, lights, bell, mirror and so on are replaced by an integrated unit, putting the rider at ease. The whole appearance of the bike changes from a functional assembly of disparate components to a professional, classy design. With a Smartbar as the 'dashbar', SRAM hope that bike manufacturers will be inspired to make their frames live up to the standard it sets – and they have created the concept model shown here as an example of the radical re-thinking required.

The Smartbar is more than a nice-looking design: on bikes, in particular, low weight and excellent functionality are essential. Keywords are Ergofit and Ergofunction – the Smartbar is highly adjustable, for tilt, height and reach: the 'Flip Flop' stem flips right over to give a huge range of positions, allowing riders of widely different dimensions or riding requirements to get comfortable on the same bike. It also offers a wide range of upgradeability with computer, lights, bells, mirrors, baskets and who knows what for the future – maybe a GPS or cell-phone holder?

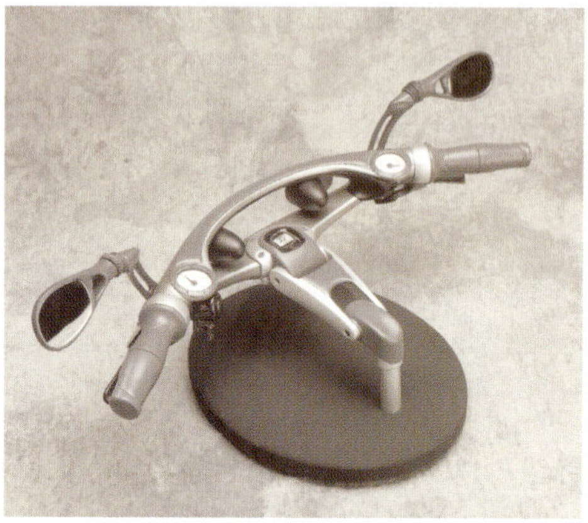

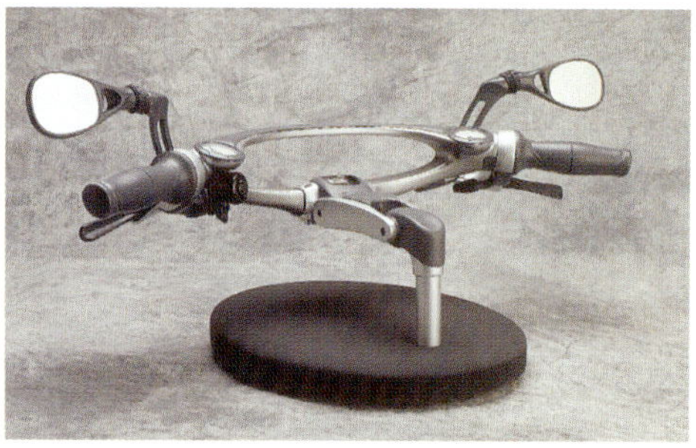

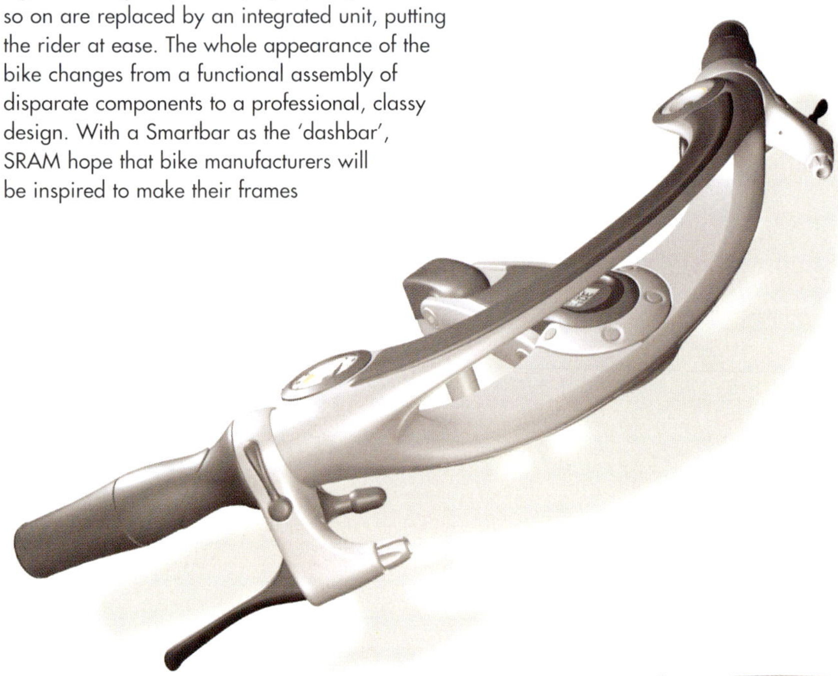

Although the Smartbar is the first component to catch the eye, SRAM's 2001 range covers also full groupsets, and they've applied the same philosophy: innovate continually and put the rider first. Everything is geared to easier operation – and the integrated appearance and style is a given.

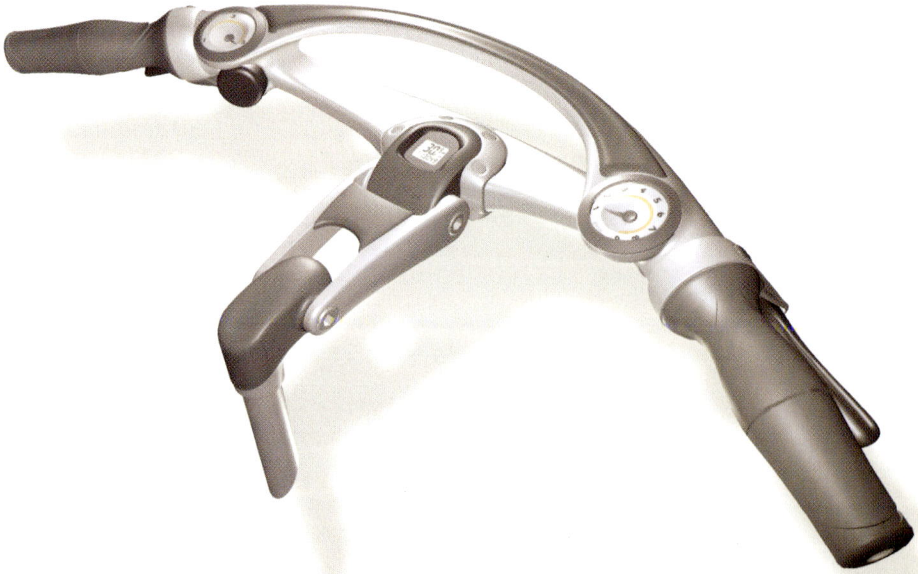

A new transmission system is described as 'DualDrive' technology: taking and refining the best elements of both internal gearhub and derailleur gearing. The shifting process is intuitive: both the hub gear and derailleur are operated from the same shifter-unit, the 'modeshifter' for the hub and the indicator window of the twistshifter show your chosen gear at a glance.

Shifting is slick and efficient, with an indexed derailleur and a load-shiftable hub that incorporates a self-energised servomechanism to reduce shifting forces to an absolute minimum. Wheel removal is no problem, with a new removable 'Clickbox', which secures the pre-installed gears for easy re-assembly.

Braking is the next area to undergo the SRAM makeover. The DualDrive-hub is disc brake-ready – but SRAM offer an elegant and consumer-friendly alternative, the new fully enclosed i-Brake. It's an internal hub brake that stops you smoothly and powerfully – without locking up – and doesn't require fiddly maintenance.

Perhaps SRAM's new Two-Axis brake levers are the best example of all of radical thinking, and of how far you can go to achieve a design with new appeal. Wide and comfortable, the lever's Ergologic function mimics the natural movement of the braking hand, moving in a slight curve as it travels towards the bar thus making braking a new 'sensual' experience.

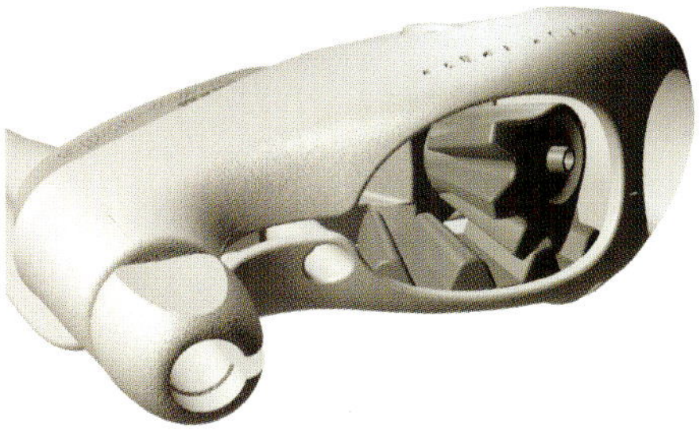

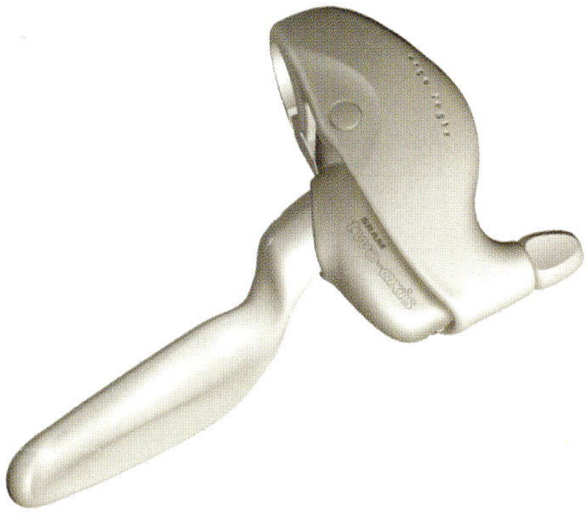

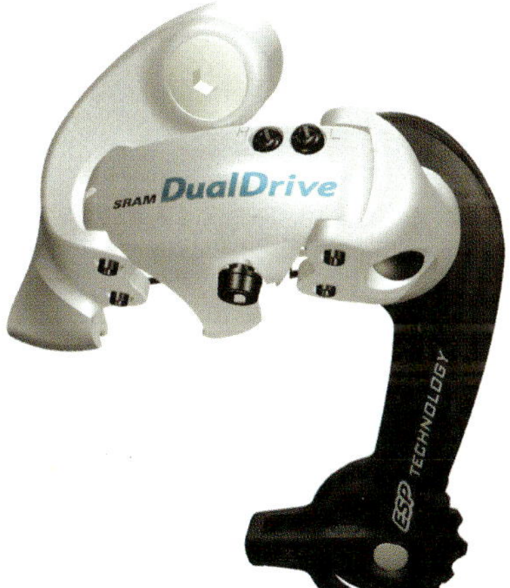

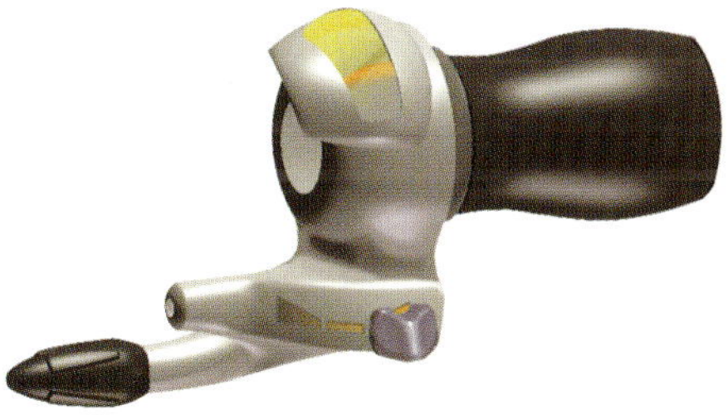

sram

SRAM was founded in Chicago in 1987 by Stan Day. The total staff was six. Today, SRAM is the second-biggest component manufacturer in the cycling world.
The product that made SRAM's name was Grip Shift. By 1992 SRAM had produced one million shifter sets, and in 1995 every winning bike in the Men's World Cup Cross Country and NORBA National Championships Cross Country was equipped with Grip Shift shifters.
In 1997, SRAM acquired Sachs Bicycle Components, a European company dating from 1895 and famous for its hub gears. A year later, SRAM sold their 34 millionth shifter set, and in 1999 they opened their Internal Hub Factory in Germany. Today they sponsor Team Cannondale, Giant, Rocky Mountain and Tomac.
SRAM's name, incidentally, belies their big company status. It's simply an acronym of Scott, Ray and Sam, the names of three of the company founders; Ray is Stan Day's middle name, while Sam designed Grip Shift. They decided on an acronym for a simple reason: 'All the cool names were trademarked.'

SRAM Corporation, 361 West Chestnut Street, Chicago, Illinois 60610, USA.
Tel +1 312 664 8800. Fax +1 312 664 8826
Website: www.sram.com

SRAM Europe, Basicweg 12-05, 3821 BR Amersfoort.
E-mail srameurope@sram.com

SRAM products are available through dealers worldwide.

Sandini Child-Seat Cushion

The gentle vibration of a moving cycle often makes childseat passengers nod off. Unfortunately, many childseats do not offer good support to a sleeping child's neck, which can flop over, risking discomfort or, at worst, injury. Sandini have the answer – a comfortable, washable cushion to fit neatly between head and shoulders. The cushion is split in two, joined with hook and loop strips, so that it can be gently put in place once the child is secured in the seat.

The Sandini cushion is connected to a carefully-sized counterweight with straps via a quick-release connector. To fit the seat, undo the straps from the connector and feed them through the belt holes in the seat – then re-connect the counterweight. This keeps the cushion centred, and means that nothing can get lost.

schneider & semsch

Sandini are keen to hear from potential distributors worldwide.

Sandini: Schneider & Semsch, Postfach 1444, 89243 Senden, Germany. Tel +49 73 072 96 73 Fax +49 73 072 45 32 Email sandini@t-online.de Website www.sandini.de

In Germany, the Sandini cushion costs around DM 49, and prices will vary worldwide.

page 108

Air Zound 2

Bicycle bells are fine for alerting pedestrians, but when a car, truck or bus driver cuts carelessly in front of you, a little 'ping, ping' just won't work as a wake-up call. You need the Air Zound 2, a compressed air horn capable of a juggernaut-like 120 decibels.

Aimed at the serious urban cyclist, the Air Zound 2 is an improved version of the popular Air Zound. The new model features a quick release clamp for the horn unit, a more compact shape, and a volume control so you can honk at a pedestrian-friendly 30dB.

As with the original, the Air Zound 2 is powered only by air. You simply attach a bike pump to the Schrader valve at the top of the horn and fill it up. An 80psi charge will give up to 50 short blasts or 80 gentle honks. The air is stored in plastic bottle which fits in bottle cage, and the whole unit weighs only 100g.

Away from city streets, the Canadian manufacturers point out that the Air Zound 2 is also useful for warding off dogs, bears and other critters.

samui corporation

Samui Corporation, 61 Research Rd, Toronto, Canada M4G 2G8, Tel +1 416 425 2583 Fax +1 416 425 2178 Email airzound2@aol.com

In Canada, the Air Zound 2 costs $25 and prices will vary worldwide.

Easy-Shift Mountain-Drive

Steep Swiss roads drove Florian Schlumpf to create the Mountain-Drive, a high-efficiency, two-speed epicyclic gear built into the bottom bracket. Used with a simple 3-speed hub, it can give a wider range than a 21-speed derailleur.

Florian has been refining Mountain-Drive for more than a decade. He now offers a three-year guarantee, plenty of guidance on fitting, and advice on use with various hub gears and rear derailleurs. There are two versions of Mountain-Drive. Type I, with direct drive and a 2.5:1 reduction ratio, gives the widest range, lowest gears and no overlaps. With a Shimano 7-speed hub, for example, it provides a range of 611%. If you want higher than normal gears, or to avoid a huge chainwheel on your small-wheeled bike, go for Type II, which offers direct drive and a 1:1.65 ratio increase. With a 20" wheel and 11-28 tooth freewheel, it gives a 430% range.

Shifting gear on the Mountain-Drive has always been simple – to change from high to low gear or vice versa, you just push a button with the heel of your shoe on the right or left end of the crank axle. Now shifting is even easier. The new Easy-Shift lever is a cover-plate that fits over the crank arm, attached under the pedal axle, and you shift by pushing anywhere along its length. Easy-Shift levers are available in four colours and can be retrofitted to older Mountain-Drives.

florian schlumpf spezialmaschinenbau

Florian Schlumpf Spezialmaschinenbau, Dorfstr. 10, CH-7324 Vilters, Switzerland.
Tel +41 817238009
Fax+41 817238364
Email schlumpf_ing@bluewin.ch
Website www.schlumpf.ch

page 109

The Indicator Glove

Being seen is the key to being safe when cycling at night. Yet while motorists may see your rear light, they may miss your hand signals in the dark. The Indicator Glove is the answer: four flashing Ultra-Bright LEDs in the back of the hand make signalling effective in poor visibility or at night, and can alert drivers to your presence whether they're behind, ahead, or to one side of you, depending on how you angle your hand. Independent tests have shown that drivers change their attitude towards cyclists using the indicator gloves.

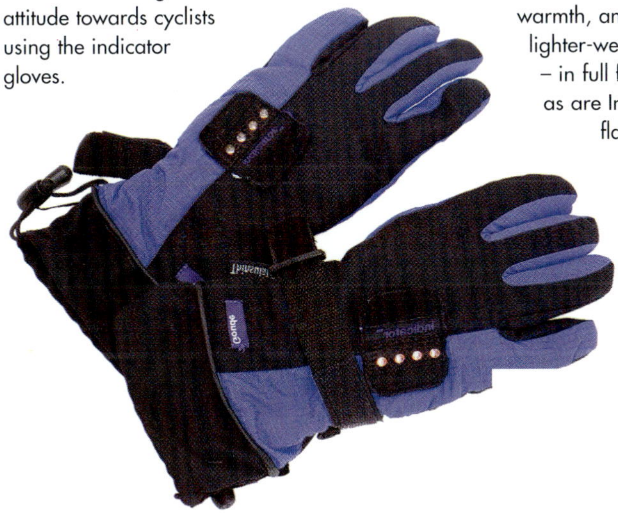

A hidden button in the forefinger lets you switch the LEDs on or off while riding, and a flap on the back of the glove conceals and protects the LEDs during the day. The LEDs are powered by a 3V watch-style battery stored in a pouch inside the glove. Rain and perspiration aren't a problem, as the 'Flextronic' circuit board is sealed against moisture.

The glove comes in S, M, L and XL sizes. The winter gloves have an outer shell of coated Teflon Microfibre for durability, a Thinsulate lining for warmth, and a Pittards leather padded palm. A lighter-weight summer glove is also available – in full finger glove or fingerless mitt style – as are Indicator Strips: velcro-backed flashing LED and battery units in a fabric pouch that can be attached to clothing, panniers, childseats or whatever else you like.

goude design

Goude Design Group, Business & Technology Centre, Bessemer Drive, Stevenage, Herts, SG1 2DX.
Tel +44 462 452852 Fax +44 870 0520 727
E-mail enquiries@goude.demon.co.uk. Website www.indicator-glove.com

In the UK, a pair of winter Indicator Gloves costs approximately £34.95, and summer gloves around £25.95.
Prices will vary worldwide

Jancho

All the best points of a stylish outdoor jacket and a traditional cycling cape come together in the Jancho, an ingenious way to keep dry without sacrificing style.

Until it starts raining, it's a stylish outdoor jacket, which doesn't shout 'cyclist!' at all. Even off the bike, it's a highly-effective, breathable waterproof, with welded seams. It's 100% windproof, so keeps you warm, too.

But when the clouds open, the Jancho comes into its own. Unzip the side zips, and the front of the jacket folds out, making a protective cover over your legs. Velcro loops attach the cape to the handlebar ends, and incorporate an elastic element to avoid restricting handlebar movement. There are three colours: yellow/black, marine blue or red; and three sizes: S, M and L.

innoway

Innoway, Hindemithstr. 20, D-48282 Emsdetten, Germany. Tel +49 2572 98 83 17 Fax +49 2572 859 35 Email innoalex@aol.com Website www.jancho.de

In Germany, the Jancho costs around DM 249, and prices will vary worldwide.

page 110

SON Nabendynamo

A gearless hub dynamo is the ultimate fit-and-forget lighting source for bicycles. It never runs down, it's always there, it won't slip in rain or snow, and it won't wear out your tyres. One of the first hub dynamos around, Schmidt's Original Nabendynamo (SON) is still the most efficient – as proved regularly in independent tests. At 15km/h (9.3mph) it consumes less than 5 Watts of your pedalling energy, and even at 30km/h (18.6mph) it only takes 7 Watts. When the light isn't on, the drag at 30km/h is an insignificant 2 Watts, the equivalent of riding half a metre uphill over one kilometre.

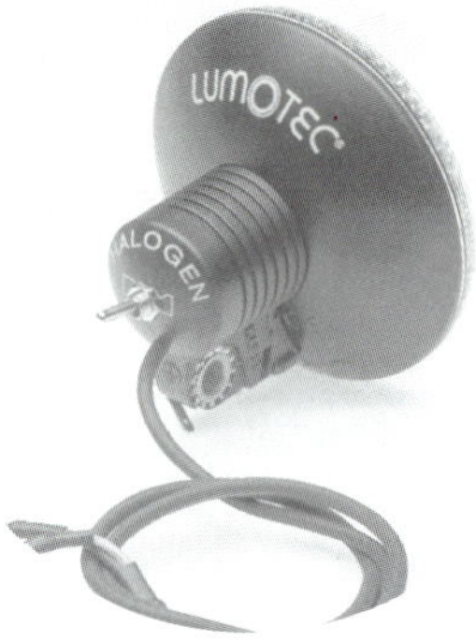

The SON is quiet and durable, being designed to give 50,000km of trouble-free riding in between servicing. It is available in 32- to 48-hole versions for 26" and 700C wheels, and with 24 to 36 holes for 16-20" wheels. A disk brake version is also available.

The SON hub is rated at 6 volts and 3 Watts. It comes with quality Lumotec lights from Busch and Müller, which have been adapted for use with the SON. The hub unit weighs 580g (1.28lb), and has a hollow axle fitted with Allen-key operated skewer.

Wilfried Schmidt Maschinenbau

Wilfried Schmidt Maschinenbau, Aixer Strasse 44, 72072 Tübingen, Germany. Tel +49 7071 3887 0, Fax +49 7071 3887 6. Email info@nabendynamo.de Website www.nabendynamo.de

The SON costs from DM 319, including a Busch and Müller Lumotec front light.

Front racks rarely fit recumbents, and rear ones often put the load too far back. Radical Design have a solution: dedicated recumbent panniers.

Radical's side bags, which range in size from 25 to 70 litres, hang from the seat and rear carrier. For recumbents without a rear rack the 25-litre Lowracer panniers hang only from the seat. Compression straps on all the panniers keep loads secure.

Radical also offer six rack top bags, ranging from 10 to 35 litres; the larger bags have twin pockets for water bottles. Specific bags are available for BikeE-style recumbents and for recumbents with wide mesh seats, while office workers will appreciate the Commuter bag, which fits a rugged Samsonite briefcase inside.

To transport and protect your panniers when they're off the bike, Radical offer a wrap-around duffel bag called the Undercover. They also make conventional panniers, and can make specially-adapted bags to order.

radical design

Radical Design, Hoofdstraat 8, 9514 BE Gasselternijveen, Holland. Tel/Fax +31 599 513 482
Website www.radicaldesign.nl

In Holland, prices range from f 69 to f 369 and will vary worldwide.

CYCLONE TRAILER

When is a trailer not a trailer? When it's a duffel bag! The Cyclone trailer switches from one to the other in seconds. The tow bar and wheels can be removed with a twist of the hand and stowed inside the bag, leaving you with conventional-looking luggage that can be taken on a train or 'plane.

On or off the bike the bag's capacity is 100 litres, and it's rated for 50kg loads. The loaded size is 36x24x20", though this flattens down to 2" high when empty. Trailer and empty bag together weigh 5.5kg.

The trailer's 16" wheels have durable sealed bearings, and high-pressure tyres for minimal rolling resistance. From late 2000, quick release axles will be fitted. The hitch is made from stainless steel and Delrin, an engineering plastic. It can be attached or detached in a second using one hand, and it fits any bike with a conventional rear axle. Radical Design also make a fine range of cycle luggage.

radical design

Radical Design, Hoofdstraat 8, 9514 BE Gasselternijveen, Holland. Tel/Fax +31 599 513 482. Website: www.radicaldesign.nl

In Holland prices range from f 799, and will vary worldwide.

For many people, the Brompton would be the perfect folder, apart from just one thing: it's not a recumbent. Now even that can be taken care of, with the Brompton Recumbent Conversion kit from Juliane Neuss in Germany.

This ingenious kit clamps to the frame, leaving the basic Brompton intact, and able to be converted back to an upright position. The seat moves to adjust for leg length, and fits riders between 160cm and 195cm tall. All parts are powder-coated in black, or are of aluminium or stainless steel. The back of the seat is fitted with a small rack.

The converted bike is very easy to ride and it retains the good handling and tight cornering of the original Brompton. The folded package is a little larger than the original Brompton, but still a tidy bundle at around 36x73x67-83 cm, depending on the leg-length adjustment. The kit adds about 4.5kg to the bike.

The kit is sold through bike shops, and over 50 are already on the road worldwide. Shops who stock the kit are listed on pages 144-145, or contact the company direct.

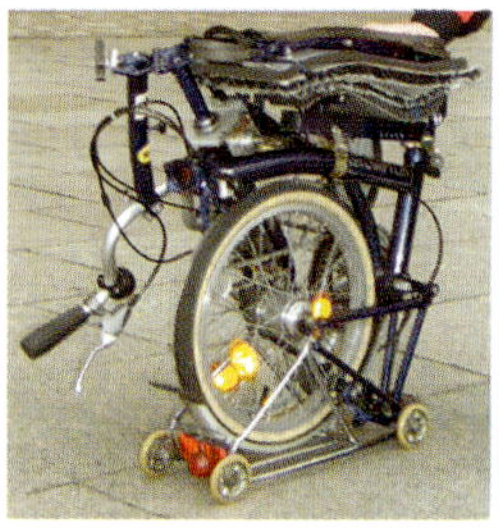

firma juliane neuss

Firma Juliane Neuss, Haferberg 2, 21509 Glinde, Germany. Tel/Fax +49 40 710 951 04 Email info@junik-hpv.de Website www.junik-hpv.de

In Germany, the Conversion Kit costs around DM 1550, and prices will vary worldwide.

SPORK BELTS

Bike tyres make perfect belts – so why didn't someone think of it before? Generator Radsport, a dynamic Leipzig collective – who make their own 'Rotor' bikes, run a bike shop, bar and more – made the connection with their 'Spork' belts. The holes don't 'spread', the material won't warp or dry out, it's completely waterproof and it will last for ever. Spork belts are pleasant to wear, as they're slightly elastic. Belts are made from unused tyres, and to make sure the belt threads through easily, only the flattest, least-curved profiles are chosen.

There are two widths – 4cm for jeans and 3.5cm for smarter trousers. A huge number of combinations of tyre profiles and solid, plated-steel belt buckles from Italy and Spain is possible. Because everything is made by hand, individual wishes can be easily accommodated. Strong quality control and development work continues, and Spork are keen to see their belts raising the fashion stakes in quality dealers worldwide, and would welcome dealer enquiries.

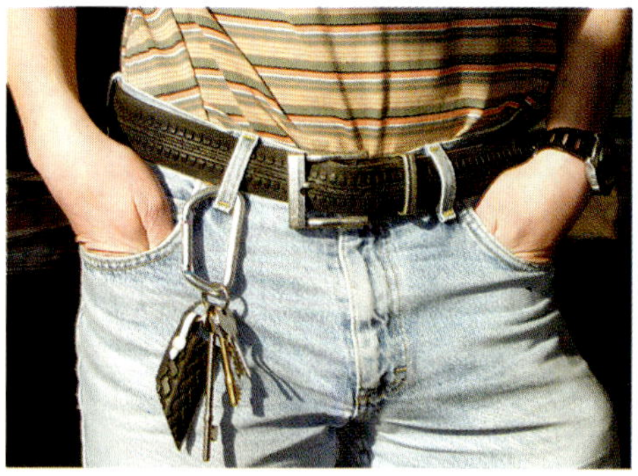

generator radsport

Generator Radsport, Spinnereistr. 7, 04179 Leipzig, germany. Tel +49 341 4980 244 Fax +49 341 49 80 240 Email info@generator-radsport.de Website www.generator-radsport.de

In Germany, a Spork belt costs from DM 59, and prices will vary worldwide.

Tubus Racks

Any frame builder knows that fatter tubes resist bending loads better – it's why mountain bikes and tandems have oversized frames. Tubus racks adopt the same principle. Rather than the 8mm diameter aluminium rod used on most racks, Tubus use 10mm steel tube. The larger diameter adds stiffness, but walls just 0.5mm thick mean the racks are light, too. Stainless steel versions are also available.

All four hand-made racks in the Tubus range will fit wheel diameters ranging from 26 to 28". The Cargo rear rack will cope with loads up to 40kg. The seatstay attachment arms pivot, so the rack will fit almost any frame.

For bikes without seatstay bosses, Tubus offer the Fly, which attaches to the seatstay bridge. Weighing a mere 325g, it enables road and audax bikes to carry up to 18kg. For front panniers, Tubus have two low-rider racks: the Tara and Duo.

Tubus' latest innovation is a front rack to fit almost any suspension forks: it attaches to the fork crown, so the load benefits fully from the suspension.

tubus

TUBUS-Gepäckträger, Borkstraße 20, 48163 Münster, Germany
Tel: +49 251 76 19 68 8
Fax: +49 251 76 19 68 9.
E-Mail : info@tubus-de.de Website: www.tubus-de.de

Bike Hod

page 113

With its narrow, upright profile, the Bike-Hod goes where other trailers can't – through doorways, and even right up to the shop checkout. One of Britain's largest supermarkets, Tesco, has had a fleet of Bike-Hods at one of its stores for several years; the trailers are loaned to shoppers.

The Bike-Hod attaches and detaches from the bike easily: you simply push a pin through the patented hose-hitch. The tow arm can be used for wheeling the bike along or it can be detached to make the trailer compact for public transport or storage.

The Bike-Hod is easy to tow and carries up to a 50kg load. There are three models: the original British handmade Bike-Hod, known as the Carryall, weighs 5.5kg and comes with a 75 litre Carradice Carradura bag (orange or red). Two new German-made models are available: Standard and Deluxe. Both have side and internal zipped pockets; the Deluxe also has an external document pocket and has a capacity of 84 litres; the Standard has a 65 litre capacity.

two plus two

Two Plus Two, 31 Western Road, St Annes, Lewes, Sussex BN7 1RL, UK.
Tel/Fax +44 1273 480479
Email info@twoplustwo.uk.com Website www.twoplustwo.uk.com

In the UK, the Bike Hod costs from £119.95 and prices will vary worldwide.

Newk Bar Ends

A long ride in the Rocky Mountains inspired Joel Newkirk to invent Newk bar-ends. Riding an off-the-peg hybrid with straight bars, his hands and wrists ached, and he suffered in the headwinds, with no way to change the riding position. The Newk dropped bar extension was his response, and proved so popular that he went into production.

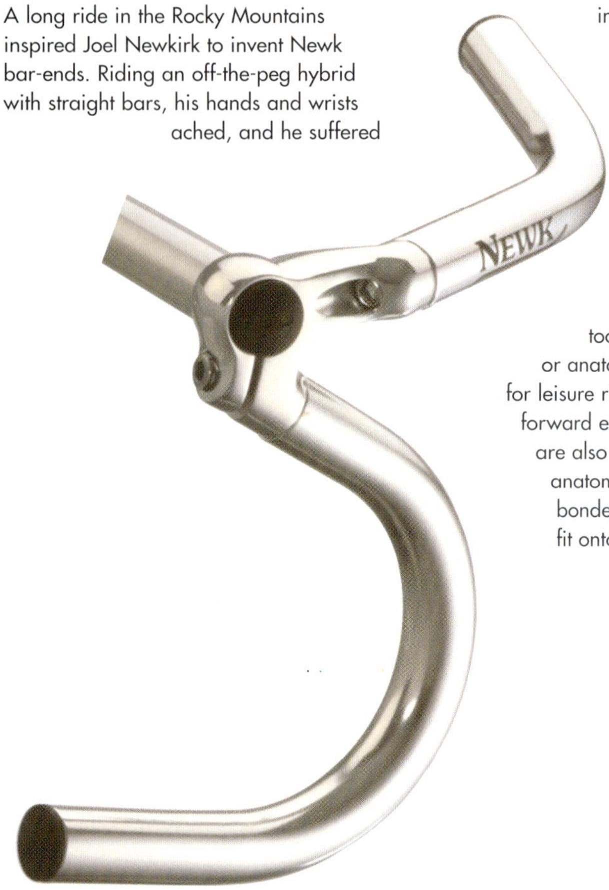

As time went on, customers began requesting other bar shapes, and Newk bars are now available in many patterns – and a custom service is available, too. You can get racing drops, classic or anatomic, deep drops, and shallow drops for leisure riding, all with an L-bend or ski-bend forward extension. The L-bend and ski-bends are also available separately, as are anatomic drops. The clamps are forged and bonded to T-6061 aluminium tube, and all fit onto 22.2mm MTB bars.

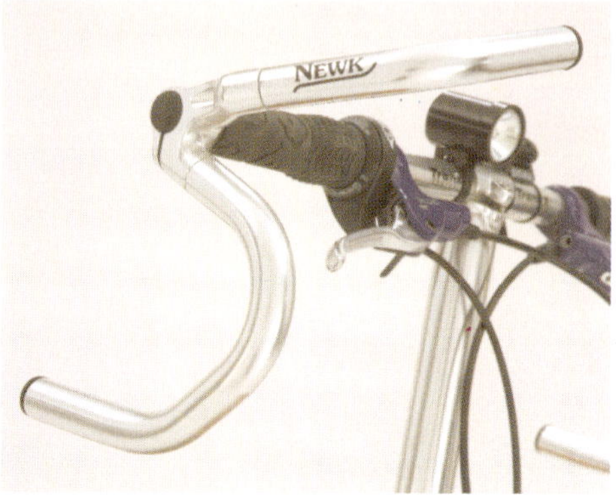

The bar-ends shown here are the latest model, with the angle of the forward extension adjustable to the rider's taste.

newk bike products

Newk Bike Products, 17452 Revello Drive, Pacific Palisades, CA 90272, USA. Tel +1 310 230 2725 Fax +1 310 230 2625 Email NewkBike@aol.com. Website www.newkbike.com

In the United States, Newk bar ends cost from $15 to $65.

Foot Pump

The Bikers Dream tackles an old problem: track pumps aren't very portable – but are powerful, while convenient hand pumps often struggle to reach high pressures. The Bikers Dream takes the best of both: it fits into a 15x9.5x7.5cm pouch and weighs just 250g, yet it's comfortable and easy to use and will inflate to 10 bar (over 140psi) with a proper pressure gauge.

As it's a foot pump, you don't need to bend over at an awkward angle while you're inflating your tyres and you never have an unpleasant pump handle digging into your palm. With one foot on the fold-out support and the other on the plunger, it's easy to inflate either mountain bike tyres, which require a lot of air, or road tyres, which need high pressure inflation. Presta and Schrader valves are provided, as well as valves for footballs and airbeds.

The Bikers Dream bag can be velcro-fastened to your bike, and is also available without the pressure gauge.

bikers dream

Bikers Dream, Tiroler Straße 34, D-87459 Pfronten, Germany. Tel +49 83 6392 4660 Fax +49 83 6392 4664. E-mail sepp.kanzian@talknet.de Website www.bikersdream.de

The pump with pressure gauge costs DM 49,90 in Germany, and prices will vary worldwide.

The ones you missed

Encycleopedia is the guide to the most interesting bicycles from around the world. Each edition is crammed with innovative cycling ideas, products and other editorial. Few products, apart from some classic designs, are repeated issue on issue.

Since its inception in 1993/94, Encycleopedia has featured colour-feature descriptions of around 550 different cycling products from 450 small and imaginative manufacturers. Here's just a small selection of products you may have missed.

Bernds

Manufacturer: Bernds zeitgemäße Mobilität
Country of origin: Germany
Publication: Encycleopedia 4

New Series Moulton

Manufacturer: Alex Moulton Bicycles
Country of origin: UK
Publication: Encycleopedia 99

Kleine Fiets

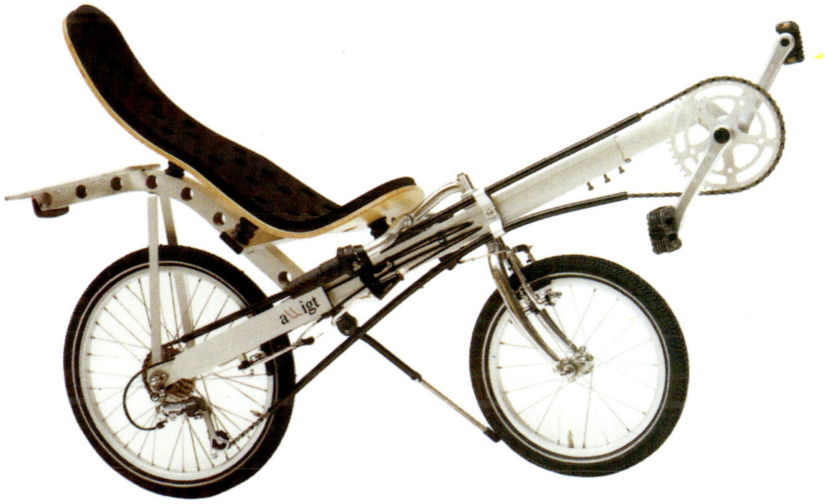

Manufacturer: Alligt Ligfietsen
Country of origin: Netherlands
Publication: Encycleopedia 99

The ones you missed

PREVIOUS ENCYCLEOPEDIAS

A complete set of Encycleopedias is an astonishing reference work to the best ideas in cycling, from many countries, over the last seven years. The majority of the products that appear in them are still available, although prices are likely to have changed, and in some cases contact details will have done so as well. For more regular updates visit our website.

The Encycleopedias published to date are named: Encycleopedia 93/94, Encycleopedia 94/95, Encycleopedia 96, Encycleopedia 4 (covering 97/98) and Encycleopedia 99. All are still available; see pages 134-135 for details.

GlobeTraveller

Manufacturer: Koga B. V.
Country of origin: Netherlands
Publication: Encycleopedia 4

Santana Tandem

Manufacturer: Santana
Country of origin: USA
Publication: Encycleopedia 4

S327 Trike

Manufacturer: A. S. Engineering
Country of origin: Russia
Publication: Encycleopedia 4

Mesicek High Bicycle

Manufacturer: Mesicek
Country of origin: Czech Republic
Publication: Encycleopedia 4

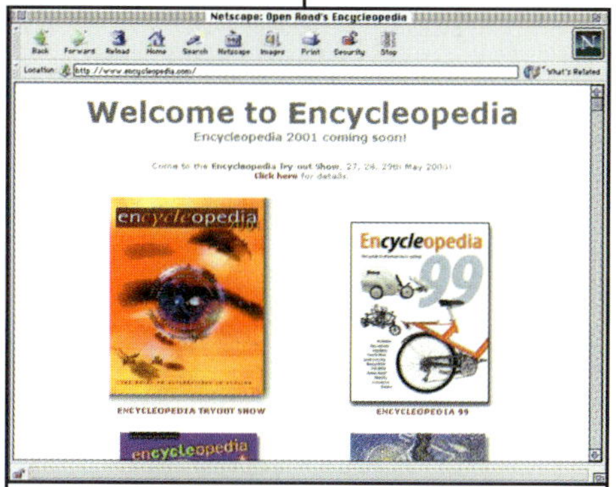

ENCYCLEOPEDIA ON THE WEB

With an annual guide, it's hard to keep pace with rapid developments in the cycling world. In order to keep Encycleopedia as the definitive guide to alternatives in cycling, we're completely revamping our website, so that it's as up to date as possible. New products will be added to the site throughout the year and we'll keep contact details and prices as up to date as we possibly can.

Bookmark the site today: www.encycleopedia.com

Traffic

Manufacturer: Valdenaire
Country of origin: France
Publication: Encycleopedia 4

Cantilevered wheels may look odd, but they make sense for many bikes. In an extract from his book, Bicycle Design, **Mike Burrows** examines the monoblade alternative

Standing on one LEG

For most cyclists the 'monoblade' and the cantilevered wheel are an anathema. This I suppose is only natural, growing up in a world of forks and stays, with the wheel always perfectly central. And woe betide any frame-builder whose wheels did not line up perfectly.

But although as cyclists we are used to seeing the wheels supported on both sides, we are of course surrounded by a world where most of the wheels are cantilever – that is, supported on one side. Indeed, there are very few vehicles other than our bicycles, their motorised cousins and wheelbarrows that still have forks. And nowadays even some of the motorised machines are abandoning forks...

Most famously, the Lambretta and Vespa scooters of the Sixties were cantilever front and rear, and carried a spare wheel under one of the side covers. Historically, though, it is a much older idea. I first saw the idea on a bicycle when visiting the Museum of British Road Transport, Coventry in 1985, in the form of the Invincible produced by the Surrey Machinists' Company in 1889. And even this machine had borrowed the idea from an earlier Coventry-built velocipede!

The idea did not catch on, and the first commercially successful use of the cantilever principle on a two-wheeler was the scooter.

GOING MONO

I first consciously used the idea on the Mk2 Speedy, as a way of simplifying the frame design. By mounting the single rear wheel on one side I was able to run the main 2" diameter aluminium tube right through from the bottom bracket to the rear axle, and not have to graft on a rear triangle. It looked very strange at first – although it wasn't really any different from the cantilevered front wheels – but worked extremely well. I decided that maybe a bit of asymmetry would not be a big thing. In practice this turns out to be true.

Despite having made this small mental leap in 1982, it was not until I saw the Invincible in '85 that I began to understand the possibilities for two wheelers. I had by then developed the original monocoque racer, which was what I was riding as part of the Rover Centenary ride when we stopped off at the museum in Coventry. On the way home on the train the pieces dropped into place. This time I did not need the cantilever for convenience but for its aerodynamics – biplanes are bad and monoplanes are good. So one big fat-but-aerofoil section blade would be a lot better that a pair of regular, or even aero-section, blades.

My first blade was machined and filed from a length of 2" square 6061 aluminium. But it was another four years and a lot more 'triggers' to finally hang the rear wheel on one side as well. Again, it was out of line, but by only 16mm this time. It was this Mk2 that was adapted by Lotus for Chris Boardman to use so successfully in the '92 Olympics.

ONE-LEGGED EVOLUTION

Having got this idea of cantilever wheels and monoblades as an option stuck firmly in my mind, I built a series of bikes of different types in an attempt to discover the advantages and disadvantages of the system. I had already built a short-wheelbase recumbent bike as part of the Mk2 development programme, again using the same 2" alloy tube as on the Speedy. This again had considerable wheel offset. It worked well and was eventually sold on to a friend who successfully raced it in HPV races.

I then built a shopper in answer to a request from Jim McGurn who, at the time, was Editor of New Cyclist magazine. He actually only wanted me to write an article on city bikes, but I was not in writing mood. And so Amsterdam was built, brazed from largish steel tubes and with the most offset rear wheel yet: 60mm. This you could notice when you first rode it, but after ten minutes or so it was just like a bicycle. This was followed by Vienna, a carbon fibre/aluminium tube rear suspension touring bike. This was more interesting than successful.

Then came San Andreas – well, what else can you call a mountain bike with offset wheels? It was similar to Vienna but rather better built. Not exactly a great bike, but a lot of fun to ride, it was also sold on to a friend who has since used it three times to complete the Polaris Challenge.

FROM AMSTERDAM TO CAMBRIDGE

Having got a job with Giant, and now that I am an 'official' designer, I don't do quite so many funny bikes. But I have done a couple of mono designs. Amsterdam evolved into Cambridge. This was built from aluminium tube and castings, and

had the multi-sprocket transmission completely encased in the frame. This was built to sell the idea of a purpose-built city bike to Giant.

It has now reached Paris, which is moulded in one piece from glass-reinforced plastic. It has what I describe as an 'internal direct transmission system'. Currently it is being used for a comprehensive market survey. Assuming that everyone likes it, and that we can find a cost-

effective way of moulding the frame, it should be in production soon.

I played around with ATBs, adding a glass-fibre monoblade (complete with disc brake) to the front of my hardtail – very light and very strong. I also built a single leg suspension version with 110mm of travel and employing the oleo leg principle, as used on virtually all the world's aeroplanes – monoblades every one!

NOT ALL ONE-SIDED

So what have I learned after 15 years of monoculture? 'Swings and roundabouts' is the answer. It is a matter of understanding the reasons and advantages, but also the trade-offs.

First, and easiest to understand, are the aerodynamic reasons. If air resistance is your big problem, either on the velodrome or in a time trial, then a monoblade in place of a fork is almost a must. It will add weight, and the fact that it tends to flex sideways, rather than fore and aft, does not encourage cornering at the limit. But it will impress the man with the stopwatch.

It also makes sense to have a cantilever rear wheel in these situations. This is not an add-on option, but for those intent on designing the best it's the only way to go. You can even fit gears, as on the Speedy.

For road racing , however, it makes no sense at all. You are mostly in the bunch, so get little aero advantage – just poor handling, extra weight and a front wheel that you can't change easily if you puncture. For time trialling, of course, you have no outside help and you have to change your own tube, which is easier with a cantilevered wheel.

A cantilever can also make sense for structural reasons, as on the rear end of the Speedy. Here the offset rear wheel is a small price to pay for a very strong simple frame.

Also, for structural reasons of a different sort, it makes sense on the front end of a mountain bike, where it is stronger and lighter than a conventional fork. This might sound strange, as I have already dismissed the idea for road bikes. But we do not do to road bikes what we do to mountain bikes. Quite simply, we abuse them. We ride them into tree stumps (collar bone!), down boulder-strewn mountain sides, not to mention the steps outside the local C&A – and we expect them to survive!

Now it is in the nature of things that, as they get bigger, they get stiffer and stronger, and that they do this faster than they get heavier. Suffice to say that, as you double the diameter of a tube, its weight doubles but its stiffness will increase some four and a half times – really nice numbers. This means that if you were to swap your two 25mm diameter fork legs for one 50mm diameter leg, you would have doubled the critical fore and aft strength without any increase in weight. You will also have increased the torsional stiffness, but that is already many times higher than necessary.

For suspension legs there can be even more advantages, as there is only one set of parts. And one big set is cheaper, and should work better, than two small ones. You will have to use disc brakes, as there is nowhere for the 'other' canti to go. But that is no bad thing.

Despite having thought long and hard about it, and even built one, I can see no good reason for a mono rear on an ATB – and quite a few reasons not to. But I have not given up completely.

The last and probably best reason for going mono is for the sheer convenience of it. Firstly, tyre changing for punctures. Not for racers – they have quick-release wheels – but for commuter/city use, where a QR is an invitation to someone to walk off with your wheels. And anyway, it is a bit tricky if you have a chainguard, hub gear and drum brake. With a single-sided shopper you don't take anything apart. The drum brake need never be disturbed. And the chain and gears are inside the bike, running in oil rather than wiping it off on your clothes.

Bicycle Design is published by Open Road, who also publish Encycleopedia. More details on pages 135-136 and 138-139.

Cycling Planet

A hundred years after motors drove horses off the road, promising the dream of unfettered, effortless travel, inner city rush-hour traffic is still inching along at 6mph. The 20th century has seen an exponential growth in car use, but at the end of it all, where has it actually got us?

Our countryside grows tarmac. Village life is cut in half and killed by fast roads. Fearful parents keep kids trapped indoors, where they degenerate in front of the television. City streets are 'safe' only for cars, their zoned-out occupants cocooned in hotel-style luxury — with GPS, talking dashboards and built-in coffee cup holders and pollution intake filters. Cyclists, pedestrians and other 'irrelevants' are encouraged to get off the streets, or suffer the consequences.

But this doesn't have to be the future. The alternatives are already around us.

In communities all around the globe, there are both active and accidental cycle advocates who are pedalling against the flow, refusing to accept that all good things come car-shaped. These are enlightened communities for whom the bicycle is an unquestioned part of their culture. Their voices are beginning to be heard, and their message is: "You can do it by bike!"

THE AMISH

The sound of a one-horse buggy passing by at a canter quietens the atmosphere. There is no engine noise, no horn or blaring radio, just the natural rhythm of an animal working for its keep. It is the sound of simplicity and modesty – it is the sound of the Amish lifestyle.

The Amish are a religious farming sect, founded in 1693 in Switzerland by Jacob Ammann. The group now lives mainly in North America, particularly in Indiana and Pennsylvania. They regard all their possessions and property as having religious significance, and have little regard for labour-saving devices. A tool that inspires patience is more highly valued than one which will get the job done faster. You may see an Amish person in a car, but it won't be his or her car. They choose not to own cars – ownership implies a duty to use for spiritual growth, and they decide that they cannot do that with cars. Instead they use their bicycles and their buggies for most of their transport needs.

The humble bicycle fits perfectly into the Amish way of life. Men, women, children and babies are all equally represented aboard the quiet wheel. Their bicycles are simple, utilitarian machines – locally built and locally maintained – ridden calmly by people going about their daily tasks, with no thought of cycle advocacy. Many roads around Amish communities are built with lanes just for buggies and bicycles, making cycling a pleasure.

Amish traditions make a virtue of being humble and ordinary. Tell an Amish man that his bicycle is the finest around and he'd probably argue with you.

U.S. BIKE MESSENGERS

Grow more eyes. Be aware of everything in a 360-degree circle around you. That's the advice of bike messenger J-Bone, a veteran of 20 years' hard-won experience riding the streets of San Francisco and Denver. "Don't focus solely on what's ahead," he says. "It's a matter of intuition and experience – once you get a feel for it, you'll know what's behind without looking. It's a sixth sense that develops over time." But even the most careful, experienced messengers admit that to do their job you have to plunge yourself daily into organised chaos.

Packages have been carried by bicycle for more than a century, but the bike messenger as a cultural icon is a more recent phenomenon. Its combination of high risk and low pay-off make bike messengering the quintessential youth-culture job. The urban anti-hero image has attracted many a would-be road warrior. But the realities of the job mean that few stick at it for more than a matter of months. "The job is dangerous as hell," says San Francisco bike messenger Mike Mitchell. "We aren't well compensated, there's no sick leave, no paid holidays, no anything."

Most couriers are drawn to the profession because they love two things: bikes and independence. Messengering was custom-built for gearheads who love feeling their quadriceps burn, and hate sitting at desks or wearing suits.

The advent of fax machines and modems cut into the bike messenger business, and the numbers on the streets fell. But gadgets can only help so much – packages still need to be moved, and speed remains critical. The swiftness of delivery depends largely on the street knowledge and guts of the messenger. Cutting corners brings messengers a lot of bad press about their unlawful road antics. J-Bone insists that "good riders always obey traffic signals. Blowing lights isn't professional and the fines cut into your profit." Besides, he adds, "it's a very good way to die."

Bike messengers are here to stay. World and European cycle messenger Championships are now an annual event, and messengers the world over are organising themselves into unions to improve their working conditions.

Picture credits: (Opposite) Sue Darlow; (top right) Doyle Yoder; (right) Sue Darlow

DANISH COMMUTERS

Denmark is the home of the Pedersen, the Leitra all-weather recumbent and the Christiania trike, which gives some clue to the cycle-friendliness of the country. Indeed, Denmark could have been designed and built from the ground up by cyclists. It has the right terrain, a host of cycle facilities in towns and cities, and a network of quiet lanes and cyclepaths. In short it has all that the cyclist could wish for.

Some of the quietest of country lanes have their own smooth, two-lane mini-roads running alongside just for cyclists. Cycling is widely used for travelling to work and to the shops. The typical Danish bike might be a smart hub-geared machine equipped with mudguards, chainguards, kickstands and a wheel lock. These bikes indicate a common-sense, unpretentious approach to life. The Danes generally opt for functional, easily maintained bicycles, rather than all-singing, all-dancing, glow-in-the-dark hi-tech.

The capital, Copenhagen, has possibly the first free bike scheme that actually seems to work. You put your 20 crowns in a slot and you can borrow a bike for as long as you need. You get your money back when you return the bike to any one of the free-bike parking racks around the city. Using a car in Copenhagen has been made more difficult since the city's car parking space was reduced to discourage motoring.

On the tiny island of Bornholm, Allan Hedegaard, director of the Nexøhuset institute for the mentally and physically handicapped, organises a unique annual cycling event. The 'Handicap Tour de Bornholm' attracts hundreds of cyclists – disabled and able-bodied – from all over Europe to take part in the 107km tour of the island.

As with Holland, travelling by bike in Denmark carries no status implications. You ride a bike to get across town, not because you're too poor to run a car or to try to save the planet.

BIKES AT WORK IN IOWA

Frustrated by the increasing volume of traffic in his small Iowa community of Ames, Jim Gregory, decided to improve matters by starting up a pedal-powered grocery delivery service. He called it Fresh Aire Delivery.

The small business took off. The demand grew, and the variety and size of load to transport grew too! Unable to find commercially available trailers adequate for carrying large or heavy cargo, Jim set up a sister company, Fresh Aire Trailers, to manufacture suitable equipment. Having developed the trailers, Jim and his partner Joan soon found them to be indispensable for their own car-free household, too.

The two companies now operate under the one name of Bikes At Work, and the business employs two people full-time, Jim and Joan, as well as fifteen part-time workers. The range of goods that is now transported includes everything from airline tickets and pizzas up to washing machines, furniture and children's play houses.

Bikes At Work also run a recycling service. Jim recalls, "We got started in the recycling business in 1993, collecting recyclables from a handful of households in Ames and transporting them to the Ames Area Recycling Centre. That business grew until we were serving over 200 homes and businesses. In 1996, we begin providing recycling services to all of the residence hall buildings at Iowa State University, serving some 8000 students."

This involves transporting huge loads of recyclable waste, such as newspaper, plastic and metal. Since the plastic is light, they try to cram on as much as possible and carry it on two trailers pulled in tandem – making a formidable vehicle of about 8 metres (25 feet) in length.

In 1998, serving both the growing residential customer base and the University got too much to manage, and the residential portion of the recycling business was sold to Second Generation Curbside Recycling, who also do all their work by bike.

Just how much can you carry with one bike? "A surprising amount!" says Jim. "We routinely transport cargo using our trailers that would challenge a typical automobile."

GRONINGEN, CYCLING CITY

When you cycle in most towns, you quickly learn which routes are safe and which routes to avoid. This isn't the case in Groningen; you simply pick a route from A to B in the certain knowledge that it'll be perfect for cycling.

With a population of 170,000 people, Groningen is the Netherlands' sixth largest city. Fifty-seven per cent of the citizens travel by bicycle. Nearly half of all city trips are by bicycle compared with only 30 percent by car.

"We ride because it's fun, it's faster, it's convenient," explains Groningen city planner Gerrit van Weryen. "This is not an environmental programme, it is an economic programme. We are boosting jobs and business. It has been proven that planning for the bicycle is cheaper than planning for the car." Requests regularly arrive from shopkeepers in streets where 'cyclisation' is not yet in force to ban cars from their area. "Businesses, once in revolt against car restraint, are clamouring for more of it," says van Weryen.

The city centre is divided into four sectors. Cars can drive in and out of sectors but not from one sector to another, forcing cars to take long detours, while bicyclists travel easily between adjacent sectors.

A vital threshold has been crossed. Through sheer weight of numbers, the bicycle now makes the rules, slows the traffic and determines the attitudes of drivers. Motorways have been dug up, roads are being narrowed or closed to traffic, miles of bike lanes and special bike overpasses weave through the city and there are tens of thousands of bike parking places. New houses are built to which the only direct access is by cycle, while out-of-town shopping centres are banned.

Dutch bicycle planning shows that if cyclists are given their own rights of way and priority in transport planning, the elegant simplicity of riding a bicycle is still popular after many years of motorisation.

CAMPAIGNERS IN MONTRÉAL

Despite long, hard winter months, Montréal enjoys a rich cycling culture. A Canadian city with a European charm of cafés and cobbled streets, it's home to large numbers of French, Italian and Belgian immigrants, all of whom come from cultures that take bikes for granted as both transportation and recreation.

The cycling die-hards have got their way, and Montréal is entering its cycling prime. Bicycle racks are as common as parking meters and bicycle parking is a requirement for new buildings. With over 40 full-time employees, the non-profit Velo Quebec has the weight to get things done for cyclists. "Bicycles are now integrated in the pattern of the city," according to Velo Quebec's Robert Boivin.

Montréal has nearly 200 miles of bike paths and lanes, with funding for the construction of more. Crucially, many on-street bike lanes are marked by concrete barriers and permanent pylons rather than ineffective painted lines.

Every June, the city plays host to Le Tour de l'Ile. More than 45,000 cyclists cruise a 40-mile loop through city streets in the largest organised bike ride in the world. All proceeds go towards the city's bike programs. But even that isn't Montréal's most impressive mass ride. The weekend before Le Tour de l'Ile is Le Tour des Enfants, a 12-mile ride just for kids. "Ten-thousand children on bicycles in the streets of Montréal – the first time I saw it, I cried," says Boivin.

Anyone looking to escape urban life can connect to the trans-Québec bicycle path, Route Verte. Provincial government provided the money to create this a 1,800-mile web of bike paths and lanes due for completion around 2004.

Those who use climate as an excuse why cycling isn't big in their city should look to Montréal for inspiration.

Picture credits: (Top left) Sue Darlow; (middle left) Earth Cycles; (bottom left) Bikes at Work; (top right) Sue Darlow

EAST AFRICAN HEALTH WORKERS

"Egaali momaso!" (Ahead with the bike) – that's the message Youth Aid East Africa are spreading among the nurses, birth-attendants, midwives and community health workers in Uganda.

Rose Kaneene, a nurse and midwife at one of Uganda's hospitals explains: "The problem we face is transport. Transport to monitor patients at home, to have vaccination outreaches or to hold health seminars in the villages. People can't afford to go by car. They need their little money for treatment. In an emergency case, you have at least to reach the patient in time. The bicycle is the appropriate means on the narrow paths in rural areas."

In East Africa, the bicycle is traditionally the most common means of transport. Local bike-taxis – 'boda-boda' – use extra-strong carrier racks to transport passengers, or heavy loads to market. Nurses and midwives carry their passengers, 'boda-boda' style, to the nearest hospital, which can be 20km away. The experience that motorised transport is neither affordable or suitable in many rural areas has led to the idea of subsidising bicycles for East Africa's rural poor.

Youth Aid East Africa is encouraging individuals and businesses in the West to sponsor bikes for social initiatives in East Africa. To date, about 5,000 locally bought bikes have been sponsored, mainly through private donations in Germany. New Indian or Chinese bicycles are bought; the sophisticated technology of Western bikes is considered inappropriate due to lack of spare parts. It is also important to the project that the recipients do not receive second-hand goods.

A workshop and training centre has been set up to assemble and maintain the bicycles. The project's most recent initiative has been to set up the First African Bicycle Information Office to provide literature and videos and to run national and international seminars on bicycle awareness.

Meanwhile, four young women in Musha, Rwanda, decided that anything the men could do they could do too. So they started the 'Bikes for Rwanda' project. This is something really special in a country where women don't usually cycle or do any mechanics.

KEIRIN RACERS

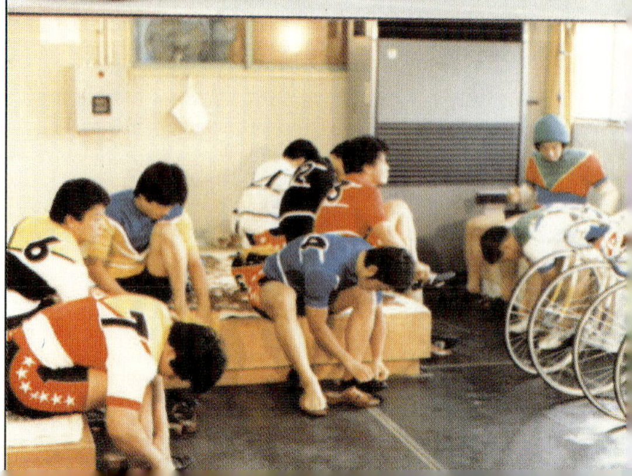

Keirin racing originated more than 50 years ago in Japan, where it is still the predominant form of competitive cycling. It's a high-speed track racing event held on a banked track, or velodrome, in which the competing cyclists jockey for position behind a pacer. In the Japanese version, riders follow in the wake of a pacer on track racing bike, while in the international version a motorcycle known as a 'derney' is used to pace the riders. It's the human equivalent of greyhound racing.

Up to eight riders race at a time, riding in single file and pursuing the pacer in a pack. For the first 1500 metres of the 2000 metre race the riders manoeuvre for the best position behind the pacer, who leads them faster and faster around the track. Spectators bet on the outcome, then watch as their rider chooses where to position himself – immediately behind the pacer to lead from the front, or further back in the line where he can launch a surprise attack as they sprint to the line. With 500 metres to go, the pacer now travelling at around 45kph, leaves the track and the riders battle it out over the final lap to be the first to cross the line, sometimes at speeds of up to 70kph.

The word Keirin, pronounced 'kay-rin', is a combination of two characters literally meaning 'racing wheels'. Keirin was held for the first time in 1948 in Kokura City, Kyushu. The very idea of racing with bicycles was novel at the time and, as the four-day event also provided the opportunity of betting, it sparked great public interest. Over 55,000 people attended the first meet. Since then Keirin has become hugely popular in Japan, tens of millions of people go to watch and to bet at Keirin meets every year. The sport has spread around the world and, for the first time, will be entered in the Sydney Olympics in the year 2000.

MOBILE MUSIC MAKERS, BRITAIN

Every month in London a Critical Mass of celebrating cyclists winds through the streets, bringing motor traffic to a standstill. Somewhere in among the throng all you'll hear Velorevolution, the mobile sound system that – leaderless though the Mass is – everyone tends to follow. It's a focus for the event, and an imaginative way to help spread the message in the face of a traffic system that marginalises cyclists.

Velorevolution isn't unique. At various festivals around the UK, Rinky-Dink makes an appearance. It's a colourful bike-train bedecked with huge flowers and big speakers. The sound system is pedal-powered. It was invented by a collective of creative technicians, artists and performers from Stroud, England, to explore and demonstrate bicycle power as non-polluting energy source.

Dan Smythies, one of the collective, explains: "In about 1990, 'Dink grew out from the realisation that a wind generator was not practical for running a sound system. Initially, it was used on civil rights rallies in London. It was good for stopping rioting and stuff: we got a good name from all sides for that. It's always had a good vibe round it. Rinky-Dink is direct, hands-on and participatory. We see it as a unique mix of science and art, serious purpose and sheer fun. It's a hugely accessible educational tool which is mobile, so that it has maximum impact at festivals we go to." The group is also moving into education work in schools, in order to teach children about sustainable power.

Velorevolution is a different machine entirely: it's Brox quadricycle fitted with a CD player, tape deck, 100W amplifier and big speakers. Yet there's much common ground between the two mobile music systems. Velorevolution technician Daniel James says the upgraded Brox is "an effective way of getting a big sound to the centre of a hectic, fast-moving street party." The sound system is currently run from pre-charged batteries; a prototype generator bike to keep the batteries topped up is under construction.

BANGLADESHI RICKSHAW RIDERS

Dhaka, in Bangladesh, is the rickshaw capital of the world. The streets teem with over a third of a million rickshaws, their bells ringing as they weave between buses, auto-rickshaws, trucks and cars. They are a colourful sight, decorated with plastic flowers, streamers, embroidery and ornately painted in elaborate designs reflecting popular culture. Film stars, futuristic cities, humanised animals, and even Saddam Hussein add colour to the city's transport. With these contraptions taking up three-quarters of Dhaka's road space, rickshaw jams are common. And accidents are part of daily life, with up to ten lanes of rickshaws all jostling for space on a busy street.

There is a hierarchy in the culture of the rickshaw. Rickshaw pullers are at the bottom and fleet owners, or maleks, are at the top. Between the two are thousands of manufacturers and spare parts vendors, managers, mechanics, mess hall workers and artists to decorate the rickshaws. This vast business network which supports one-in-five of Dhaka's city-dwellers. One taka in every three spent on transport goes to the rickshaw business, which is twice as big as Bangladesh Biman, the national airline.

The city is a maze of streets and lanes with small shops, tradesmen, and bustling commercial activity. This is not a city of Walmarts or similar emporia, but a huge collection of specialised enterprises, all trying to survive. Need a rickshaw of your own? Go to Bicycle Street and, depending on how well you can bargain and how much decoration you need to impress your customers, a new one could set you back 11,000 taka (US$300).

Perhaps the highest cost is paid by the 600,000 men who cycle heavy loads of people and goods around the streets, working in shifts to keep the city moving. "I was a healthy man three years ago but now my muscles crumble," says one 41-year-old puller, who has ten children and two wives to care for. "Only those who need money and have the strength drive rickshaws."

Picture credits: (Top left) Richard Kisamadu; (bottom left) Tim Potter; (bottom right) Lonely Planet

MIT DEM RAD ZU DEN PLANETEN
MIT DEM RAD ZU DEN PLANETEN
MIT DEM RAD ZU DEN PLANETEN
CYCLING THE SOLAR SYSTEM
LE SYSTÈME SOLAIRE EN VÉLO
LE SYSTÈME SOLAIRE EN VÉLO
LE SYSTÈME SOLAIRE EN VÉLO

Heavenly journeys

Jim McGurn, co-publisher of Encycleopedia, finds that we often travel further than the distance we cover.

I ride past Saturn on my way to work, missing Neptune and Pluto a mile or so ahead. In the other direction I can rocket past the inner planets before scorching past the Sun itself at ten times the speed of light – to scale. A group of cyclists interested in astronomy built a replica of the solar system along my stretch of bike path near York. The sun is the width of my outstretched arms, and the earth the size of my thumb. I live, apparently, in the asteroid belt. The distances between the planets are to scale, guaranteeing that bike rides become a celestial experience, if they weren't one already.

Sometimes I listen to music on this path, although not the Planets Suite as yet. Other times it's current affairs. One morning my planetary musings were interrupted by a scientist explaining how, over trillions of years, the material universe will go through five great and inevitable changes of state, before resolving into nothing more than protons and electrons. Time began, a few things happened, time ceased. For a short while, on a minor planet of a minor solar system, a certain species had its brief day, inventing the flint axe, the steam train and MTV. At one particular point, in a rare moment of sanity, that busy life form invented the bicycle: just before the industrial revolution popped its boiler. If I feel fortunate being part of that split second of human life, sandwiched between trillions of years of cosmic confusion, I feel doubly blessed being around just after mankind invented its most perfect machine.

I feel lucky in other ways. Even before the planets came to punctuate my daily bike ride, my route was more than a journey through space. It was also a journey through time, with history alive on all sides. Bishopthorpe, where my ride begins, is named after the stately palace of the Archbishop of York, who was forced to this rural retreat by Henry VIII. Soon I pass the site of mediaeval gallows and cross an old Roman road, before I hit the bike path: a railway line built by Victorians and closed 20 years ago. The path takes me across the river bridge, whose engine was kept permanently in steam to swing the bridge open for tall-masters heading for the ancient city of York. Down below you can still see where the wartime anti-aircraft guns were housed, keeping the route safe for the Flying Scotsman which once thundered along the very track I now ride. Then, with headphones off, I crank up my speed through the still pretty village of Fulford (foul-ford) where King Harold's army defeated the invading Scandinavians in 1066, before rushing south to lose it all at Hastings. Where Harold's warriors slew Tostig's I come across that modern metaphor for powerlessness and futility: a mile-long queue of almost static traffic, which I overtake in top gear, on the outside. They see me do it every morning.

Your bike ride is no doubt as interesting as mine, because on a bike the physical and historical landscapes surrounding you are so much closer. I've always believed that, even on the most familiar routes, cycling lets you travel further than the distance you cover.

I've nothing against a change of scene. It's good for any cyclist's soul. But I no longer yearn to appropriate exotic destinations like an obsessive stamp collector. Almost every cyclist, in the western world at least, has already reinterpreting leisure in their own individual way, rather than buying into a dubious packaged paradise, where the only action is the walk between hotel and bathing beach. The off-road rider, the world-tourer, the city rider, the country lane meanderer: these are the people redefining leisure. They travel to enjoy but not consume, and even when they're lost they know where they're going. They'll still be faced with that perennial question from non-cyclists: why? Maybe it's best to accept that all rationales are futile on a planetary scale. Cycling in the sun is its own justification, and the only one we need.

For more information about the cycle path solar system, see www.solar.york.ac.uk

Istory

PEDAL PROSE

IN THE 19TH CENTURY THE BICYCLE BECAME THE FASTEST VEHICLE ON THE ROAD, AND ONE OF THE TECHNOLOGICAL MARVELS OF ITS AGE. IT AMASSED COLUMN INCHES IN BOOKS, NEWSPAPERS AND MAGAZINES AROUND THE GLOBE. WITH THIS SELECTION OF PERIOD CLIPPINGS WE PRESENT THE BICYCLES OF THE PAST AS THEY APPEARED TO THE PEOPLE OF THE TIME.

Von Drais's running machine

The velocipede of Monsieur le Baron de Drais was given a trial yesterday morning in the garden of the Luxembourg, and the experiment showed an improvement upon the Célérifère of 1790… The machine can never be of any utility as it can only be used in the garden or a park on a well kept walk or road… If the numerous spectators were not satisfied with the result the curious were well repaid by the presence of a number of pretty women in their most brilliant dresses. A nut being lost, it was no longer possible to use the machine.

Le Petit Chronique de Paris . April 7 1818

…………………………

On Thursday 12 July 1818, according to reliable witnesses, the baron Karl von Drais journeyed from Mannheim to the Schwetzinger relay house and back on the latest version of his horseless carriage in one hour, a journey that would have taken the post coach four hours. On the same machine he covered the steep hill path from Gernsbach to here, which normally takes two hours, in one hour

The idea of the invention is simple: using one's feet, one propels along the ground a seat resting upon two wheels. The design is ideal as, there being only two wheels, one if front of the other, it is possible to travel about on all footpaths and country roads, which are usually very good the whole summer through. The rider maintains his balance by resting his arms on a small upholstered board in front of him. He steers by holding a small control in front of this with one hand. Good distances can be covered using this machine, which weighs less than 50 pounds and is well produced and durable. One can be bought for, at most, 4 Carolins, with travelling bags and other accessories.

Badwochenblatt (local newspaper), Baden, July 28, 1818

…………………………

"Thank you, my dear friend, for your letter informing me of the new machine, of which you already make use and that was entirely unknown to me; from what you tell me, it could become very useful, in the country especially, or on roads which are well surfaced. I imagine that, with the exercise and on a good path, one can travel quickly; one must however, as we have said, look rather odd on it.

"I think that someone with long legs… can go very fast: it would appear that the longer one's legs, the further one can go without getting tired.

"I look forward with great pleasure to learning of fresh details of this new invention… I firmly believe, as you do, that one could achieve great distance on one and I imagine that this kind of exercise must be very agreeable. I compliment you on your success. It is astonishing enough, that this invention is not already widespread in the country."

Extracted from two letters written by a certain Claude to his brother, Nicéphore, in the November and December of 1818 concerning a velocipede.

…………………………

The Velocipede

The craze jumps from house to house, country to country, and then from continent to continent – everything goes velocipedal.

Johann Wolfgang von Goethe

…………………………

In 1868, a London magazine reported that every alternate Sunday or so velocipede races have taken place in the environs of Paris – at St. Cloud, Vincennes, Eughien, Pantin, and elsewhere. Mounted, too, upon these flying horses, amateurs dash along the crowded thoroughfares of the capital, while adepts risk of their lives by driving their two-wheeled velocipedes along the narrow stone parapet at the side of the Seine, and down the hundred and one steps of the Trocadero; rising up in their seats, lying down on their hacks, letting go the handle of the vehicle, and throwing both legs over it while performing these daring feats.

Government employees living in the suburbs ride to their offices every morning on the new iron horse… You may see them on their return journey at night, steering in between the throng of carriages with lighted lanterns swinging in front of them, and with other velocipedes sent out by enterprising tradesmen displaying illuminated advertisements.

London Society, vol 14, pp408-414, 1868

…………………………

Fox, Sheridan, Pitt and other notables of the period patronised the velocipede in St. James' Park, taking their constitutional daily on the Dandy Horse, after a hard night spent in the House of Commons or around the gaming tables.

English Mechanic, 1868

…………………………

The Ministers of Instruction and of War have authorised its (the bicycle's) adoption in Public Schools and in the Army. It combines three indispensable qualities for the exercise of Mankind Utility, Health, and Pleasure – and being for all, is the real 'Omnibus'. Skill in its management may now be classed with riding, fencing, swimming and gymnastics, and no liberal education is complete without it.

Veloces, distinguished by their elegance and beauty, are used by the rich in their parks and gardens, in Town and Country; on it they accompany Ladies, who, unable to use the Veloce, are condemned to carriage exercise; for fishing and other excursions it is most useful.

The Clerk obliged to come early and leave late, was compelled at great pecuniary loss, to live near his place of business. Now master of a Veloce, a distance of 10 or 15 miles is nothing, and he saves 75 per cent in house rent.

The Veloce (UK), 1869

During the winter months nothing has been more common than to see a party of 'wheelers' trundling along the hard frosty roads at a clipping pace to some favourite pond – their skates dangling from the guiding-bar, or strapped along the spring. Gentlemen have come home on them from evening parties in the clear moonlight, the rider merely changing his shoes before starting. Leaving the hot, close dancing rooms, he has arrived at home still warm with the glow of wholesome exercise.

Wheels and Woes, written by 'a Light Dragoon', 1870 or 1871

....

High Wheelers

The bicycle atrocity is avenged, and riders now may go their way, feeling assured that they have an equal right with all others on the Queen's highway, and that ruffianism such as Messrs. Gee and Mitchell experienced will not be looked over and cannot be excused. On Saturday week, while riding peaceably along the Edgware Road, Mr. Gee and his friend, Mr. Goulbourn, in attempting to pass the Watford and St. Alban's coach, were nearly run down, and the former gentleman received a severe lashing from the driver. Another rider, of the name of Mitchell, just behind, when trying to pass the coach, was pulled to the ground and dragged along for some few yards by a rope, which, with a weight attached, had been flung by the conductor across the front wheel of the bicycle, and caught in the spokes.

The Bicycle Journal, London, September 8, 1876

....

A case just tried at the North Shields Police Court has proved that the fact of his being a bicyclist himself did not prevent a spirit merchant named Lamb, when in his trap, from running down a fellow cyclist, Mr. John Snowdon, the well-known B.T.C. Consul. Mr. Lamb was sentenced to pay £3 and costs, or go to gaol for a month.

The Cyclist – July 13 1881

....

In the United States, the Charlestown riders speak quite hopefully of the day when the roads will he 'fixed' to such an extent that the Charlestown Bicycle Club will have from 8 to 10 miles available for decent riding.

The Cyclist 1882

....

I was jolting along a very bad road, and happening to overtake an old man, I enquired if the road got any better further on. He replied in the negative, and on my asking how it was the road was so bad, he expressed himself thus: "It used to be a very good road, but since they've bin an' took the toll gates off, well – it ain't fit for a pig!" Quite so. The railways having now entirely superseded the old coaches and every other means of conveyance for passengers and goods, the roads of the kingdom connecting the different towns are not now used as in former times... Therefore, as bicyclists, it behoves us to bestir ourselves and prepare to look after our own interests in the matter.

The Cyclist 1882

The Munich Velocipede Club has a good track (five laps to the mile), and races are fixed for 30th May. The open events are a 3 kilometre (1 mile 7 furlongs) handicap, and a 10 kilometre (6 miles) scratch race, for both of which the best riders are entered, so that some good racing may be expected. Royalty is also taking to the sport, and Prince George of Saxony (nephew of the King of Saxony), and Prince Leopold of Prussia (great nephew of the Emperor of Germany), now ride bicycles purchased of The Howe Machine Co., Limited, in Berlin. Neither bicycles nor tricycles are allowed in the streets of Berlin, although the streets in the West End of the city are well paved, and many of them laid with asphalt. As some riders have been fined for riding, the Berlin B.C. has resolve to try and obtain redress in the law courts

The Cyclist, May 31 1882

One great feature of this new (bicycling) school is the complete privacy with which the lessons are given. No two ladies are allowed to learn together. This is a great attraction to those novices who have a horror of making their first floundering attempts with any eyes to watch them, and see their failures. Many women have remarked to me that they would like to learn the safety, if they had any chance of doing so without public observation; so I feel sure that this chance will be appreciated by any who are able to avail themselves of it.

C.T.C. Gazette , 1882

The only place the Philadelphians have to ride in is the Fairmount Park, which took them some considerable time to get the privilege of. It is impossible to ride in the streets, as they are paved with cobble stones. I rode my monster in the procession and the roads were so bad that before I had got any distance seven spokes had drawn from the hub. My next trip was to Washington... which is the best city in America for bicycling; they have 45 miles of asphalt pavement. In this city I made a great success. The proprietor... told me to ride through the city, which I did at a pretty good rate, and the monster caused quite a sensation.

One high bicycle rider reports from the saddle of his 52inch 'monster', in The Cyclist, June 1882

"A slave of the enemy, on a bicycle, tried to ride through our ranks, but the Lord upset him and he fell on his head."

An event which occurred during a Salvation Army procession in Birmingham recorded in the War Cry in 1882

Within the next few years we are certain to see comfortable inns spring up along all the roads which are suitable for bicycle-riding. The wheelman cannot carry much luggage, and is especially unable to find accommodation for food. His ability to travel easily fifty or seventy-five miles a day makes comfortable lodging-places at night and comfortable eating-places by day great desiderata along his pathway. There are old inns within a radius of fifty miles of New York city that have known scarcely more than a customer a week for years which are now overrun with wheelmen, and are adapting themselves rapidly to the new situation...

The bicycle is, in fact, the agent of health and of a wider civilisation. It will give stronger bodies to the rising generation than their fathers have had, and it will bring the city and the country into closer relations than have existed since the days of the stagecoach.

Scribener's Monthly (USA), circa 1885

Safety Bicycles

As for the bicycling itself, it was exceedingly clever. To guide a bicycle with one hand and trundle a hoop with the other does not look very easy; and the riding with linked hands was the cause of a disaster – two ladies falling down just in front of the Royal circle. A musical ride was especially graceful, and the tortoise race was quite the most amusing. Some of the ladies sat very high on their machines, a few were almost upright, and this, of course, did away with a great deal of the knee action, which is so very ugly; but it did not suggest ease.

Vanity Fair, June 11, 1896

Few men have urgent need either of a new machine for enforcing exercise or occupying the mind; yet there is many a middle-aged or elderly professional man who is exchanging flabby fat for firm muscle, increasing his breathing-space, toning up his circulation, and putting old age five or ten years farther ahead, by discarding the carriage, buggy, or street-car for the bicycle. The wheel is also effecting a radical change in the lives of many poor artisans. ...The bicycle allows the working man to reach home for a good warm dinner during a nooning too brief... the bicycle, by annihilating distance, makes it possible to seek a home in the suburbs, or at least in a thinly populated portion of the city, remote from the noise, dust, and crowding of the business centre.

It is no exaggeration to say that the bicycle is making self-respecting householders and property owners of men who would otherwise become the victims of tenement life.

The Bicycle and the Tenement-House, Century Magazine, USA, 1897

There are four of them. Their legs, like giant levers, will power onwards for sixty hours; their muscles will grind up the kilometres; their broad chests will heave with the effort of the struggle; their hands will clench onto their handlebars; with their eyes they will observe each other ferociously; their backs will bend forward in unison for barbaric breakaways; their stomachs will fight against hunger, their brains against sleep. And at night a peasant waiting for them by a deserted road will see four demons passing by, and the noise of their desperate panting will freeze his heart and fill it with terror.

Henri Desgrange reporting on the 1901 Paris-Brest-Paris race

More details on Jim McGurn's book are on pages 135 and 138.

ANDERS SEIN
ANDERS SEIN
ANDERS SEIN
BEING DIFFERENT
VIVRE LA DIFFÉRENCE
VIVRE LA DIFFÉRENCE
VIVRE LA DIFFÉRENCE

Everyday revolutions

It's absurd, really. You stick together some metal tubes and a pair of skinny wheels. Then you learn to balance on it, make a few refinements, and become the most beautiful mover in the known universe. Then you're comprehensively ignored because it was all too simple.

I recall an American cycling cartoon from the early '80s. The traffic planners in city hall were desperate for a fast solution to city's traffic problems. They needed something cheap and available which could use existing roads. It had to give independent mobility but leave the community and environment unharmed. And as they wrestled with their complex search for the mega-solution, a single cyclist passed by the building, unseen, unacknowledged, and smiling.

What is it about bikes that makes them so right that they become invisible? Perhaps they're too harmless for their own good. Perhaps we should fit them with noise generators and fake exhausts. Perhaps we should make them cost a fortune to buy and license their use – so everyone wants one.

Perhaps the problem is that cycling requires us to make our bodies do something useful. And bodies were given us to enjoy, not to put to work. We've spent a century scrapping manual jobs, and turning sport into a spectator activity. Physical fitness is packaged as a consumer item, to be enjoyed in private gyms and expensive leisure centres. To keep fit while you have fun just transporting yourself around is so sensible it verges on the subversive in many societies. The loud politics of industrial power cannot take in the quiet power of the cyclist as a biomechanical engine of change.

It's hard to repress a good idea, and cycling is returning to the cultural agenda in many Western countries. But it's in danger of falling into the hands of the same package leisure industry which gave us the fitness gym. Beware the smiling family on mountain bikes wearing slick cycling gear, and riding on a scenic, safe and undemanding cycle path somewhere not near you. Beware the muscular young males in the cycle mag adverts, dealing big dirt on an impossible descent. Good for them, but the real cycling world can be even more fun than that.

Most cyclists I know are individualists. They lead interesting lives, of which cycling is an important but integrated part. They can pedal all dressed-up to the theatre of an evening, then put on their serious cycling gear next day for an 80 mile ride with a few friends. Their lives are as diverse as the cycles they own. They're not necessarily interested in transport politics, and many simply enjoy the ownership of fast metal. They prize independence, and the joy of moving fast and free, anytime, and almost anywhere.

They're not freaks. They're fully-paid up members of society. They also often drive cars, work in big business and worry about their children staying out late. They are also the ones who by being regular cyclists are changing the world from the inside, and having a lot of fun in the process.

The ideas you have seen in this book show that there are few corners of our lives which are not open to pedal-power in one way or another. Perhaps we have inspired you to take off in a new direction, or to tell a friend or two about some cycling ideas which might change their lives. This is a book of exciting and enjoyable solutions, and we hope we have helped make the world a happier place. **Jim McGurn**

Open Road Publications

Encycleopedia CD-ROM

We have been producing a video to accompany each edition of Encycleopedia for several years. The video contained in-depth analysis of a number of the featured bikes. The rapid expansion of domestic computer markets has now allowed us to move on from pure video to producing a multimedia CD Rom. The CD format has several advantages: words, pictures, video and sound can be brought together, and it's much easier on a CD to make a large body of information easily navigable and accessible. We can also put lots more information and features onto a CD than can go into either the printed book or a video. The CD will also give easy access to our website, where even more new and regularly updated material can be enjoyed. And it will give fast access to the websites of participating cycle manufacturers. Being a new departure, requiring additional preparation time, this CD will not be available at the time of going to press, so please check out our website on www.encycleopedia.com for release date information. You can place an advance order using the order form on page 138.

Bycycle Magazine

Bycycle is our subscriptions magazine for UK readers, but is read in many countries. It gives you the latest cycling news, bike tests, technology reports, riders' reports, touring suggestions and hard-hitting columnists. The emphasis is on leisure, family and commuting cycling, and not so much on sport. No hype, no nonsense, but a lively, entertaining read for any open-minded cyclist, male or female. Bycycle appears six times a year, with 64 large-format pages, mostly in colour.

Bike Culture Quarterly

There's never been a cycling magazine like this before. BCQ is read by bicycle lovers worldwide, carries no adverts and no conventional bike tests. There's even a full German-language edition. It's pure editorial: hard news, powerful ideas, astonishing technology, and remarkable people-stories. We're proud that it has become a forum for a worldwide community of free-thinkers, campaigners, inventors, visionaries and people who simply love bicycles. BCQ was shortlisted in America for the title of best new magazine from a small publisher. In fact, we've been going since 1994, and all back issues are available in bound sets - BCQ is like a book published in parts. It's mainly by subscription and has 64 large format pages, mostly in colour.

BCQ Bound sets

Your chance to enjoy what will soon be one of the most sought-after collector's items: the first 19 issues of Bike Culture Quarterly (Summer 94 to Winter 99/2000) in two purpose-made maroon and gold binders, each of which will hold 12 issues. It's virtually a book in nineteen parts, with over 1000 adverts-free pages (most of them in colour) of the best cycle writing, making it, we believe, the biggest, most comprehensive cycling reference works ever compiled. It's timeless stuff – as fresh now as when it was written. You can read it as a book, or you can remove and replace each issue individually, in seconds. It's an ideal gift for any cyclist, with life-long value.

Bicycle Design, by Mike Burrows

The long-awaited masterwork from the world's most famous and irreverent cycle designer and inventor. Bicycle Design is the essential handbook if you love cycle technology, or simply want to know how to go faster. It's written in Mike's usual lively style, matched by explanatory cartoons from Jo Burt (Mint Sauce) and others. Published June 2000.

On Your Bicycle:
The Illustrated Story of Cycling

The high-riding clubmen, the society ladies awheel during the great cycling boom, the thrills of cycle sport. This social history describes the bicycle's rollercoaster of popularity. Sometimes it was a sad, neglected toy, other times the darling of the age. The bicycle did more for morals and manners than almost any other invention, and this richly illustrated book takes a lively look at its ups and downs. 208 pages, 16 in colour. On your Bicycle is written by Jim McGurn, one of Open Road's publishers. Originally published in 1987: this new edition is considerably updated with many pictures.

David Eccles Prints

We commissioned David Eccles, one of Britain's foremost cycling illustrators, to produce original images of 19th century cycles in the form of a limited edition set of four linocuts. Conceiving an image and printing it from a block of cork linoleum is a rare and delicate craft. A linocut has a limited capacity for printing due to the fragility of the material. David produced 75 individually numbered and signed sets of the four prints before cancelling each block.

Because both the printing and the inking are done by hand no two prints will be exactly the same.

The paper, made entirely from 100% cotton and acid-free, has been specially made by hand for this edition by Chris Bingham of Ruscombe Valley Paper. It replicates exactly paper made in the mid-to-late 1700s. For our purposes we had the making hot-pressed by the Wookey Hole Mill.

These prints are offered individually and, subject to availability, also in sets of all four prints. Each print is numbered, signed and dated by the artist.

The prints have all been window-mounted on 46cm x 41cm acid-free conservation board.

For practical reasons, we cannot supply the prints ready-framed.

1. Dursley Pedersen Tandem

2. Mergamobile

3. Alpha Bantam circa 1898

4. Bicycle racing, mid 1880s

Binders

Both Bike Culture and Bycycle have specially-made binders, which contain 12 issues; the former in maroon, the latter in blue, and both with gold lettering.

Open Road Events

Bike Culture Weeks

Every year, Open Road, the publishers of Encycleopedia, organise Bike Culture weeks for our readers. Previous holidays have taken place in York and Northumberland in Britain, as well as in France. All Bike Culture weeks are very international events, with a unique atmosphere.

The exact holiday programme varies from event to event, but always includes:

- guided rides
- a programme of evening talks, films, and live entertainment
- fix-your-bike and maintenance classes
- a wide selection of interesting recumbents and other unusual bikes, supplied by Open Road, to try out
- the chance to meet and ride with other cyclists from around the world
- ... and much more besides.

You may still have time to book the Bike Culture York holiday in 2000, which takes place from August 5th to 12th. If you wish to attend, contact Open Road's office on +44 1904 654654, or email melanie@bcqedit.demon.co.uk. For information of Bike Culture Weeks in 2001, visit our website: www.bikeculture.com

The visitors' verdicts

"We enjoyed the holiday very much, having no preconceived ideas of how it would go. We have met some lovely people and seen and ridden many interesting bikes. I will certainly recommend it to friends."
Nicola Green & Ian Maunders, UK

"All the Open Road crew were exceedingly friendly and helpful...beyond reasonable expectations. The school staff were wonderful, they went out of their way. Everyone was delightfully willing to share cycles, stories, meals and much more."
Ross Lowell, USA, on the York Holiday

"The atmosphere was superb, the rides were great, and everyone felt included. We made so many new friends."
Horst Alt, Germany

"The ride leaders were great! They were all willing to adjust their speeds for a variety of cycling abilities. I enjoyed the juggling, the slide show and video show very much. I got more than expected. The people were great, mostly open to new experiences - a wonderful group."

Other publications from Open Road

Publications	USA / Mexico / Canada (US $)	Postage	Australia	Postage	Germany / Austria	Postage	Switzerland	Postage	UK / Rest of World	UK Postage (except Northern Ireland)	Other European Postage	Rest of World Postage	Choices	Quantity	Total Price
Encycleopedia 2001	$ 20.00	$ 4.00	A$ 30.00	A$ 7.00	DM35,-	DM8,-	SFr30,-	SFr7,	£ 12.00	£ 2.50	£ 3.50	£ 5.00			
Encycleopedia 2001 CD	$ 16.00	—	A$ 25.00	—	DM29,-	—	SFr24,-	—	£ 9.50	—	—	—			
Encycleopedia 99	$ 12.00	$ 4.00	A$ 22.00	A$ 4.00	DM17,-	DM8,-	SFr23,-	SFr7,-	£ 7.00	£ 2.00	£ 3.00	£ 4.00			
Encycleopedia 96 or Encycleopedia 97/98	$ 12.00	$ 4.00	A$ 22.00	A$ 4.00	DM17,-	DM8,-	SFr23,-	SFr7,-	£ 7.00	£ 2.00	£ 3.00	£ 4.00	Specify edition(s)...		
Encycleopedia 94/5 (inc BCQ3)	$ 12.00	$ 4.00	A$ 22.00	A$ 4.00	DM17,-	DM8,-	SFr23,-	SFr7,-	£ 7.00	£ 2.00	£ 1.25	£ 2.00			
BCQ 1 – 18 set in two binders	$ 118.00	—	A$ 170.00	—	DM192,-	DM12,-	SFr161,-	SFr10,-	£ 64.00	—	£ 15.00	£ 20.00			
On your Bicycle, history book	$ 27.00	$ 5.00	A$ 42.00	A$ 5.00	DM51,-	DM8,-	SFr45,-	SFr7,-	£ 16.95	£ 2.50	£ 1.50	£ 2.50			
Cycle Design, Mike Burrows	$ 27.00	$ 5.00	A$ 42.00	A$ 5.00	DM51,-	DM8,-	SFr45,-	SFr7,-	£ 16.95	£ 2.50	£ 1.50	£ 2.50			
Subscriptions															
Bike Culture Quarterly, (4 issues)	$ 38.00	—	A$ 50.00	—	DM75,-	—	SFr65,-	—	£ 24.00				Start at BCQ Issue...		
Bycycle (6 issues)	$ 39.00	—	A$ 55.00	—	DM54,-	—	SFr44,-	—	£ 18.00	—	£ 5.00	£ 9.00	Start at Bycycle Issue...		
Open Road Art															
David Eccles limited edition print	$ 64.00	$ 24.00	—	—	DM120,-	DM30,-	SFr100,-	SFr25,-	£ 40.00	£ 5.00	£ 10.00	£ 15.00	Print 1/2/3/4		
David Eccles limited edition (set of 4)	$ 256.00	$ 24.00	—	—	DM480,-	DM30,-	SFr403,-	SFr25,-	£ 160.00	£ 5.00	£ 10.00	£ 15.00			
													Total		

(For how to pay see opposite page)

Prices as at 1/1/99, and subject to alteration.

* The Encycleopedia published in 97/98 is known as just Encycleopedia in the USA (published there by the Overlook Press) and as Encycleopedia 4 elsewhere.

Note: We also have agents in Norway, the Netherlands and New Zealand
See the page opposite for prices and how to contact them.

Visit our Website: www.encycleopedia.com On-line ordering services are available

Date ☐☐/☐☐/☐☐

If cheque enclosed please tick ☐

Your unique reference number (if you have one) ☐☐☐☐☐☐☐

DELIVERY ADDRESS

Name Mr / Mrs / Ms

Address

Post Code

Telephone (daytime)

CREDIT CARD DETAILS (Not available in Germany)

Name Mr / Mrs / Ms

Address (if different)

Post Code

Signature

Visa/Delta ☐ Access/Mastercard ☐ Eurocard ☐

Card Number ☐☐☐☐ ☐☐☐☐ ☐☐☐☐ ☐☐☐☐

Issue Number ☐☐ Expiry Date ☐☐/☐☐/☐☐

Switch ☐

Switch Number ☐☐☐☐☐☐☐☐☐☐☐☐☐☐☐☐☐☐☐

Issue Number ☐☐ Valid From ☐☐/☐☐/☐☐ Expiry Date ☐☐/☐☐/☐☐

How to order

1. Make your choice from the ordering table opposite.

2. Add up the prices. Choose the price column for your country.

3. Check on this page for details of where to send your order and how to pay. Note that you can usually order by telephone if you wish.

4. Finally, fill out the form with your details, and send off your order and payment. We'll get the goods to you within 28 days, but usually a lot sooner.

USA, Mexico and Canada

Orders directly from individuals, including all subsbcriptions, are handled by the publishers in the UK: Open Road, The Danesmead Wing, 33 Fulford Cross, YORK, YO10 4PB. Tel +44 1904 654654. Fax +44 1904 654684. E-mail: melanie@bcqedit.demon.co.uk. Website www.encycleopedia.com.

This book can be ordered through North American bookstores, who are supplied by the Overlook Press (see masthead on page 3 for full details). Bike stores are supplied by AlpenBooks. 3616 South Road, C-1, Mukilteo, WA 98275 USA Tel 425-290-8587 (extension 301) Fax 425-290-9461.

Deutschland, Österreich und die Schweiz

Alle Bestellungen aus Deutschland, Österreich und der Schweiz für Einzelausgaben (BCQ oder Encycleopedia), Jahresabonnements, T-Shirts, Videos usw. werden von Kalle Kalkhoff, KGB, Donnerschweerstr. 45, 26123 Oldenburg bearbeitet. **Tel:** 0441 8850389 **Fax:** 0441 8850388

Für weitere Informationen und Preise von Einzelexemplaren, rufen Sie KGB an und sprechen Sie mit Kalle.

Zahlungsmodus

Soweit Sie über ein Konto in der Bundesrepublik verfügen, senden Sie bitte mit Ihrer Bestellung einen Verrechnungsscheck an KGB in deutscher Währung.

Die Schweiz

Unsere neue Postscheckkontonummer für Schweizer Abonnenten ist 87-601949-5 KGB Kalle Kalkhoff

Senden Sie bitte Ihre Bestellung an KGB und den Betrag in Schweizer Währung an dieses Konto. Verwenden Sie andernfalls einen Euroscheck. Bitte denken Sie daran, 'Oldenburg' als 'Ort' anzugeben und Ihre EC-Kartennummer auf der Rückseite des Schecks zu vermerken. Euroschecks müssen ebenfalls in DM notiert werden. English versions of Bike Culture and Encycleopedia can be sent by KGB on request.

Dieses Plakat (DIN A2) von David Eccles im Fin-de-Siècle-Stil ist auf hochwertigem Papier gedruckt und für DM25,- plus DM10,- Versandkosten ausschließlich von KGB erhältlich.

Netherlands

Danny Siepman, Korenbloemlaan 11, 2343 VA Oegstgeest, Den Haag. Tel: +31 (0) 71 5174368. Info@zephyr.nl Website www.zephyr.nl/bcq

Encycleopedia 2001 - fl 42,00. **Encycleopedia 1999** - fl 25,00. **Encycleopedia 1994/1995** - fl 22,00 (inclusief Bike Culture nr. 3). **Encycleopedia 1996** - fl 24,00, compleet met videoband van 35 minuten. **Encycleopedia 4 (97/98)** - fl 29,00 compleet met videoband van 35 minuten **Encycleopedia 1993/1994** - fl 19,00. **Alle vijf voorgaande nummers van de Encycleopedia compleet**: f 99. **Bike Culture Quarterly oude nummers 1-18** f11,00. **Alle achttien voorgaande nummers van Bike Culture compleet**: f169. **Alle voorgaande nummers van Bike Culture en Encycleopedia compleet:** f 245

Alle bestellingen exclusief F5 Postzegel. U kunt on-line bestellen.

New Zealand

Orders are handled by:

Bikedirect, Scott Clavis, 2/45 Riddell Rd, St Heliers, Auckland, New Zealand

Phone 09 5755462 **Fax** 09 5755406 **Email** anniescott@clear net.nz

Website www.nvo.com/bikedirect

Australia

All Australian orders are handled by:

Ian Sims, Greenspeed, 69 Mountain Gate Drive, Ferntree Gully, VIC 3156.

Tel: (03) 9758 5541 **Fax:** (03) 9752 4115 **Email:** ian@greenspeed.com.au

Website www.greenspeed.com.au

Ian accepts credit cards, cheques or money orders made out to Greenspeed.

UK and Rest of the World

Please direct all subscriptions, orders and subscription enquiries to:

Open Road Mail Order, Unit 1, East Riding Business Centre, Annie Reed Road, Beverley, East Yorkshire, HU17 OLF, UK **Tel:** +44 1482 880399 **Email:** openroad@nite-direct.demon.co.uk

UK customers can use the FREEPOST address:

Open Road Mail Order, FREEPOST NEA 3279, Beverley, East Yorkshire. HU17 OBR

If the automatic answering service is running, please speak slowly and clearly and make sure you include relevant card details. We accept almost all credit and debit cards. If you want us to phone you back, tell us how. We always aim to phone back within 24 hours.

All cheques and Eurocheques must be payable to Open Road Ltd. If using a Eurocheque, please send your order in Pounds Sterling, putting 'Beverley, England' as the 'Place'. Credit card payments must be made in Pounds Sterling only. When using your card by post please indicate the type of card, expiry date, registered card address, the name as it appears on the card, the card number, and the name and address for delivery. For debit cards please add issue number and 'valid from' date.

We do not accept cheques from non-UK bank accounts made out in Pounds Sterling. If you are paying in a currency other than Sterling, please ensure that you are sending enough money at the current rate of exchange.

Editorial enquiries, and enquiries about Bike Culture Weeks and shareholdings should go to:

Open Road Ltd, The Danesmead Wing, 33 Fulford Cross, York YO10 4PD, UK

Tel: +44 1904 654654 **Fax:** +44 1904 654684 **Email:** melanie@bcqedit.demon.co.uk

Norway

Penny and Chris Heymans, PedalNor, Kløverveien 10, 4300 Sandnes, Norway.

Tel: 51 66 40 60 **Fax:** 51 66 48 70

Email: pedal@robin.no **Website:** www.robin.no/pedal

Keeping bike culture in your neighbourhood

When you buy a bicycle you take home a machine which will become either a personal friend or an expensive liability, or, more likely, something between the two.

For anyone who rides regularly, a cheap bike is never exactly that, because it will soon bring you big repair bills and personal disruption as components begin to give up the ghost. For long periods this 'cheap' bike sits at home, until the time can be found to buy and fit a replacement part, or to take it (by car?) to the bike shop. Then the day comes when the owner decides that cycling wasn't much fun anyway: the bike was a heavy beast, and might as well stay out of sight and unrepaired. Besides, it had begun to rust...

Good specialist bike shops are essential to the fabric of a society which values cycling. This is why Encycleopedia supports such shops strongly. A good bike shop is part of the local community. We list on the following pages some of the bike shops which stock Encycleopedia. They are in many different countries, and reflect their local cycling cultures, but the simple fact that they sell such a book as this is a reasonable indication that they are caring shops.

It is the specialised shops who are taking an interest in the kind of bikes you see in Encycleopedia. These machines are often expensive to keep in stock and take considerable knowledge to explain. It also usually takes many times longer to demonstrate and sell an unconventional cycle than it does to sell a cheap mountain bike from the Far East. Some of the shops listed will stock quite a few of the products which you see in Encycleopedia, others will stock hardly any, but they all have details, from us, the publishers, of how to source the products in Encycleopedia. However, a shop may decline, for very understandable reasons, to source a product for you. After all, they have no prior knowledge of which products we will put into Encycleopedia. They may suggest you try sourcing from a different shop. If all else fails, contact us.

A few manufacturers prefer to deal with customers directly. This is usually because their products are too specialised, or may require a degree of custom building, or perhaps, being big and bulky, they take up too much space in the average shop. However, you or the manufacturer may prefer to have the machine delivered to your local bike shop for assembly, final fitting and after-sales service.

We hope you will support the cycle shops listed over the following pages, or any local bike shop which makes an effort.

AUSTRALIA

CANBERRA
Canberra Cycles Pty Ltd
70 Newcastle Str., Fyshwick, Canberra, 2609.
Tel 02 6280 4984 Fax 02 6239 1257
Email canberracycles@canberracycles.com.au
Website www.canberracycles.com.au
Mo-Fr 8.00-18.00, Sa 8.00-16.00, Su 10.00-15.00
All kinds of bikes from $100 to $6,000, including dual-suspension MTBs and recumbents.

MITCHAM
Cycle Science Mitcham
478 Whitehorse Road, Mitcham, VIC 3132. Tel 03 9874 8033 Fax 03 9874 8442
Email freedhpv @connexus.apana.org.au
Mo-Th 9.00-18.00, Fr 9.00-21.00, Sa 9.00-17.00
A wide range of accessories and bicycles including recumbents for sale or hire. We custom build in steel or aluminium.

PERTH
Quantum
64 Farmer Street, North Perth, WA 6006.
Tel 089 443 3407 Fax 089 443 8687
Hrs Mo-Fr 9.00-18.00, Sa 9.00-12.00

VICTORIA
Greenspeed
69 Mountain Gate Drive, Ferntree Gully, VIC 3156.
Tel 03 9758 5541 Fax 03 9752 4115
Email ian@greenspeed.com.au
Website www.greenspeed.com.au

SYDNEY
Cheeky Monkey Cycle Company
456 Pitt St ,Sydney, NSW 2000.
Tel/Fax +61 2 9212 4460,
Email www.cheekymonkey.com.au
Citybike and touring specialists! Loadcarrier, recumbent, folder and trailer enthusiasts. Service, sales and rentals near Sydney's Central Station. Cheeky!

BELGIUM

BRUSSELS
Velodroom
Van Arteveldestraat 41, B -1000 Brüssels
Tel 0032 / 2 513 81 99 Fax 0032 / 2 513 81 99
Email velodroom@hotmail.com
Website www.velodroom.com
Mon-Sat 10.00 to 18.30
City, folding, touring, transport, retro and other bikes. Comfortable, high-quality, low-maintenance, easy-to-operate, bikes made by leading European manufacturers. Friendly, reliable and competent advice in English, Dutch, French or German. Excellent service. Most of our product range is exclusive in Belgium.

CANADA

VICTORIA
Fairfield Bicycle Shop, Ltd.
1275 Oscar St., Victoria, BC V8V 2X6.
Tel 250 381 2453 Fax 250 384 2453
Email fairbic@islandnet.com
Practical bikes for the real world. Commuters' oasis in an MTB desert. Frame building, cycle repair courses, cycling coalition involvement.

VANCOUVER
Reckless: the bike store
1810 Fir St @ 2nd Ave., Vancouver, BC V6J 3B1. Tel 604 731 2420 Fax 604 266 9090
110 Davie Street @ Pacific Tel 604 648 2600
Fax 604 648 2601
Email dragan@rektek.com Website www.rektek.com
Quality rentals, guided or independent tours, full service repairs, and unrelentingly friendly service! We speak French, Italian, Spanish, Japanese, German & Cantonese. Free air and free oil any time!

TORONTO
Bikes on Wheels
309 Augusta Avenue, Toronto, Ontario M5T 2M2
Bikes and accessories. We advocate the use of human-powered vehicles. Burley, Ibis.

TORONTO
Curbside Cycle & Inline
412 Bloore St. West, Toronto, M5S 1X5.
Tel 416 920 4933 Fax 416 920 3354
Email curbsidebike@eol.ca
Webstie www.curbsidebike.ca

DENMARK

COPENHAGEN
Christiania Cykler
Oster Port Open Mo-Fr 10.00-17.30, Refshalevej 2, DK-1432 Copenhagen K.
Tel 032 954 520 Fax 031 544 593
A highly professional, enthusiastic shop within the famous Christiania commune, yet attracting customers from all over Copenhagen. Specialisms: Pedersens and MTBs.

COPENHAGEN
Dansk Cyklist Forbund
Rømersgade 7, DK-1362 Copenhagen K.
Tel +45 33 32 31 21 Fax +45 33 32 76 83
Email dcf@inet.uni-c.dk
Website www.dcf.dk

FRANCE

PARIS
Bicloune (Le Comptoir du Cycle)
7 Rue Froment, 75011 Paris. Tel 0148 054775
Fax 0148 054770
Specialists in international bikes, particularly Dutch bikes and parts, eg Gazelle, Batavus, also for Schwinn and Scott. Antiques department: complete bicycles, spare parts, catalogues and postcards.

GERMANY

D -06108 Halle / Saale
Fahrradies GmbH
Bernburger Str. 25 Tel 0345-2909727 Fax 0345-2909728 Email fahrradies.halle@t-online.de
Very scenic shop not far at all from the Saal cycle route in a millennia-old town. Townies and tourers, transporters and recumbents, child trailers. VSF-member; Manufaktur, Diamant, Cannondale.

D -10119 Berlin
Velo.B
Gipsstr. 7 Tel 030-28390809 Fax 030-28390815
Email velo.b@vsf.de Website www.vsf.de/velo.b
Trailers, folders, transport bikes, Reha-bikes, strollers and joggers.

D -10405 Berlin
Ostrad GmbH
Winsstr. 48 Tel 030-44341393 Fax 030-44341394
Email OstradGmbH@aol.com Website www.ostrad.de
Master craftsmen, Shimano Service Center, bikes of all sorts,m accessories of every description and almost any repair you can imagine.

D -10555 Berlin
Velophil
Alt-Moabit 72 Tel 030 / 39 9021 16
Fax 030 / 39 90 21 17

D -13347 Berlin
Radhaus Wedding oHG
Liebenwalder Str. 1 Tel 030 / 455 10 41
Fax 030 / 455 70 16 Email radhaus.wedding de
Town and touring bikes, trekking-bike, trailer-bikes, fun-trailers, baby joggers, spares and repairs.

D -18055 Rostock
Radhaus Rostock
Goetheplatz 1 Tel 0381 / 45 52 03
Fax 0381 / 45 52 04

D -21029 Hamburg
pro velo
Serrahnstr. 1-2 Tel 040 / 721 31 09 Fax 040 / 721 29

D -22087 Hamburg
Die Luftpumpe Hamburg
Lübecker Str. 114 Tel 040 / 25 49 28 00 Fax 040 / 25 49 28 01 Email lupu-hh@t-online.de
Website www.luftpumpe-hamburg
Bremen Manufaktur, Votec, Patria, Maxcycles, Special bikes for teh disabled from several manufacturers, Göricke, Bergamont.

D -22765 Hamburg
Rad & Tat
Am Felde 2 Tel 040-395667 Fax 040-392154
With its enthusiastic team RAD & TAT in Hamburg has become one of the institutions of the cycle industry. Our speciality are bikes from FahrradManufaktur Bremen. Highlights include bikes from riese & müller, and Wanderer bikes.

D -22765 Hamburg
Zweirad und Zukunft
Gaußstr. 19 Tel 040 / 39 52 85 Fax 040 / 39 03 221

D -23552 Lübeck
Sattelfest
Kanalstr. 70 Tel 0451 / 70 46 87 Fax 0451 / 706 37 42

D -24106 Kiel
Fahrradies
Adalbertstr. 11 Tel 0431 / 33 20 16 Fax 0431 / 33 63 81 Email fahrradies-kiel@t-online.de
Website www.fahrradies-kiel.de

D -24118 Kiel
VeloCenter
Knooper Weg 165 Tel 0431 / 80 39 91
Fax 0431 / 8 50 53 Website www.velocenter.de
Manufaktur, Ortlieb, Topeak, Riese und Müller, Wanderer, Stevens, Puky, Gore, Shimano etc..

D -26721 Emden
Transvelo
Boltentorstr. 30 Tel 04921-26913 Fax 04921-27557
Small but perfect! Manufaktur, Diamant, Riese und Müller, Giant, Utopia

D -28857 Syke
per Pedal
Herrlichkeit 36. Tel 04242 929 5090
Fax 04242 9295091

D -28203 Bremen
Radschlag GmbH
Humboldtstr. 16 Tel 0421 / 70 41 05
Fax 0421/ 76 120

D -29549 Bad Bevensen
Fahrradhaus Bevensen
Medingerstr. 20 Tel 05821 / 13 05
Fax 05821 / 413 53
Email fahrradhausbevensen@t-online.de
Everything to do with cycling!

D -30171 Hannover
Räderwerk GmbH
Marienstr. 28 Tel 0511-717174 Fax 2832140
Email raederwerk@com link.org
Website www.raederwerk-gmbh.de
Customers tell us we're a real museum - of the future of cycling. Bike to ride more as you drive less: folding bikes, trailers, load-carriers, recumbents, tourers, trikes, tandems, hobby-horses.

D -30175 Hannover
Drahtesel GmbH
Volgersweg 58 Tel 0511 / 348 15 12
Fax 0511 / 31 16 38

D -30451 Hannover
Radgeber Linden GmbH
Limmerstr. 32 Tel 0511 / 44 26 94 Fax 0511 / 44 26 96

D -31785 Hameln
Fahrradies
Thietorstr. 27 Tel 05151 / 92 34 55
Fax 05151 / 92 34 56
Email carsten@fahrradies-hameln.de
Website www.fahrradies-hameln.de
Our offer includes, alongside the good service, customer-oriented advice and fulfilling individual wishes (only cycle-related!): trekking and touring bikes, recumbent bikes and trikes, city and racing bikes, trailers for all purposes.

D -33102 Paderborn
Pigal Fahrradladen
Bahnhofstr. 31 / Im Hauptbahnhof Tel 05251 / 37 284
Fax 05251 / 37 07 59 Email erst ab März 2000
Website erst ab März 2000
Bike hire at the main rail station. New bikes: Bremen Fahrradmanufaktur, Puky, Riese und Müller, Radius.

D -33602 Bielefeld
Freilauf
August-Bebel-Str. 33
Tel 0521 / 638 11 Fax 0521 / 17 28 53

D -33790 Halle
Avanti Halle
Lange Str. 34 Tel 05201 / 57 07 Fax 05201 / 66 51 36

D -34134 Kassel
Fahrradhof VSF GmbH
Frankfurter Str. 285 Tel 0561 / 47 11 32
Fax 0561 / 47 33 38 Email info@fahrradhof.de
Website www.fahrradhof.de
MTBs, Racers, tourers, children's bikes, child and load trailers, tandems, recumbents, special shop for shoes, helmets, glasses, clothing.

D -34576 Homberg
Liege-Rad Treffpunkt
Oderweg 8 Tel 05681 / 91 062 Email: in preparation
Website: in preparation
Recumbents from Anthrotech, HP Velotechnik, Ostrad (planned), VSF Fahrradmanufaktur. Trailers from 2 + 2. Accessories, repair, self-help workshop..

D -34582 Borken
radstop
Kernstr. 10 Tel 05682 / 71 011 Fax 05682 / 73 07 50

D -37073 Göttingen
ultra Rad
Nikolaikirchhof 12 Tel 0551 / 48 41 13
Fax 0551 / 48 41 13 Email ultrabauer@t-online.de
We offer Patria, Utopia, Spezialräder: Ostrad, Bevo, Streetmachine, Kettwiesel, Alligt, Brompton, Flux V200, ADD-Bike, Christiania load-carriers. Speciality: child-trailers. We are truly independent, and work and advise with enthusiasm.

D -37073 Göttingen
Velo Voss GmbH
Nicolai Str. 21 Tel 0551 / 48 42 36 Fax 0551 / 562 37

D -38106 Braunschweig
Radhaus
Heinrichstr. 25 Tel 0531 / 33 96 50
Fax 0531/ 33 71 46

D -40217 Düsseldorf
Rad ab
Friedrichstr. 112 Tel 0211 / 33 66 61
Fax 0211 / 31 62 26 Email Rad_Ab@t-online.de
Website www.radab.de (in preparation)

D -41239 Mönchengladbach
Räderei rapid
Dahlener Str. 22 Tel 02166 / 40 447
Fax 02166 / 61 14 22
Bikes: Giant, Manufaktur, Kettler. Trailers: 2 + 2. Folders: Birdy, Brompton. Recumbents: Radius.

D -42285 Wuppertal
Radfinesse
Haspeler Str. 10 Tel 0202 / 81 512 Fax 0202 / 81 512
Email Radfinesse@t-online.de
Website www.radfinesse.de
"Where you can still get a real bike" is the word that's spread in and around Wuppertal... advice and service of well-known quality. Very scenic shop, in sight of the unique Wuppertaler suspended railway. Worth the trip!

D -44135 Dortmund
Das Rad Fahrradspezialgeschäft GmbH
Brüderweg 14 Tel 0231 / 52 93 24
Fax 0231 / 55 13 20 Email info@das-rad.com
Website www.das-rad.com
Everything to gladden the heart of any cyclist. From children's bikes to Pedersens. Master workshop and Multi-Service-Center.

D -47051 Duisburg
Radwerk Fahrradladen
Oberstr. 42 Tel 0203 / 24 032 Fax 0203 / 288 116
Bikes with maximum utility; touring, trekking, recumbents, large tandem department, large trailer department, hire, spares, repair. Brands: Riese + Müller, Fahrradmanufaktur, Zwei + Zwei, Santana, Maxcycles, Steppenwolf, Brompton.

D -48151 Münster
1 2 3 Rad
Sentmaringer Weg 113 Tel 0251 / 97 45 890
Fax 0251 / 97 45 891

D -48653 Coesfeld
High Tech Radsport Coesfeld
Citadelle 20-22 Tel 02541 / 69 09 Fax 02541 / 69 91

D -50678 Köln
Stadtrad
Teutoburgerstr. 19 Tel 0221 / 32 80 75
Fax 0221/ 93 22 258
Manufaktur, Riese & Müller, Flux, Ortlieb, Wanderer, Gazelle.

D -51427 Bergisch-Gladbach
Veloladen Liegeräder
Stegerwaldstr. 1 Tel 02204 / 61 075
Fax 02204 / 61 076 Email mega@veloladen.com
Website www.veloladen.com
The recumbent specialists with a wide range! Know How and objective advice go without saying. Proprietors: Ortwin Kürten & Klaus Schröder, VSF and HPV Club members.

D -53111 Bonn
Stahlroß GmbH
Dorotheenstr. 1-3 Tel 0228 / 69 42 09
Fax 0228 / 65 87 94
Manufaktur, Guderreit, Maxcycle, Wanderer, Specialized, Steppenwolf, recumbents, folders, transport and child trailers, parts and accessories, full selection. And a second shop: Velocity, Belderberg 18, 53111 Bonn.

D -53173 Bonn
Liegeraddatbi, Andreas Pooch
Heidestr. 8. Tel 02241 75344

D -53840 Troisdorf
Vam Bike
Alte Poststr. 21 Tel 02241 / 786 45
Fax 02241 / 833 57

D -55116 Mainz
Fahrrad-Laden
Albinistr. 15 Tel 06131 / 22 50 13 Fax 06131 / 23 00

D -57076 Siegen
ExtraRad
Auf den Hütten 20 Tel 0271 / 72 387
Fax 0271 / 790 823 Email m.goebel@extrarad.de
Website www.extrarad.de
The multifaceted bike shop in Siegerland. From sporty mountainbiks to recumbents, you can get everything you need on one, two or three wheels for non-motorised existence at Extrarad. Brands: Stevens, Riese + Müller, Schmidt's hub dynamo.

D -58452 Witten
pro velo
Winkelstr. 1 Tel 02302 / 96 33 66
Fax 02302 / 96 33 69 Email pro.velo.witten@cww.de
Website www.pro-velo.de

D -60389 Frankfurt
Radschlag GmbH
Hallgartenstr. 56 Tel 069 / 45 20 64
Fax 069 / 45 32 84

D -60437 Frankfurt
Fahrradscheune
Alt Harheim 27 Tel 06101 / 48 958
Fax 06101 / 403 521 Email info@fahrradscheune.de
Website www.fahrradscheune.de
Anthrotech-Trike, Adagio from Ostrad, Lorri from Kemper, S-60, S-RX, V200 & V220 from Flux, Kettwiesel and Pino from Hase, SL4L and SL1 from Nöll, C4 and Hornet II from Radius, Streetmachine GT, Speedmachine from HP-Velotechnik, Brompton, Turn-a-Round, folding tandems.

D -60487 Frankfurt
Per Pedale GmbH
Leipziger Str. 4 Tel 069 / 707 23 63 Fax 069 / 77 20 84
Email info@perpedale.de Website www.perpedale.de
Town and touring bikes from Bremen Fahrradmanufaktur; Individual bikes from Utopia; comfort bikes from Riese + Müller; Brompton folders; trailers from Zwei plus zwei; recumbents and other special bikes; Bico plus dealer with exclusive products.

D -61231 Bad Nauheim
Erstrad
Zander Str. 7 Tel 06032 / 47 91 Fax 06032 / 92 01 34
Email erstrad@t-online.de
Bremen Manufaktur, Winora, Hartje Manufaktur, Utopia, child trailers, recumbent mobility trikes, Specialising in everyday bikes and cyclists.

D -64287 Darmstadt
WoogRad
Soderstr. 85 Tel 06151 / 420 580

D -64293 Darmstadt
Luftpumpe GmbH
Liebigstr. 52 Tel 06151-291884 Fax 06151-292739

D -64521 Groß-Gerau
Fahrrad Fuchs - zeitgemäße Fahrradkultur
Am Schlag 17 Tel 06152 / 557 95 Fax 06152 / 511 95
Email fahrrad-fuchs@t-online.de
Website www.fahrrad-fuchs.de
Fahrradmanufaktur, Wanderer, Riese & Müller, Pedersen, Specialists in child and load trailers.

D -65468 Trebur
Fahrrad Claus
Astheimer Str. 58 Tel 06147 / 79 15 Fax 06147 / 13 29
Family business since 1920 - from children's bikes to tourers, recumbents, folders, hire bikes, trailers. Master workshop. Test rides welcome. Special requests? Ask! Child's bikes: Enik, Puky. Folders: Bernds, Birdy, Brompton, Hercules. Recumbents: Flux, Hase, HP.

D -66111 Saarbrücken
Der Fahrradladen
Nauwieserstr. 19 Tel 0681 / 37 098
Fax 0681 / 39 77 71
Email fahrradladen.saarbrücken@t-online.de
Bread + Butter! High quality touring and town bikes, not much racing and MTBs. More and more full-suspension everyday and touring bikes.

D -69115 Heidelberg
Das kleine Radhaus
Kaiserstr. 59 Tel 06221 / 18 37 27
Fax 06221 / 18 27 53
Bikes: Manufaktur Bremen, Villiger, Diamant, Chemnitz, Cannondale.

D -71254 Ditzingen
Pedalkraft Spezialräder
Hirschlander Str. 2 Tel 07156 / 83 69
Fax 07156 / 340 34 Email info@pedalkraft.de
Website www.pedalkraft.de
Bike E German importer, RANS, Radius, Optima, Flux, Horizont, Anthrotech, Challenge, almost every folder, special accessories, mail order with online-catalogue.

D -71272 Renningen
RADieschen Zweiradtechnik
Lange Str. 24/1 Tel 07159 / 90 29 48
Fax 07159 / 90 29 47
Email info@RADieschen-Zweiradtechnik.de
Website www.RADieschen-Zweiradtechnik.de
Small but perfect! Town, folding and recumbent bikes and custom service. Everything for children, trailers, accessories, hire and service.

D -72764 Reutlingen
Transvelo
Kaiserstr. 52 Tel 07121 / 47 07 26
Fax 07121 / 47 07 27 Email info@transvelo.de
Website www.transvelo.de
MTBs, andn a wide range of folders and trailer brands: Cannondale, Utopia, Votec, VSF-Manufaktur, Trek, Stevens, Sundance, Bergamont.

D -73433 Aalen
Rundum - der Fahrradladen
Schafgasse 32 Tel 07361 / 791 52 Fax 07361 / 792 35

D -76133 Karlsruhe
Rad & Tat GmbH
Waldstr. 58 Tel 0721-22238 Fax 0721-26458
Rad & Tat has the following brands: Brompton, Riese & Müller (full range), HP Velotechnik (Street-machine), Flux (V200 & V220), KGB-Pedersen.

D -76275 Ettlingen
Radial
Karl-Friedrich-Str. 14 Tel 07243 / 126 14
Fax 07243 / 155 12

D -76726 Germersheim
Haasies Radschlag
Marktstr. 22 Tel 07274-4863 Fax 779360
Email haasies@haasies-radschlag.elch.net
Website www.haasies-radschlag.elch.net

D -77933 Lahr
rad & tat
Werderstr. 65 Tel 07821 / 2 94 58
Fax 07821 / 984 407 Email radunt@t-online.de
Utopia, riese und müller, Diamant , Patria, Brompton, Bevo, Ortlieb, Every possible trailer. .Specialities: Touring and town bikes.

D -78462 Konstanz
Radial Radsport GmbH
Konradigasse 13 Tel 07531 / 225 32
Fax 07531 / 292 74 Email Radial@t-online.de
Town and touring bikes from Fahrradmanufaktur, Wanderer, Centurion, Maxcycles, Gudereit. Sport tourers from Fahrradmanufaktur, Steppenwolf, Centurion, Gudereit, Bergamont. MTBs: Steppenwolf, Trek, Centurion, Bergamont, Cycle Wolf. Racing bikes, too.

D -79106 Freiburg
Radhaus
Münchhofstr. 4 Tel 0761 / 28 08 32 Fax 0761 / 28 08 38 Email radhaus-freiburg@t-online.de Website www.radhaus-freiburg.de
City and trekking bikes, MTBs, recumbents, folders, special bikes.

D -79106 Freiburg
Duett Räder am BHF
Wentzingerstr. 15 / Fahrradwerkstatt: Habsburgerstr. 9, Tel.: 0761 / 5 27 29 Tel 0761 / 29 27 670
Fax 0761 / 29 27 671
New bikes: Utopia, Fahrradmanufaktur Bremen, Velo de Ville, Tornado. Accessories: Ortlieb, Uvex, Jeantex... Cycle literature.

D -80538 München
Fidelio
St. Anna Str. 18 Tel 089 / 21 86 90 16
Fax 089 / 21 86 90 17 Email mail@fidelio-mobil.de
Website www.fidelio-mobil.de
Product range:: bike trailers, trailerbikes, scooters, folders, baby-joggers.

D -81241 München
Cycle
Josef-Retzer-Str. 47 Tel 089 / 83 41 612
Fax 089 / 83 42 145

D -82362 Weilheim
Radl Bimbo
Rathausplatz 13 Tel 0881 / 41 79 980
Fax 0881 / 41 79 981 Email radlbimbo@aol.com
MTB, racers, tourers and commuters, to recumbents, folders, Pedersens, trailers. Special equipment for tourers and commuters, clothing to tents.

D -83093 Bad Endorf
mbf - muskelbetrieben Fahrzeuge
Poststr. 1 Tel 08053 / 23 74 Fax 08053 / 23 97
Website www.mbf-spezialrad.de
Amazing range at "mbfs": recumbents, trikes, Pedersens, Wanderer, Moulton, folders, transport bikes, trailers, trailerbikes, scooters, tandems, rehabilitation - for any model long-lasting, smart accessories.

D -88250 Weingarten
BICI
Liebfrauenstr. 39 Tel 0751 / 486 71 Fax 0751 / 430 74
Email bici-weingarten@t-online.de
The southern Germany tandem specialist. Always at least five models in stock. Also tandems to hire (DM 50,00 / day).

D -90419 Nürnberg
ride on a rainbow
Adam-Kraft-Str. 55 Tel 0911 / 39 73 37
Fax 0911 / 39 60 78
Manufaktur, Utopia, Riesig and Schneller, Bergamont, recumbnets, hire, 24 h repair service, free loan bike, Espresso machine and all other VSF requirements.

D -90762 Fürth
Zentralrad
Moststr. 25 Tel 0911 / 74 60 90 Fax 0911 / 77 05 79
Trailers (Chariot, Ritschie, Kindercar, Leggero). Recumbents: Liegeräder (Flux, HP-Velotechnik) City- and trekking bikes (VSF-Fahrradmanufaktur, Hercules, Giant). Child bikes (Puky, Falter), Racers (Giant, Cannondale).

D -91054 Erlangen
Freilauf GmbH
Lazarettstr. 4 Tel 09131 / 20 22 20
Fax 09131 / 20 17 10
Email 09131202220@t-online.de
Website www.freilauf.de
High-quality bikes for everyday and sport. Fahrradmanufaktur, Cannondale, Wanderer, Riese + Müller, Stevens, Principia. Trailers: Zwei plus zwei service centre dealer, Tandems and Pedersens.Folders a speciality: Brompton, Birdy, Moulton, Bernds.

D -91522 Ansbach
Fahr' Rad!
Reuterstr. 3 Tel 0981 / 13 501 Fax 0981 / 13 501
Recumbents (Flux, HPV, Anthrotech, Optima, Aeroproject, any other to order), folders (Brompton, Birdy, Bernds), Trailers (Burley and 2 + 2, touring trailers, transport trailers, trailerbikes), scooters, Like a Bike, touring bikes (Nöll, VSF, Patria).

D -91564 Neuendettelsau
Rad mit Hand und Fuß GmbH
Windsbacherstr. 10 Tel 09874 / 18 35
Fax 09874 / 687097 Email radmithuf@vsf.de
Website www.radmithuf.de
Integrated orthopaedic technology centre and bike shop: all 'normal' bikes as well as specials for disabled, rehabilitation, wheelchair users, tandems, etc.

D -93053 Regensburg
Feine Räder
Furtmayrstr. 12 Tel 0941 / 700 03 65
Fax 0941 700 05 46

D -97070 Würzburg
Fahrradstation
Bahnhofplatz 4 Tel 0931 / 57 445 Fax 0931 / 57 465
Bikes: Manufaktur, Pedersen, Wanderer-Service station, Velotraum child- and transport-trailers, Service, bike hire, recumbent hire, VSF-shop.

D -97816 Lohr / Main
Radsport Marschall
Jahnstr. 9 Tel 09352 / 702 55 Fax 09352 / 708 55

D -99097 Erfurt
Radscheune
Haarbergstr. 19 Tel 0361 / 41 33 86
Fax 0361 / 41 33 86

REPUBLIC OF IRELAND

DUBLIN
Square Wheel Cycleworks
Temple Lane South, (Off Dame Street) Dublin 2.
Tel 01 6790838
Hrs Mo-Fr 8:30-6:30 Sat 10:30-6:30
A centre of Cycle Culture, with a full repair and bike parking service. Occasional holidays.

NETHERLANDS

EINDHOVEN
De Liggende Hollander,
Postbus 1831, 5602 CA Eindhoven.
Tel 040 2424368
Sale and hire of recumbents, trailers and folding bikes. Open days for potential customers. Organises recumbent cycling holidays.

DEN HAAG
Kemper
Piet Heinstraat 42, 2518 CJ Den Haag.
Tel 070 345 9696
Folding bike and recumbent specialist, trailers and tandems. Also hire of recumbent and folding bikes. Accompanied try-out touring runs for those interested in recumbents.

UTRECHT
Wim Kok Fietsplezier
Nachtegaalstraat 51, 3581 AD Utrecht.
Tel 030 2315780 Fax 030 2316675
All-round excellent cycle shop for touring, recumbents, ATB, hybrids, tandems, scooters. Folding bike and trailer specialist. Many unusual lines, clothing, helmets, etc.

NORWAY

SANDNES
Pedalnor
Kløvereien 10, 4300 Sandnes, Norway.
Tel 066 40 60 Fax 066 48 70
Email pedal@robin.no
Website http//www.robin.no/ped
Agents for Bike Culture. Arrange Cycle tours in Lofoten Islands and West Norway.

SWITZERLAND

CH -6010 Kriens
Velociped
Luzernerstr. 16 Tel 0041-41-320 53 51
Fax 0041-41-311 2077 Email velociped@tic.ch
Velos nach Maß, Elektrovelos, Falträder, Trotinett, Comfortbikes, Kinderanhänger, Trailerbikes, Tandems.

UNITED KINGDOM

CHANNEL ISLES

GUERNSEY
Ian Brown Cycle Shop
Route Militaire, St Sampsons, Guernsey, Channel Isles GY2 4DZ. Tel 01481 241308 Fax 01481 241309
Email ianbrowns@aol.com
Website www.ianbrownsshop.co.uk
Hrs Mon-Sat 8:30-5.30
We offer the world's finest products at the world's best prices. Try us for service youll find we are first class.

JERSEY
Mark Pickford Cycle Shop,
13 La Motte Street, St Helier, Jersey, JE2 4SY.
Tel 01534 832280 Fax 01534 832281
Specialists on all cycling products and services. VAT free. Try us for service we are the professionals.

ENGLAND

BARNSTAPLE (N. DEVON)
Biketrail Cycle Hire
Estuary business park, West Yelland, Barnstaple, Devon, EX32 3EZ. Tel 01271 861424
mobile 0771 31582 Email info@biketrail.co.uk
Website www.biketrail.co.uk
The Tarka Trail is a scenic traffic-free cycle route. With bike 'n' bus and bike 'n' boat services for car-free days out. Hire trailers, special needs bikes, tag-a-longs, U+2s, trikes, tandems, and top quality GT MTBs. Special needs and group discounts.

BATH
Avon Valley Cyclery
Rear of Bath Spa Train Station, Bath, Avon BA1 1SX.
Tel 01225 442442/461880 Fax 01225 446267
Hrs 9-5.30 seven days a week.
Email Info@bikeshop.uk.com
Web www.bikeshop.uk.com, www.foldingbikes.co.uk
Makers of unique Caribou Road mountain bikes, racelite bikes, folding bike experts, recumbents, hire and big workshop.

BERWICK-UPON-TWEED
Brilliant Bicycles
17a Bridge Street, Berwick-upon-Tweed, Northumberland, TD15 1ES. Hrs 9-5:30 Tel 01289 331476 Fax 01289 302345
Email enquiries@brilliantbicycles.co.uk
Website www.brilliantbicycles.co.uk
A brilliant range of cycles, tricycles, special needs products and cycle hire.

BIRMINGHAM
Feet First
170 Widney Manor Road, Solihull, W Midlands. Open 6 days per week – please phone first Tel 0121 7044412 Fax 0121 2339928
garyh@compuserve.com or gary7@dial.pipex.com
Specialist offering demonstrations, hire and sales of a wide range of UK and European recumbents, folding bikes and special needs.

On Your Bike
From July 2000, 33/36 Bradford Street B5 6HX
Hrs Mon-Fri 10-6 Sat 9.30-6
Tel 0121 627 1590
Situated in the centre of the city and staffed by enthusiastic knowledgeable staff, the store is a mecca for cyclists in the Midlands.

BRISTOL
Comfort Cycles (Recumbents)
4 Cossham Street, Mangotsfield, Bristol.
Tel 0870 7878736 Fax 08707878739.
Email info@comfortcycles
We buy, sell, p/ex recumbents, test rides available. Special trailers and bags. Radical Design UK agent.

CAMBRIDGE
Ben Hayward Cycles
69 Trumpington Street, Cambridge CB2 1RJ. Hrs Mon-Sat 8.30-5.30 Tel 01223 352294
Fax 01223 573989 Email robturner@dial.pipex.com
Website www.benhaywardcycles.com
Now in its 85th year, we hope to balance traditional high standards of service, with a forward looking attitude tampered by experience. Pop in and see us.

CAMBRIDGESHIRE (NR. ELY)
D. Tek HPVs
Main Street, Little Thetford, Nr. Ely, Cambridgeshire CB6 1BR. Tel 01353 648177 Fax 01353 648777
March-Oct. 7 days a week 9.30 to 5, Winter Mon-Fri 10-4. Bookings essential other hours by arrangement. Outstanding range of recumbents for hire or sale. Unique one-stop trailer shop. Solutions for the disabled We wont say can't!

CHESTER (CHESHIRE)
The Bike Factory
153-161 Boughton, Chester, CH3 5BH.
Hrs Mon-Sat 9.30-5.30 Sun 10-4.
Tel 01244 317893/320173 Fax 01244 317916
Website www.the-bike-factory.com
We pride ourselves on good advice and quality service. Try us, you wont be disappointed.

Davies Brothers Cycles Limited
5 Delamere Street, Chester CH1 4DF.
Hrs Mon-Sat 9.30-5.30 Sun 10-4
Tel 01244 371341/381177 Fax 01244 381175.

CROMER (NORFOLK)
Pedal Pushers Of Norfolk
9 Station Road, West Runton, Cromer, Norfolk, NR27 9QD. Tel 01263 837 675. Web www.pedalpushers.net
Trailers a speciality, luggage, children, whatever. Hire and demonstration models.

DISS (NORFOLK)
Madgetts Cycles
8 Shelfanger Rd, Diss, Norfolk IP22 3EH. Hrs 9-5:30, Mon-Sat, half day Tues. Tel 01379 650419
Fax 01379 642735 Email madgettscycles@aol.com
Website www.madgettscycles.com
75 years of expert experience in all cycling, from the ordinary to the extreme. High-tech stock with traditional service.

EAST SUSSEX (FOREST ROW)
FutureCycles
Friends Yard, London Road, Forest Row, Sussex RH18 5EE. Hrs Mon 10.30-5.30 Tues-Sat 9.30-5.30. Half day Wed. Tel 01342 822847 Fax 01342 826726
Email bikes@futurecycles.prestel.co.uk
Website www.there.is/futurecycles
Specialising in recumbents, we offer a complete range of conventional bikes including folders. Traffic-free test-ride area in rural location.

ILKLEY (WEST YORKSHIRE)
JDs Bicycle Workshop
42A Nelson Road, Ilkley, West Yorkshire LS29 8HN.
Hrs 9 - 6pm Mon - Sat.
Tel 01943 816101 Fax 01943 601829
Email jdscycles@aol.com Web www.jdcycles.co.uk
Stockists of Dawes, Brompton, Yamaha, Schwinn, Ridgeback, Saracen, Univega, Newport, Peugeot. Cobra and ACT members.

LEYLAND (LANCS)
Paul Hewitt Cycles
25 Turpin Green Lane, Leyland, Lancs. PR5 3HA.
Hrs Mon-Sat 9.30-6 Tel/Fax 01772 424773
Website www.hewittcycles.co.uk
Custom-built frame specialist, full frame measuring, top quality wheel builder and cycle repair service. Race, Audax, touring, and trikes.

LIVERPOOL
Liverpool Cycle Centre
9-13 Berry St., Liverpool L1 9DF. Hrs 10-6.
Tel/Fax 0151 7088819
Providing a helpful service to everyone from the first-time buyer to the seasoned professional, regardless of age or gender.

LONDON SE1
On Your Bike
52/54 Tooley Street, London Bridge, London SE1 2SZ.
Tel 020 7378 6669
Hrs Mon - Fri 9-6 Sat 9.30-5.30
Sun (summer only) 11-4.
Since 1983, OYB have catered for the city cyclist, also keeping the latest components & clothing in stock for the avid mountain biker and enthusiast.

London Bicycle Tour Company
1a Gabriels wharf, 56 Upper ground, London, SE1 9PP. Hrs Mon-Sun 10-6
Tel 020 79286838
Email london.bicycle@btinternet.com
Website www.londonbicycle.com
Londons leading bicycle tour and rental company. We cycle for fun.

LONDON SW11
London Recumbents
Battersea Park, London, SW11 4NT, opening times seasonal, ring for details. Tel 020 72232533
Come and enjoy a day in the park, we've got the funkiest machines to hire or buy, including the seven seater Octos, recumbents, family bikes and special needs bikes.

LONDON SW19
Wheelie Serious Cycles
124-126 The Broadway, Wimbledon, London, SW19 1RH. Hrs Mon-Fri 10-7 Sat 10-6 Tel 020 8545255
Email info@wheelie-serious.com
Website www.wheelie-serious.com

LONDON SE24
London Recumbents
Rangers Yard, Dulwich Park, College Road, London SE21 7BQ. Tel/Fax 020 82996636 Opening times ring for details. Email recumbents@aol.com
Website www.londonrecumbents.co.uk
Pederson, special needs bikes, recumbents and more, for hire or sale.

LONDON W1
Wheelie Serious Cycles
63 George Street, London, W1H 5P.
Hrs Mon-Fri 8.30-6 Sat 10-6.
Tel 020 74873233
Email info@wheelie-serious.com
Website www.wheelie-serious.com

LONDON WC2
Wheelie Serious Cycles
2 Nottingham Court, Covent Garden, London, WC2H 9AY. Hrs Mon-Fri 10-7.30 Sat 10-6.
Tel 0207 8361752, Fax 020 74873210
Email info@wheelie-serious.com
Website www.wheelie-serious.com

LONDON W11
Bicycle Workshop
27 All Saints Road, Westbourne Park, London W11 1HE. Hrs Tue-Sat 10-6 (closed 2-3) Tel 020 7229 4850
Email ninon@copuserve.com
Website www.bicycleworkshop
Specialises in repairs, including jobs many shops don't like, supplier of sturme-archer hubs. Sells spares and accessories. Has a strong base in the local community and a wider catchment area.

LONDON W14
Cyclecare-Olympia
30 Blythe Road, London W14 0HA.
Hrs Mon-Fri 10-6,30 Sat 10-5 Tel/Fax 020 7602 9757
Brompton since 1988. All bikes, repairs, parts and advice. Pederson, custom build, Dawes for city, Giant for race. We service what we sell.

LONDON WC1
Bikefix
48 Lambs Conduit Street, London WC1N 3LJ. Hrs Mon-Fri 8.30 - 7 Sat 10 - 5.
Tel 020 74054639
Email bikefix@bikefix.co.uk
Website www.bikefix.co.uk/humanpower/
The complete Encycleopedia shop, with recumbents, trailers and folding bikes.

LOUGHBOROUGH (LEICESTERSHIRE)
Beacon Cycles
88 Derby Road, Loughborough, Leicestershire, LE11 5AG. Tel 01509 215448Hrs 9,00-5.30pm
Bikes, spares (and repairs), everything for happy cycling.

LYMINGTON (HAMPSHIRE)
The Bicycle Barn
Leagreen Farm, Christchurch Road, Lymington, Hampshire, SO41 0LA.
Tel/Fax 01590 644441
Email Bicyclebarn@talk21.com
Website www.bicyclebarn.co.uk
Huge and diverse selection with something for the whole family. Test rides around the farm. Friendly, qualified and knowledgeable staff. Great atmosphere and easy parking.

LYNTON (DEVON)
Bike Trail (Exmoor National Park , N. Devon)
19 Queen St. Lynton, Devon, EX35 6AA. Tel 01598 753987 Fax 01598 752490 mobile 0771 3158227
Email info@biketrail.co.uk Web www.biketrail.co.uk
Top quality bikes for sale and hire. Spares, repairs, and accessories. Electric bikes & trikes, tandems, U+2s, trailor bikes and brilliant special needs bikes. Free planned route maps and guided tours through the National Park. Group and special needs discounts.

MANCHESTER
Bicycle Doctor
68-70 Dickenson Road, Rusholme, Manchester M14 5HF. Tel 0161 2241303 Fax 0161 257 3102
Hrs Mon-Fri 10-6 Sat 10-5.30
Email sales@bikedoc.demon.co.uk
Website www.bicycledoctor.co.uk
High quality tourers, mountain, city bikes, folders, top class workshop.

The Bike Factory
Manchester Velodrome, Stuart Street, Manchester M11 4DQ
Hrs Hrs 9.30 - 5.30 Mon to Sat, 10.00-4.00 Sun.
Tel 0161 230 7100

NEWCASTLE-UPON-TYNE
Cycle Logical
37 St. Georges Terr, Jesmond, Newcastle-Upon-Tyne.
Mon-Sat 10-6, Sun 10-2.
Tel 01912 818383 Fax 01912 810681
Website www.cyclelogical@pashley.co.uk
Over 50 years of combined experience and service. We cater for all cyclists, both young and old.

NORWICH (NORFOLK)
Specialised Cycles
80 Connaught Road, Norwich, Norfolk, NR2 3BS. Hrs Mon-Sat 8.30-6. Tel/Fax 01603 665668
Email specycle@line1.net Web www.specycle.co.uk
Lightweight sales, spares, repairs, wheelbuilding, refinishing, clothing, shoes, Alsys, Dawes, Bromptons.

NOTTINGHAM
Freewheel,
34-36 Goose Gate, Hockley, Nottingham, NG1 1FF.
Hrs Mon-Fri 9.30-5.30 Sat 9-5.15
Tel 0115 9520200. Fax 0115 9520111.
Email us@freewheel.cc Web www.freewheel.cc
The bicycle specialists, with an extensive range of bikes and accessories to suit all your cycling needs. Folders, touring, city and family bikes, trailors and MTBs. Shimano service centre.

POULTON-LE-FYLDE (LANCS)
Wyre Wheels
15b Lower Green, Poulton-le-Fylde, Lancashire, FY6 7JL. Hrs Mon-Sat 9-5.30, closed Wed.
Tel/Fax 01253 896554
For the keener recreational cyclist, road bikes, hybrids and MTBs and a large selection of accessories to match.

SHIPLEY (W. YORKSHIRE)
Ellis Briggs Cycles
18 Otley Road, Shipley, W/Yorks. BD17 7DS. Hrs Mon-Sat 9-5.30, Sun10-4, closed Wed.
Tel/Fax 01274 583221
Established 1936, still family run business, offering a personal service for all your cycling needs.

SOUTH SHIELDS (TYNE & WEAR)
Norman Faye Cycles Ltd.
134 Dean Road, South Shields, Tyne & Wear, NE33 4AW. Hrs Mon-Sat 9-5.30.
Tel 0191 4561055 Fax 0191 4569011
Email nfay@faycycle.demon.co.uk
Family run business for over 35 years, genuine friendly service, specialists in touring and commuting, stocks Brompton and Birdy folders, Busch and Muller dynamos, Carradice and Ortlieb bags. Members of the Electric Vehicle Network.

STRATFORD UPON AVON (WARWICKSHIRE)
Pashley
StoreGuild Street, Stratford upon Avon, CV37 6QZ Hrs Tues-Sat 9-5 Tel 01789 205057 Email sales@pashley.co.uk Website www.pashley.co.uk Different by design. Distinctive by nature. Bicycles, tricycles, clothing and lifestyle accessories for all the family. Cycle hire also available.

TAUNTON
Westcountry Recumbents
23 Hamber Lea, Bishops Lydeard, Taunton, Somerset, TA4 3NJ. Tel 0870 7401227. Fax 07050 695561. Email sales@wrhpv.com, Website www.wrhpv.com. Trike specialist, choose from Greenspeed, ICE and Anthrotech. Carradice recumbent panniers, Comp-Pool tyres, spares and advice. Test rides available, booking essential.

TIPTREE (ESSEX)
Pedal Partners
91 Church Road, Tiptree, Essex, CO5 0HB. Hrs Tues-Sat 9-6, Sun 10-4, closed Mon. Tel/Fax 01621 815690. Website www. pedalpartners.co.uk Almost everything cycleable and associated. Special needs and able bodied. Sales, hire and information.

WORCESTER
Peddlers
46-48 Barbourne Road. Worcester, Worcestershire, WR1 1HV. Hrs Mon-Sat 9.30-6, Sun 9.30-4.30 Tel 01905 24238 Dedicated to enhancing cycling: Moulton and Brompton sales & servicing.

WORTHING
Michaels Cycles
21 Southfarm Road, Worthing, BN14 7AD. Tel 01903 232884 Email barmi@bigwig.net Hrs Mon-Fri 8.30-5.30 sat 8.30-4.30 Closed Wed/Sun Consistent trading since 1901, we offer an efficient, friendly service. Spares, repairs, and accessories. Racers, road bikes, and hybrids are our speciality.

YORK
Cycle Heaven
2 Bishopthorpe Road, York YO23 1JJ. Tel 01904 651870/636578 Fax 01904 672059. Now also opening Sunday Email cycleheaven@enterprise.net Website www.cycle-heaven.co.uk Featuring Dawes, Scott, Kona, Brompton, Birdy and Gazelle. Cycle Heaven is also a Shimano Service Centre.

SCOTLAND

ABERDEEN
St. Andrew Street Cyclery
34 St. Andrews Street, Aberdeen, Scotland, AB25 1JA. Hrs Mon-Sat 8.30-6 Thurs 8.30-8pm Tel 01224 658156. Email info@cyclery.co.uk Website www.cyclery.co.uk A little shop with a lot of honest knowledge. We like to serve how we like to be served.

EDINBURGH
Bike Trax
11 Lochrin Place, Edinburgh EH3 9QX. Hrs 10-5.30 Tel 0131 2286333 Fax 0131 2286333 Email biketrax@btinternet.com Website www.biketrax.co.uk Folding bike, trailers, touring bikes, family and leisure. Quality and service with a smile.

GLASGOW
Gear of Glasgow
19 Gibson Street, Hillhead, Glasgow G12 8NU. Hrs Mon-Sat 10-6 Tel/Fax 0141 3391179 Email j.allan@btinternet.com Website www.gearbikes.com Shimano service centre, organised maintenance classes (twice per year), and wheel building. We specialise in Orange mountain bikes, Birdy folders, Orbit touring and racing bikes. If you like tea, and chatting about the sort of bike you need, then give us a try.

Kinetics
15 Rannoch Drive, Bearsden, Glasgow G61 2JW. Hrs Tues-Sun 10-6 Tel/Fax 0141 9422552 Email ben@kinetics.org.uk Web www.kinetics.org.uk We sell folding bikes, electric bikes and recumbents. We are happy to custom-build absolutely anything.

STIRLING
Stuart Wilson Cycles
44 Barnton Street, Stirling, FK8 1NA. Hrs Mon-Sat 9-5.30 Sun 12-4 Email: stewartwilsoncycles@stirling.co.uk Website www.stewartwilsoncycles.co.uk Youll find the biggest selection of cycles in central Scotland, including Giant, Valley, Marin, Specialised, Brompton and Dawes.

WALES

ABERYSTWYTH (CEREDIGION)
Summit Cycles
65 North Parade, Aberystwyth, 11Ceredigion, SY23 2JN, Hrs Mon-Sat 10-6 Sunday seasonal. Tel/Fax 01970 626061 Email mail@summitcycles.co.uk Website www.summitcycles.co.uk Wide range of bikes and accessories for sale and hire.

MACHYNLLETH (POWYS)
Centre for Alternative Technology
CAT Shop, Centre for Alternative Technology, Pantperthog, Machynlleth, Powys, Wales, SY20 9AZ. Hrs 10-5.30 pm, dusk in winter. Tel 01654 702400 Fax 01654 703409 Email mail.order@cat.org Web www.cat.org.uk Working demonstrations of sustainable technology, 50% discount off entry to the Centre for cyclists. Selection of books on transport in the shop.

USA

ALASKA
The Bicycle Department
400 West Potter Drive, Anchorage, Alaska, AK 99518 Tel 907 561 1131 Fax 907 5621433 Email tmfi@alaska.net Web www.themotorcycleshop.com 17yrs of high quality service to Alaskas cycling community. We sells custom bicycles and alternative forms of transportation, and support commuter cyclists.

CALIFORNIA
American Cyclery
510 Frederick St., San Francisco, CA 94117. Tel 415 664 4545 Fax 415 664 6353 Email KimoToguchi@americancyclery.com Website www.americancyclery.com An historic landmark of San Francisco and West Coast Cycling, specializing in custom, classic and high quality commuting bikes, and offering a unique array of European and American bicycles.

CALIFORNIA
Aquarian Bicycles
486 Washington St., Monterey, CA 93940. Tel 408 375 2144 Fax 408 375 2843 Email tbushlow@aol.com Voted the best bike shop eight years in a row by the county paper, Aquarian specializes in mid- to high-end bicycles, recumbents and tender loving care.

CALIFORNIA
Cupertino Bike Shop
10493 So. De Anza Blvd., Cupertino, CA 95014. Tel 408 255 2217 Fax 408 255 5382 Email sprocket@cupertinobike.com Website www.cupertinobike.com In 46 years we've created a positive environment for all cycling enthusiasts, focusing on all aspects of road, tandem and mountain biking.

CALIFORNIA
Open Air Bicycles
437 W. Channel Islands Blvd., Port Hueneme, CA 93041. Tel 805 985 5045 Fax 805 984 7123 Email openair12@aol.com A local store dedicated to keeping cycling fun and carefree on the beautiful south central coast of California

CALIFORNIA
Palo Alto Bicycles
171 University Ave., Palo Alto, CA 94301. Tel 415 328 7411 Fax 415 328 0323 Email paloalto@pacbell.net Family owned and operated since 1930. Located in Californias bicycle friendly Silicon Valley. Friendly knowledgeable staff, quality selection and expert service.

CALIFORNIA
Rest Stop Bicycle Accessories
3230 Folsom Blvd., Sacramento, CA 95816. Tel 916 453 1870 Fax 916 453 1005 Email pinkdog@bbs.macnexus.org Hard-to-find accessories and unusual items. Oriented to customer convenience, community involvement, bicycle event and information center.

CALIFORNIA
The Chain Gang Bike Shop
1180 Industrial Street #A Redding, CA 96002. Tel 530-223-3400 Fax 530-223-3783 Email: bicycles@c-zone.net Website www.chaingangbikeshop.com Instrumental in making all types of bicycling a part of our community's history.

CALIFORNIA
People Movers
980 North Main St., Orange, CA 92867. Tel 714 633 3663 Fax 714 633 7890 Email peoplemovers@recumbent.com Website www.recumbent.com People Movers has been open for eleven years and regularly adds new and unusual products to their line to meet the unique requirements of their recumbent customers.

CALIFORNIA
The Missing Link Bicycle Co-op
1988 Shattuck Ave., Berkeley, CA 94704. Tel 510 843 7471 Fax 510 848 5322 Web www.missinglink.org Set up as workers' co-op. Radical ideas for promoting pedal power. Free repair classes, facilities for doing your own repairs. We rent and sell bicycles.

CALIFORNIA
Bicycle Odyssey
1417 Bridgeway, Sausalito, CA 94965. Tel 415 332 3050, Fax 415 332 5344 Email bikeodyssey@aol.com Over 25 years experience, specialising in custom fitting, road bikes, MTBs, hybrids and a wide range of clothing and accessories.

CALIFORNIA
Start To Finish Bicycles
599 Second St. San Francisco, CA 94107. Tel 415 202 9830 Fax 415 243 8815 Website www.stf.com

COLORADO
AngleTech Cyclery
318 N. Hwy 67, PO Box 1893 Woodland Park, CO 80863. Tel/Fax 719 6877475 Toll Free 800 793 3038 Email anglezoom@aol.co Website www.angletechcycles.com An alternative cyclist's dream. A full line of recumbents, folding bikes and cycles for special needs. Two hours browse time recommended.

FLORIDA
Fools Crow Cycles
1046 Commercial Drive, Tallahassee, Florida 32310. Tel +1 850-224-4767 Toll Free +1 877-771-2579 Email: edde@tfn.net Website www.foolscrow.com We stock euro-bikes from Challenge, M5, HP-Velotechnik, PDQ, TRICE, Festina, ZOX and many US bikes too. We offer full service for bicycles as transport, as well as sport.

FLORIDA
LakeShore Schwinn
2108 Blanding Blvd., Jacksonville, FL 32210. Tel+1 904 388 0612 Fax+1 904 384 7945 E-mail LSSchwinn@Juno.com Website www.Bik4fun.com An old style family bike shop. Helping develop Florida's cycling community. Let us help you find what you want.

GEORGIA
Free Flite
2800 Canton Rd., Marietta, GA 30066. Tel 770 422 5237 Fax 770 422 0912 Email freflite@mindspring.com Operating since 1978, Free Flite has grown to become the area's premier bicycle shop. Dedicated to cycling enthusiasts at your service.

HAWAII
Island Triathlon & Bike
569 Kapahulu Ave., Honolulu, HI 96815. Tel 808 737 7433 Sales 808 732 7227 Fax 808 737 2399 Email itb@aloha.net Website www.aloha.net/~itb Shop staffed by experienced, knowledgeable athletes and sales professionals, serving beginners and pros alike. Your one-stop shop for swim, bike, run and fun!

ILLINOIS
Rapid Transit
1900 W.North Ave., Chicago, IL 60622. Tel 773 227 2288 Fax 773 227 2328 Website www.rapidtransitcycle.com Bikes for the year-round urban cyclist. Run by commuter cyclists. ATB Vision, Tour Easy, Rans, Bike E, Long Bikes and Lightening. Test rides available.

MAINE
Back Bay Bicycle
333 Forest Ave., Portland, ME 04101. Tel 207 773 6906 Fax 207 773 5404 Email backbaybike@netscape.net Website www.backbaybicycle.com

MARYLAND
Mt Airy Bicycle
4540 Old National Pike, Mt Airy, MD 21771, Tel 410 795 2929 Fax 301 831 5877 Website www.bike123.com/ Earth's most interesting collection. Virtual museum. All for sale. Vintage/modern. 100 tandems. 50 Recumbents. Rentals. Trades. Long test rides.

MARYLAND
College Park Bicycle
4360 Knox Rd, College Park, MD 20740. Tel 301 864 2211 Fax 301 831 5877 Website www.bike123.com/ Over 800 used bikes for sale, rapid frame repair, same-day wheel building and six types of trailers. Extensive hire service includes recumbents, tandems and folders.

MASSACHUSETTS
Lincoln Guide Service
152 Lincoln Rd., Lincoln, MA 01773-0100. Tel 781 259 1111 Fax 781 259 1722 Email farny@erols.com Everything for the self-propelled: bikes, cross country skis, snow shoes and in-line skates. APB Vision, Bike E, Burley, Easy racers, Lightening, Linear, and Trek. Cycle repair classes.

MINNESOTA
Calhoun Cycle, Recumbent Specialists
3342 Hennepin Ave. S., Minneapolis, MN 55408, Tel: 612-827-8000 Fax: 612-926-0719 Email: info@calhouncycle.com Website: www.calhouncycle.com Calhoun Cycle is Minnesotas premier recumbent dealer. Featuring the largest selction of recumbent bikes and trikes for sale and rent. They are also the worlds largest source for recumbent - specific cycling apparel. Free clothing catalog available on request.

MINNESOTA
Freewheel Bicycle Co-op
1812 South Sixth St., Minneapolis, MN 55454. Tel 612 339 2219 Fax 612 339 8268 Email freewheel@freewheelbicycle.com Website www.freewheelbicycle.com Centrally located within Minnesota's twin cities, we sell new bikes, service any brand, and offer a do-it-yourself workshop for our customers. Repair classes and a thorough parts and accessories selection. Recumbents and custom bike fit are our speciality.

NEW JERSEY
North East Recumbents
9 Wayland Dr., Verona, NJ 07044. Tel 973 239 8968 Over a dozen different recumbents for sale and rent. Good advice for novices, excellent service and facilities, custom modifications.

NEW YORK
Toga Bike Shop
110 West End Ave. New York, NY 10023. Tel 212 799 9625 Fax 212 799 9625 Email info@togabikes.com Web www.togabikes.com

OREGON
Citybikes Workers Cooperative
734 S E Ankeny, Portland, OR 97214. Tel 503 2396951 or 503 2390553 A worker-owned cooperative aimed at making bike-riding and commuting easily accessible. Specializing in 3-speeds, trailers and upright commuter bikes.

OREGON
Eugene Bicycle Works / C A T
455 West 1st Ave, Eugene, OR 97401. Tel 541 683 3397 Fax 541 6861015 Email cat@efn.org Web www.efn.org/~cat The CAT believes that bicycles are essential tools for modern civilization and builds, sells and rents utilitarian bicycles, cargo bikes, heavy-duty work trailers, recumbents and adult tricycles.

PENNSYLVANIA
Jay's Pedal Power Bikes
512 E. Girard Ave., Philadelphia, PA 19125. Tel 215 425 5111 Fax 215 426 2653 Toll Free 1888 777 JAYS Jay's is a professional shop with 20 years experience and a large selection of components and parts. Electric bikes, tandems, recumbents and folding bikes. Largest selection of bikes in PA. Will ship globally.

TENNESSEE
Mt. Moriah Bicycle Co, Inc.
5715 Mt. Moriah, Memphis, TN 38115. Tel 901 795 4343 Fax 901 795 4310 Email mtmoriah1@aol.com Oldest continuous Schwinn dealership in the world. Triathlon and other high-end cycles. Many 'alternative' bikes, inc. recumbents and portables.

TEXAS
Freewheeling Bicycles
2401 San Gabriel, Austin TX 78705. Tel 512 477 6846 Fax 512 478 3733 A caring, professional service, and a fine choice of cycles and accessories. Good advice for novices.

WASHINGTON
Elliott Bay Bicycles
2116 Western Ave., Seattle, WA 98121. Tel 206 441 8144 Fax 206 441 1815 Email ebbikes@aol.com, Websites www.davidsonbicycles.com, www.elliottbaybicycles.com Home of the Davidson line of handbuilt bicycles. A wealth of experience in racing, international touring and custom design.

WASHINGTON, D.C.
City Bikes
2501 Champlain St., N W Washington, D.C. 20009. Tel 202 265 1564 Fax 202 462 7020 Website www.citybikes.com Supports bicycling as *THE* transportation alternative. Bikes, gear, parking, etc. Everything you need to ride. Declare your autó-nomy – ride a bike!

WASHINGTON
The Bikesmith
2309 No. 45th, Seattle, WA 98103. Tel 206 632 3102 Speciality: whatever no one else does. Bike and parts vintage to modern, new, used and reconditioned. Custom jobs welcomed.

WISCONSIN
Yellow Jersey
419 State St., Madison, WI 53703. Tel 608 257 4737 Office 608 257 4818 Fax 608 257 5161 Email yellowje@execpc.com Web www.execpc.com/yellowje Full service since 1971. Machining, frame service, eclectic bits, custom fabrication/modification. Real touring bikes, internal gearboxes, roadsters, Dynohubs, too!

WYOMING
Dr. Spokes Cyclery & Museum
240 South Center, Casper, WY 82601-2524. Tel 307 265 7740 Fax 307 265 7740 Buy-Sell-Trade antique bicycles, tricycles, pedal cars, related advertising samples and curios. Restoration work done. Carries new line of Harley Davidson Bicycles.

A. Winther A/S : *Dolphin, Donkey*
Rygesmindevej 2, DK 8653 Them, Denmark. Tel +45 8684 7288 Fax +45 8684 8528. win@a-winther.dk www.winther-bikes.com
Germany: Utopia Fahrradmanufaktur, Eschberger Weg 1, 66121 Saarbrücken. Tel +49 681 516506 Fax +49 681 815 098
Holland: Van Meurs & Co., Postbus 122, 4130 EC Vianen. Tel +31 34 73 51 855 Fax +31 34 73 51 334
Norway: Sport-Casa A/S, Postboks 377, 1801 Askim. Tel +47 69 88 89 10 Fax +47 69 88 52 44
Switzerland: Vitelli Velo-Bardarf AG, Dornacherstr. 101, 4053 Basel. Tel +41 61 361 7070 Fax +41 61 361 5770

Advanced Vehicle Design : *Windcheetah*
L&M Business Park, Norman Road, Altrincham, Cheshire WA14 4ES, UK Tel +44 161 928 5575 Fax +44 161 928 5585 bob@windcheetah.co.uk www.windcheetah.co.uk

Airnimal Designs: *Chameleon*
Tel +44 1223 523973 info@airnimal.com www.airnimal.com.

AnthroTech Leichtfahrzeugtechnik GmbH : *Anthrotech*
Rothenbergstr. 7, D-90542 Eckental-Frohnhof, Denmark. Tel +49 9126 288 644 Fax +49 9126 288 321

Arved Klutz Spezialraeder : *Quantum ZR*
Steinstr. 5, 25364 Hörnerkirchen, Germany. Tel +49 4127 92283 Fax +49 4127 92284 info@quantum-liegeraeder.de www.quantum-liegeraeder.de

ATP Green Gear Cycling : *Tandem Traveller, Air Friday*
3364 W 11th Ave, Eugene, OR 97402, USA. Tel +1 800 777 0258 Fax +1 541 687 0403 info@bikefriday.com www.bikefriday.com
UK: Valley Cycles, 2 Nene Court, The Embankment, Wellingborough, NN8 1LD. Tel +44 1933 271030 valley@primex.co.uk

Batavus : *Team DH*
Batavus and Be One bikes are available through specialist dealers: see www.batavus.nl and www.beone-bikes.com

Bike Best : *Bike Best*
71 Wroxham Rd, Sprowston, Norwich, NR7 8TW, UK. Tel 01603 405 918 Fax 01603 405 918 info@bikebest.co.uk www.bikebest.co.uk

Bike Hod : *Bike Hod*
Two Plus Two UK, 31 Western Road, St Annes, Lewes, Sussex BN7 1RL, UK. Tel +44 1273 480479 Fax +44 1273 480479 info@twoplustwo.uk.com www.twoplustwo.uk.com
Germany: Zwei plus Zwei, Bismarkstr. 56-62, 50672 Köln. Tel +49 221 9514700 Fax +49 221 95147020 www.zweipluszwei.com

Biker's Dream : *Biker's Dream Foot Pump*
Tiroler Str. 34, D-87459 Pfronten, Germany. Tel +49 8363 924660 Fax +49 8363 924664 sepp.kanzian@talknet.de www.bikersdream.de

Bishopthorpe Bicycles : *Dwarf Safety*
Mike West, 35 Keble Park North, Bishopthorpe, York, YO23 2SX, UK. Tel +44 1904 703 413

BK Tech AG : *Flyer*
Industrie Neuhof 9, CH – 3422 Kirchberg, Switzerland. Tel +41 34 448 60 60 Fax +41 34 448 60 61 Email info@swiss-flyer.com Web www.swiss-flyer.com

BMW AG : *BMW bikes*
BMW Mountain Bikes are distributed through BMW dealers worldwide. See www.bmw.com or www.bmw.de

Bringewald's function-bikes : *Tarpan & Muli*
Wolfsburg, Germany. Tel.: +49 177 540 74 00 bringewald@t-online.de Website www.bringewald.de

Brompton Bicycle Ltd : *Brompton*
Kew Bridge Distribution Centre, Lionel Rd, Brentford, Middlesex, TW8 9QR, UK. Tel +44 181 232 8484 Fax +44 181 232 8181
Denmark: Preben Pedersen, Sminge Cykler, Sortenborgvej 7, DK-8600 Silkeborg. Tel 8680 0411 Fax 8682 8622
Germany: Voss Spezial-Rad GmbH, D-25524 Itzehoe-Ebendorf, Tulpenweg 2. Tel 04821 78023 Fax 04821 41014
USA: CM Wasson Co, 423 Chaucer St., Palo Alto, CA 94301-2202. Tel 415 321 0808 Fax 415 321 8375

Burley Design Cooperative : *D'Lite, Piccolo, Tandems, Limbo*
4020 Stewart Road, Eugene, OR 97402, USA. Tel +1 541 687 1644 Fax +1 541 687 0436 burley@burleybike.com www.burley.com
Australia: Tandemonium!, 70 Gozett St, Katoomba 2780, New South Wales. Tel 61 4 1457 2265 Fax: 61 2 478 27961
Belgium: Now Company, Avenue Edison 5-Zoning Nord, 1300 Wavre. Tel 32 10 23 01 80 Fax 32 10 23 01 81 now.info@infonie.be
Denmark: Dansk Cyklist Forbund, Romersgade 7, DK-1362 Kobenhavn K. Tel +45 33 32 31 21 Fax 45 33 32 7683 dct@inet.uni-c.dk www.dcf.dk
Finland: Velosport KY, Kimmontie 3, 00610 Helsinki. Tel 358 9 757 1377 Fax 358 9 795 498 www.velosport.fi
Germany: Centurion Renner KG, Blumenstrasse 49-51, 71106 Magstadt Tel 49 7159 9459 30 Fax 49 7159 945 950 Gerd.Klose@Centurion.de
Japan: Tokyo Flagship Store/REI JAPAN K.K., 3-4-1 Tsuruma, Machida-Shi, Tokyo, 194-8509 Contact: Tam Mjelde, Intl. Retail Admin. Asst., Bldg. C –IHQ, (253) 437-5742 (In USA) tmjelde@rei.com
The Netherlands: Kok Better Bikes B.V., Nachtegaalstraat 51, 3581 AD Utrecht. Tel 31 (30) 2315780 Fax 31 (30) 2316675
New Zealand: Cycle Supplies, PO Box 33051, Christchurch. Tel 64-3-332-3622 Fax 64-3-332-3243 bikes@caverock.net
Norway: Sykkeldelisk, 0355 Oslo Tel 47 22 60 18 05 Fax 47 22 60 15 13 sykdel@online.no www.sykkeldelisk.no
Switzerland: Intercycle, Postfache, CH-6210 Sursee. Tel +41 41 926 65 11 Fax +41 41 926 63 52 gregor.lichtsteiner@intercycle.com www.intercycle.ch
United Kingdom: UK Trailer Co., The Camel Trail, Wadebridge, PL27 7AL Cornwall. Tel 44 1208 815715 Fax 44 1208 814407 burley@uktrailer.freeserve.co.uk
Dawes Cycles Ltd., Pete Bird, Wharfdale Road, Tyseley, Birmingham, B11 2DG. Tel 44 121 765 2000 Fax 44 121 765 2020 info@dawescycles.com www.dawescycles.com

Calfee Designs : *Calfee Tandem*
2801 Mission St. Suite C, Santa Cruz, CA 95060, USA. Tel 1-800-965-2171 or Fax (831) 466 9043 jim@calfeedesign.com www.calfeedesign.com

Christiania Bikes : *Light-Split*
Dammegardsvej 22, DK-3782 Klemensker, Denmark. Tel +45 5696 6700 Fax +45 5696 6708. contact@christianiabikes.com www.christianiabikes.com
Sweden: Christiania bikes, Postadress: Box 107, 443 31 Lerum, Sverige. Tel +46 (0) 302-131 30 Mob +46 (0)705-13 13 00 Fax +46 (0) 302-102 60
The Netherlands: Christiania bikes NL, Boslaan 10, 7875 AR Exloo NL. Tel +31 (0)591-549060 GSM +31 (0)6-53536564 Fax +31 (0)591-549324 christiania-bikes@tref.nl www.christiania-bikes.nl
England: Zero Emissions, Real Options Ltd., 66 Rossmore Ct, Park Rd, London NW 1 6XY. Tel (0)591-549060 Mob (0)411 908955 Fax (0)171 723 2409 zero@workbike.org www.workbike.org/homepages/zero
Germany: See Website for list of German dealers
Switzerland: Velociped, Veloförderungs-Werkstatt, Luzernerstrasse 16, CH-6010 Kriens/Luzern. Tel +41 (0) 41 3205351 Fax +41 (0)171 723 2409 velociped@tic.ch

Cool Breeze UK Ltd : *Prone Low-Profile*
194 Upper Street, Islington, London, N1 1RQ, UK. Tel +44 171 704 9273 Fax +44 171 354 9641

Cycles Maximus : *One Less Car Trishaw*
103 Walcot St, Bath, BA1 5BW. Tel 01225 319 414 Fax 01225 334 494 l.wood@which.net

Dahon Inc : *Gotham City*
8F-2, 6 Lane 609, Sec 5 Chunghsin Rd, ROC Sanchung, Taiwan. Tel 001 818 305 5264 Fax 001 818 305 9153 dahon@ficnet.net www.dahon.com
For details of agents in other countries please contact Dahon in the US.

Di Blasi Industriale srl : T3 *Trike*
C.da Risicone, Vizzini (CT), Italy. Tel/Fax +39 095 940 384 mail@diblasi.it www.diblasi.it
Details of agents and distributors in many countries can be found on the website.

Die Fahrradwerkstatt der Gustav Werner Stiftung zum Bruderhaus : *Transporter*
Tübinger Str. 89, D-72762, Germany. Tel +49 7121 930 7220 Fax +49 7121 930 72218 diefahrradwerkstatt@t-online.de

Draisin : *Draisin bikes*
Am Risisee 1, 77855 Achern-Gamshurst, Germany. Tel 07841-260 51 Fax 07841-260 81 info@draisin.de www.draisin.com

EPMB UK Ltd : *EP-X*
The Manor, Naseley Business Centre, Warwick, CV35 7LS, UK. Tel +44 2476 247 264 Fax +44 2476 247265 tasha@ep-x.com www.ep-x.com

Firma Juliane Neuss : *Brompton Conversion Kit*
Haferberg 2, 21059 Glinde, Germany. Tel 040 / 710 951 04 Fax 040 / 710 951 04 info@junik-hpv.de www.junik-hpv.de
Germany: Räderwerk Hannover, Radl-R München, Fahrradscheune Caspari, Frankfurt/M
Switzerland: Diverso, Ennelmoos
Holland: Simon Koorn, Zwolle
UK: Phoenix Cycles, London
USA: Channel Wasson, California, Palo Aalto

Florian Schlumpf Spezialmaschinenbau : *Easy-Shift Mountain-drive*
Dorfstr. 10, CH-7324 Vilters, Switzerland. Tel +41 817238009 Fax+41 817238364 schlumpf_ing@bluewin.ch www.schlumpf.ch

Generator Radsport : *Spork belts*
Spinnereistr. 7, 04179 Leipzig, Germany. Tel +49 341 498 0244 or 0157 Fax +49 341 498 0240 info@generator-radsport.de www.generator-radsport.de

Giant Europa B.V. : *Lafree, XTC*
Pascallaan 66, 8218 NJ Lelystadt, Netherlands. Tel +31 320 296 296 Fax +31 320 296 200 info@giant-bicycles.com www.giant-bicycles.com
Giant bicycles are distributed worldwide: contact your local dealer, or see their website.

Goude Design Group : *Indicator Glove*
Bridge House, Hollywood Lane, Mellor, Cheshire, SK6 5LR, UK. Tel +44 370 984 263 Fax +44 870 0520 727 simon@goude.demon.co.uk

Greenspeed : *Greenspeed GTO*
69 Mountain Gate Drive, Ferntree Gully, Vic 3156, AUSTRALIA. Tel +61 3 9758 5541 Fax +61 3 9752 4115 ian@greenspeed.com.au www.greenspeed.com.au
See web-page for list of world-wide dealers.

Hase Spezialräder : *Pino*
Karl-Friedrich-Str. 88, 44795 Bochum, Germany. Tel +49 234 9469050 Fax +49 234 9469099 info@hase-spezialraeder.de www.hase-spezialraeder.de
UK: London Recumbents, Bikefix, D.Tek HPVs, Pedalers Bike Shop (Lancaster), Kinetics (see Shops list for details)
Canada: Cambie Cycles www.cambiecycles.com
New Zealand: Trikes New Zealand Ltd, Levin, Tel +64 636 78272 Fax 70146 trikes.nz@xtra.co.nz
Holland: Wim Kok Fietsplezier (Tel +31 30 2315780), Flevobike (Tel +31 321 33.7200)
Switzerland: Velociped, Haso's Veloladen
USA: Recumbent People Movers CA (www.recumbent.com), The Chain Gang Bike Shop CA bicycles@c-zone.net, 21st Century Bikes, MA Tel +1 781 659 2991, Mt. Airy Bicycle MD Fax +1 301 854 6876, Bikesmith WA Tel (0 01) 206-632-3102.

heintz-bike : *Velocross*
Mergentheimer Str. 18, 97082 Würzburg, Germany. Tel +49 931 409 731 or 84816 Fax +49 931 781 1522 or 408 438 Mobile: +49 171 871 0335 or 880 8270

Heinzmann : *Estelle*
Am Haselbach 1, D-79677 Schönau, Germany Tel +49 76 73 82 08 122 Fax +49 76 73 82 08 194 info@heinzmann.de www.estelle.de

HP Velotechnik : *Speedmachine*
Goethestr. 5, D-65830 Kriftel, Germany. Tel +49 6192 41010 Fax +49 6192 91 02 18 mail@hpvelotechnik.com www.hpvelotechnik.com
A full international dealer list appears on the website.

Hubert Meyer GmbH : *Culty, Pacy*
Thomas Poreski Spezialfahrräder, Charlottenstr. 39, D-72764 Reutlingen, Germany. Tel +49 177 277 7592 Fax +49 7121 204 085 culty@liegerad.com www.culty.de, www.pacy-faltrad.de

Innoway : *Jancho*
Hindemithstr. 20, D-48282 Emsdetten, Germany. Tel +49 2572 98 83 17 Fax +49 2572 859 35 innoalex@aol.com www.jancho.de

Inspired Cycle Engineering : *ICE trike*
Unit 9b.Spencer Carter Works, Tregoniggie Industrial Estate, Bickland Water Road, Falmouth, Cornwall, TR11 4SN. Tel +44 1326 378848 Fax +44 1326 378848 sales@ice.hpv.co.uk www.ice.hpv.co.uk
See web-page for list of worldwide dealers

J & S Fietsdiensten : *Quest*
De Vecht 28, NL-8253PH Dronten, Netherlands. Tel +31 321 332717. ymte@ligfiets.net www.ligfiets.net/j-en-s

Jesper Sølling Cykelproduktion : *Pedersen and Woodguards*
KGB, Donnerschweerstr. 45, 26123 Oldenburg, Germany. Tel +49 441 8850389 Fax +49 441 8850388 kgb.kalle@nwn.de www.pedersen-fahrrad.de

Karbon Kinetics : *Mako TR*
18613 Honeysuckle Way, Monument, Colorado 80132, USA. Tel Fax karbonkinetics@hotmail.com

Heinz Kettler GmbH & Co. : *CityShopper*
Postfach 1020, D-59463 Ense-Parsit, Germany. Tel +49 02938 810 Fax +49 02938 2022 alu-rad@heinz-kettler.de. www.heinz-kettler.de
UK: Kettler GB Ltd, Merse Rd, North Moons Moat, Redditch, Worcestershire B98 9HL, UK. Tel +44 1527 591 901 Fax +44 1527 62423 kettler@btinternet.com
Austria: Kettler Austria, Halbach 221 5321 Koppl/Sbg, Tel. 06221/7050-0 Fax 06221/705020
Benelux: Kettler Benelux: Indumastraat 18, NL-5753 RJ Deurne Tel. 0493/310345 Fax 0493/310739 kettler@xs4all.nl
Spain: Kettler sa Aragón 316, 08009 Barcelona. Tel. 93/4879090 Fax 93/4879066 info@kettal.es

France: Kettler sarl, 5, Rue du Château, Lutzelhouse 67133 Schirmeck Cédex. Tel. 0388/475580 Fax 0388/473283 comm@kettler-france.fr
Italy: Strada per Pontecurone 5, 15053 Castelnuovo Scrivia (AL) Tel. 0131/855848 Fax 0131/826436 kettlersrl@comm2000.it
Poland: Kettler Polska: ul. Kossaka 110, 64-92 Pila, Tel. 67/2122103 Fax 67/2135737
USA: Kettler International P.O. Box 2747. Virginia Beach, VA 23450 USA. Tel. (757)427-2400 Fax (757)427-0183 kettler@pro.onet.pl

KHW GmbH : *Allround Fahrrad Set*
Kunststoff- und Holzverarbeitungswerk GmbH, Alte Lage, 98716 Geschwenda, Germany. Tel +49 36205 76301/2 Fax +49 36205 74934 khw-geschwenda@t-online.de www.khw-geschwenda.de

Kinetics : *Toucan Tandem*
15 Rannoch Drive, Bearsden, Glasgow, , G61 2JW, UK. Tel +44 141 942 2552 Fax +44 141 942 2552 ben@kinetics.org.uk www.kinetics.org.uk

Kokua Holzspielzeug : *Like-a-Bike*
Wallstr. 15-17, D-52064 Aachen. Tel +49 241 406 497 kokua@t-online.de

Kool Stop International Inc : *Koolite, Brake Blocks*
1061 S. Cypress Street, La Habra, CA 90632, USA. Tel +1 714 738 4971 Fax +1 714 992 6191 www.koolstop.com

Lightfoot Cycles : *Roadrunner*
179 Leavens Road, Darby, Montana 59829 USA. Tel +1 406 821 4750 Fax +1 406 821 0963 info@lightfootcycles.com www.lightfootcycles.com

Linear Manufacturing Inc : *Linear LWB*
32744-MK Kestrel Ave, Guttenberg, IA 52052, USA. Tel +1 319 252 1637 Fax +1 319 252 9030 linear@netins.net www.linearrecumbents.com
UK: MICWIC, Unit 12, Oaklands Ind Est, Braydon, Swindon, SN5 0AN, UK. Tel 01793 852 484 Fax 01793 852 484

Lynch Motor Company : *Lynch Motor*
PO Box 919, London, N1 1DE, UK. Tel 0171 607 8141 Fax 0171 709 3625 info@lynchmotor.com www.lynchmotor.com

MIC WIC : *Delta*
Unit 12, Oaklands Ind Est, Braydon, Swindon, SN5 0AN, UK. Tel 01793 852 484 Fax 01793 852 484

Nauticraft, Inc : *Escapade*
5980 Grand Haven Road, Muskegon, MI 49441, USA. Tel 1-888-709-7097 or(231)798-8440 Fax (231)798-7739 gwen@nauticraft.com www.nauticraft.qpg.com

Newk Bike Products : *Newk bar ends*
17452 Revello Drive, Pacific Palisades, CA 90272, USA. Tel +1 310 230 2725 Fax +1 310 230 2625 newkbike@aol.com www.newkbike.com
See web-page for list of world-wide distributors

Nihola : *Nihola Transporter Trike*
Vesterbrogade 137, DK-1620 Kobenhavn V, Denmark. Tel 0045 3322 7905 Fax 0045 3322 7907 nihola@nihola.dk www.nihola.dk

Nokian Tyres Ltd : *Tyres*
Box 20, 37101 Nokia, Finland. Tel 358 313407601 Fax 358 313407694 www.nokian.com
USA, Sun Metal Products Inc., T +1-219-267 3281, F +1-219-267 2446, sales@sunrims.com
UK, Wind Wave, T +44-1705-521912, F +44-1705-522 625, office@windwave.co.uk
Japan, Kuwahara International , T +81-6 6971-1601, F +81-6 6971-8722, kuwabike@osk3.3web.ne.jp
Germany, Cool Down T +49-2337-270 122, F +49-2337-270 123, cooldown@cooldown.de
Switzerland, Agentur Felix AG, T +41-71-9116 616, F +41-71-9116 629, agenturfelix@access.ch
Austria, Funbike GmbH, T +43-662-6362 450, F +43-662-6362 455, funbike@funbike.at
Sweden, Hallman Sports Ab, T +46-18-15 1600, F +46-18-50 0322, anders.lindgren@hallmansport.se
Norway, Stians Sport, T +47-67 11 00 20, F +47-67-11 00 42, office@stians-sport.no
Denmark, Verner Aadal Aps, T +45-65-961 284, T +45-65-961 283,
Netherlands, Koch Kleeberg B.V., T +31-36-5320 504, T +31-36-5322 548, cycleparts@koch-kleeberg.nl

One Dot Pty: *Ant*
113 Anzac Hwy, Ashford, Australia 5035. Tel: +61 8 8371 4439 Fax: +61 8 8371 1686 info@one-dot.com

Optima Cycles : *Lynx/Aerorider*
Industriestraat 3A, 1976 Central Station, Eumuiiden, Netherlands. Tel +31 255 514 215 Fax +31 255 524 757 info@optima-cycles.nl www.optima-cycles.nl
Germany: Tom Tours, Herbertstr. 10, 45661 Recklinghausen. 0049-2361-656797
Belgium: Velo futura, 3 Rue Louis Lamothe, Andernos les Bains, 0033-557702944
UK: Comfort Cycles UK, 279 Sundridge Park, Yate, Bristol BS37 4HA. Tel 01454-320319 and Bikefix, 48 Lambs Conduit St, WC1N 3LJ London.

Pashley : *Brilliant Bicycles, Harrods Bike*
Masons Road, Stratford-upon-Avon, Warwickshire, CV37 9NL, UK. Tel +44 1789 292 263 Fax +44 1789 414 201 info@pashley.co.uk www.pashley.co.uk

PBW : *PBW Road bike*
PO Box 2809. Athens, GA 30612, USA Tel/fax: +1 706 548 1179 info@PBWbikes.com, www.pbwbikes.com *Germany:* Voss Spezialrad GmbH, Tel +49 4821 7 80 23 Fax +49 4821 796 93, voss-spezialrad@t-online.de www.voss-spezialrad.de

Rabbit Tool USA : *Electric folding bike*
105 – 9th Street, Rock Island, Illinois 61201, USA. Tel +1 309 793 43 75 Fax +1 309 793 4632 rabbittool@revealed.net www.rabbittool.com

Radical Design : *Bags, Trailer*
Hoofdstraat 8, 9514 BE Gasselternijveen, Holland. Tel/Fax +31 599 513 482 www.radicaldesign.nl

Radius Liegeräder - Liegerad Münster GmbH : *Radius C4*
Borkstr. 20, D-48163 Münster, Germany. Tel +49 1805 723 487 Fax +49 215 78 03 58 mail@radius-liegeraeder.de www.radius-liegeraeder.de

Radnabel : *Radnabel ATL*
Jakobsgasse 19, D-72070 Tübingen, Germany. Tel/Fax +49 7071 23896

Rans Inc. : *Velocity²*
4600 Highway 183 Alternate, Hays, Kansas 67601, USA. Tel +1 785 625 6346 Fax +1 785 625 2795 bikes@rans.com www.rans.com

riese und müller : *Birdy, Equinox*
Erbacher Str. 123, D-64287 Darmstadt, Germany. Tel +49 6151 366 860 Fax +49 6151 366 8620 team@r-m.de www.r-m.de *UK dealers*: contact r&m for details. *US:* Burley Design Cooperative 4020 Stewart Road, Eugene, OR 97402, USA. Tel +1 541 687 1644 Fax +1 541 687 0436 burley@burleybike.com www.burley.com

Robert Hoening Spezialfahrzeuge : *Compagnon, Twin*
Ulmer Straße 16/2, D-71229 Leonberg, Germany. Tel +49 7152 43046 Fax +49 7152 73589 r.hoening@t-online.de www.hoening.com
Belgium, France, Euromove s.p.r.l., B-1640, Rhode St Genese, 44, chee de Waterloo, T +32-2-3585986, F +32-2-3585951
Switzerland, B & M Mobility Systems GmbH, CH-3008, Bern, Fischermättelistr. 18, T +41-31-3760001, F +41-31-3710957
Denmark, Hospitalsartikler A/S, DK-8355, Solbjerg, Hvilstedvej 16, T+45-86927955, F +45-86927027
UK, Ireland, Pashley Cycles, GB, Warwickshire CV37 9NL, Masons Road, Stratford-upon-Avon, T +44-1289-305134, F +44-1289-302345
Italy, Off. Carr. s.n.c., I-35010, Villa Del Conte (Padova), Via San Rocco, 4, T +39-049-9390122, F +39-49-9390133
Japan, Index Ltd., Japan, Tokyo 152, 2-16-24-402 Jiyugaoka Meguro-ku, T +81-3-37249901, F +81-3-37189871
Norway, Medema-Gruppen AS, N-0903, Oslo, Sven Oftedals Vei 2-8, T +47-22168100, F +47-22168190
Netherlands, Freewiel Techniek BV, NL-5521 DA, Eersel, Kerver 21, T +31-497531270, F +31-497531279
Sweden, Trident Industri AB, S-26272, Ängelholm, Metallgatan 27, T +46-431-83900, F +46-431-83937
USA, Canada, Frank Mobility Systems L.P., USA, Oakdale, PA 151071-9223, PIIP-ICM Building 1003 Int. Drive, T +1-724-6957822, F +1-724-6952922

Roberts : *Clubman Compact*
89 Gloucester Rd, Croydon, Surrey CR0 2DN, UK Tel +44 208 684 3370 Fax +44 208 665 9763

Rohloff GmbH : *Disk brake hub*
Mönchebergstr. 30, 34125 Kassel, Germany. Tel +49 561 87 5615 Fax +49 561 87 5338 service@rohloff.de www.rohloff.de
Austria: Fun Bike, Salzachweg 1, A-5061 Salzburg –Elsbethen el 0043-662-6362450 Fax 0043-662-6362455
Australia: Rohloff Australia, Maria & Dieter Mohrholz, 38 Boyne Crescent, 4680 Gladstone QLD el 0061-749-725554 Fax 0061-749-725554
Canada: NRG Enterprice Ltd., 715 Vernon Street, Nelson BL, Canad VIL 4G3 Tel 001-250-3522099 Fax 001-250-3522038
Denmark: Bike toyz, Grenavej 646, DK 8541 Skodstrup. Tel 0045-86990058 Fax 0045-87990051
Finland: MT Bike, Koulukatu 40, SF-80100 Joensuu Tel 00358-13-224891 Fax 00358-13-224892
France: Philamy SA, 1384 Pl, St. Maurice, F-04100 Manosque Tel 0033-4-92709700 Fax 0033-4-92726070
Hungary: Lenkei Bike Components Bl., Kevehaza u. 11, H- 1119 Budapest Tel 0036-1-2042045 Fax 0036-1-2042045
Italy: Larm SpA, Via Cadell´Orbo, 36 (BO), I-40055 Villanova diCastenaso (Italy) Tel 0039-51-6053460 Fax 0039-51-6053411
Netherlands: Vertex Cycle Systems BV, Flemingstraat 100 A, NL-2041 VL Zandvoort Tel 0031-2357-18184 Fax 0031-2357-18606
New Zealand: GroundZero, 42 Quarantine Rd., Nelson, NZ, Freephone(NZ) 0800-656-900 Tel 0064-3-547-8386 Fax 0064-3-547-8388 info@groundzero.co.nz www.groundzero.co.nz
South Africa: Bruce Reyneke Cycles C.C., 275 Lynnwood Road, RSA-Pretoria, Tel 0027-12-3621628 Fax 0027-12-3621630
Spain: Bike Difusion S.L., C. Telesforo Aranzadi, 3, E- 01009 Vitoria (Alava) Tel 0034-945-200590 Fax 034-945-222512
Switzerland: Intercycle, Industriegebiet, CH-6210 Sursee (Switzerland) Tel 0041-926-6511 Fax 0041-926-6352
UK: Ison Distribution, Maltings Warehouse, 307 Millroad, Cambridge, CB1 3DF Tel 0044-1223-213800 Fax 0044-1223-568361 sales@ison-distribution.com www.ison-distribution.com
USA: ROHLOFF Inc., 1327 Richmond Street, El-Cerrito, CA 94530 Tel 001-510-232-4833 Fax 001-510-527-6650 usa@rohloff.de

Rotator Recumbent Bicycles : *Tiger & Pursuit*
4325 Montgomery Drive, Santa Rosa, CA 95405, USA. Tel 1 707 539 4203 Fax 1 707 539 5354 rotator@neteze.com www.rotatorrecumbent.com

Samui Corp : *Air Zound Horn*
61 Research Rd, Toronto, M4G 2G8, Canada. Tel +1 416 425 2583 Fax +1 416 425 2178 Email airzound2@aol.com
The Air Zound horn is available through dealers worldwide. In case of difficulty contact the manufacturers.

Schmidt Maschinenbau : *SON*
Aixer Strasse 44, 72072 Tübingen, Germany. Tel +49 7071 3887 0, Fax +49 7071 3887 6. info@nabendynamo.de www.nabendynamo.de
UK: CTC shop: shop@ctc.org.uk, St John Street Cycles: www.sjscycles.com
Switzerland: Vitelli www.vitelli.ch
Netherlands: Gerritsen & Meijers, Ingenieurs, www.tubus.nl
Denmark: Danish Cyclist Federation: www.dcf.dk
Iceland: Icelandic Mountain Bike Club www.mmedia.is/~ifhk/
USA: Peter White Cycles: www.PeterWhiteCycles.com
Australia: St. Kilda Cycles: therbst@bigpond.net.au

Schneider & Semch : *Sandini*
Postfach 144, 89243 Semden, Germany. Tel +49 7307 29673 Fax +49 7307 24532 sandini@t-online.de www.sandini.de

Skoot : *Skoot*
24 Peartree Business Centre, Stanway, Colchester, Essex, CO3 5JN, UK. Tel +44 1206 542 542 Fax +44 1206 542 www.skoot.co.uk

SRAM : *SPARC, SRAM*
SRAM Europe, Basicweg 12-05, NL-3821 BR Amersfoort, Holland. srameurope@sram.com www.sram.com
SRAM products are available through dealers worldwide – see their website.

St John St Cycles : *Thorn XTC*
91-93 St John Street, Bridgwater, Somerset TA6 5HX, UK Tel +44 1278 441500 Fax +44 1278 431107 sales@sjscycles.com www.sjscycles.com

Staller Studio : *Conferencebike*
Herengracht 100, 1015 BS Amsterdam, Netherlands. Tel +31 20 624 9198 Fax +31 20 624 9198 info@conferencebike.com www.conferencebike.com

Thijs Industrial Designs : *Rowbike*
Koorkewrstraat 10, 4331 AW Middelburg, Netherlands. Tel +31 118 634 166 Fax +31 118 612 511 thys@zeelandnet.nl www.zeelandnet.nl/thys

Tubus Transport Systems : *Tubus Carriers*
Borkstraße 20, 48163 Münster, Germany. Tel 0251 / 76 19 68 8 Fax 0251 / 76 19 68 9 info@tubus-de.de

Utopia : *Vektor*
Kreisstr. 134f, 66128 Saarbrücken, Germany. Tel +49 681 970 360 Fax +49 681 970 3611 utopia@utopia-fahrrad.de www.utopia-fahrrad.de

Xtracycle : *Xtracycle*
LLC, 14618 Tyler Foote Rd., Nevada City, CA 95959, USA Tel +1 530 470 2388 Fax +1 419 735 1427 info@xtracycle.com www.xtracycle.com *UK:* Merlin Matthews: Tel +44 1206 38 2207 Fax +44 1206 38 5729

ZEM AG : *ZEM*
Postfach 8034, Zurich, Switzerland. Tel +41 1383 6363 Fax +41 1383 6362 info@zem.ch www.zem.ch